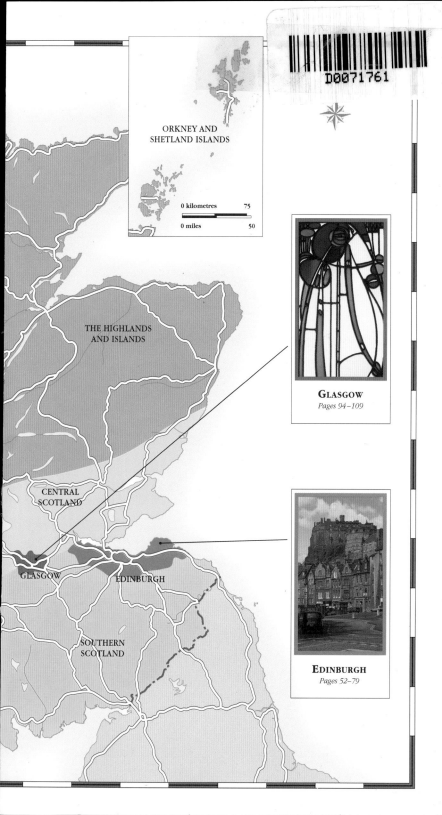

ORKNEY AND
SHETLAND ISLANDS

0 kilometres   75

0 miles   50

THE HIGHLANDS
AND ISLANDS

GLASGOW
Pages 94–109

CENTRAL
SCOTLAND

GLASGOW   EDINBURGH

SOUTHERN
SCOTLAND

EDINBURGH
Pages 52–79

DK TRAVEL GUIDES

SCOTLAND

DORLING KINDERSLEY *TRAVEL GUIDES*

SCOTLAND

Main Contributors: JULIET CLOUGH, KEITH DAVIDSON,
SANDIE RANDALL & ALASTAIR SCOTT

DORLING KINDERSLEY, INC.
LONDON • NEW YORK • SYDNEY • MOSCOW • DELHI
www.dk.com

DORLING KINDERSLEY, INC.

www.dk.com

PROJECT EDITOR Rosalyn Thiro
ART EDITOR Marisa Renzullo
EDITORS Felicity Crowe, Emily Green
DESIGNER Paul Jackson

CONTRIBUTORS
Juliet Clough, Keith Davidson, Alan Freeman,
Sandie Randall, Alastair Scott, Roger Smith

MAPS
Ben Bowles, Rob Clynes
(Colourmap Scanning, London)

PHOTOGRAPHERS
Joe Cornish, Paul Harris, Stephen Whitehorn

ILLUSTRATORS
Richard Bonson, Gary Cross, Jared Gilby,
Paul Guest, Kevin Jones Associates, Claire Littlejohn,
Chris Orr & Associates, Ann Winterbotham

Film output by Graphical Innovations, London
Printed and bound in China by L. Rex Printing Co., Ltd

First American Edition, 1999
2 4 6 8 10 9 7 5 3

Published in the United States by DK Publishing, Inc.,
95 Madison Avenue, New York, New York 10016
Reprinted with revisions 2000

Library of Congress Cataloging-in-Publication Data

Scotland. -- 1st American ed.
    p.   cm. -- (Dorling Kindersley travel guides)
Includes index.
ISBN 0-7894-4621-9 (alk. paper)
1. Scotland -- Guidebooks. I. DK Publishing, Inc. II. Series.
DA870.S364 1999
914.1104'859 -- dc21
                                            99-18500
                                            CIP

The information in every
Dorling Kindersley Travel Guide is checked annually.
Every effort has been made to ensure that this book is as up-to-
date as possible at the time of going to press. Some details,
however, such as telephone numbers, opening hours, prices,
gallery hanging arrangements and travel information are liable to
change. The publishers cannot accept responsibility for any
consequences arising from the use of this book. We value the
views and suggestions of our readers very highly. Please write to:
Editorial Director, Dorling Kindersley Travel Guides,
Dorling Kindersley, 9 Henrietta Street, London WC2E 8PS.

The dramatic, sunlit ruins of Tantallon Ca

CONTENTS

INTRODUCING SCOTLAND

PUTTING SCOTLAND ON THE MAP 8

A PORTRAIT OF SCOTLAND 10

SCOTLAND THROUGH THE YEAR 36

THE HISTORY OF SCOTLAND 40

Mary, Queen of Scots (1542–87)
of the House of Stuart

SCOTLAND REGION BY REGION

SCOTLAND AT A GLANCE 50

◁ The tranquil river, lush greenery and snowy peaks of Glencoe in the Highlands

n the southeast coast

**Royal Scots Greys Memorial to the
Scottish soldiers of the Boer War**

**Detail of the decorated vaulting in
Roslin Chapel, in the Pentland Hills**

**Skirlie – a traditional Scottish dish
of oatmeal, onions and thyme**

SURVIVAL GUIDE

**Walkers enjoying a glorious
summer's day in Glen Etive**

**Edinburgh Castle on its granite
rock above the city centre**

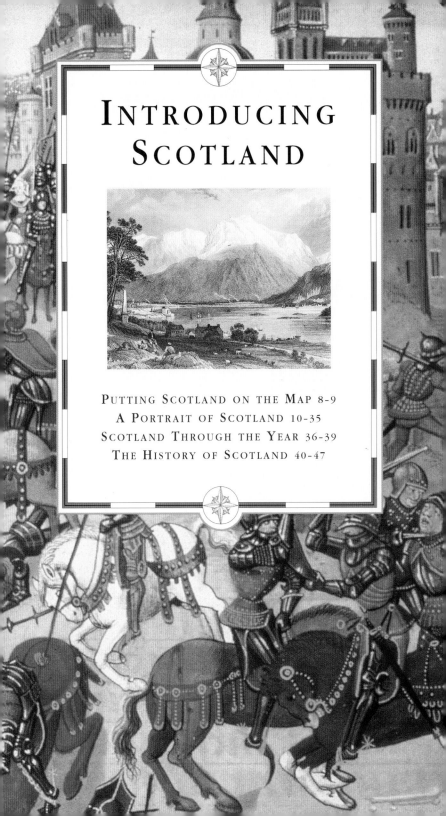

INTRODUCING
SCOTLAND

Putting Scotland on the Map

SEPARATED FROM CONTINENTAL EUROPE by the North Sea, Scotland forms the northern part of Great Britain. It is a mountainous, sparsely populated land. The highest peak is Ben Nevis, at 1,344 m (4,406 ft). The coastline is also ringed by hundreds of islands; at the farthest extreme Shetland lies just six degrees south of the Arctic Circle. Edinburgh is the historic capital, and Glasgow is the largest city with a population of 750,000. The country has good road, rail and ferry connections.

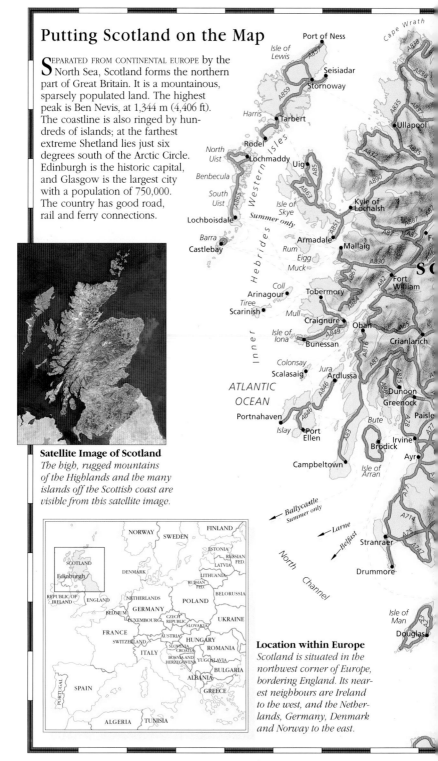

Satellite Image of Scotland
The high, rugged mountains of the Highlands and the many islands off the Scottish coast are visible from this satellite image.

Location within Europe
Scotland is situated in the northwest corner of Europe, bordering England. Its nearest neighbours are Ireland to the west, and the Netherlands, Germany, Denmark and Norway to the east.

◁ **15th-century manuscript showing King David of Scotland at the Battle of Neville's Cross in 1346**

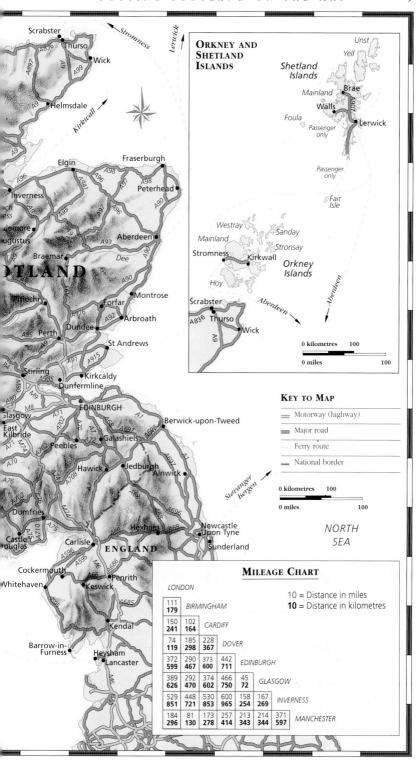

ORKNEY AND SHETLAND ISLANDS

Shetland Islands

Unst
Yell
Mainland
Brae
A970
Walls
Lerwick
Foula
Passenger only
Passenger only

Fair Isle

Westray
Mainland
Sanday
Stromness
Stronsay
Kirkwall
Orkney Islands
Hoy

Scrabster
A836 Thurso
Wick
Aberdeen

0 kilometres 100
0 miles 100

Scrabster
Thurso
Wick
A897 A9 A99
Helmsdale
A9
Kirkwall

Elgin
A96
Fraserburgh
A98
A96
A98
Peterhead
Inverness
A96
A95
A97
A96
A90
iemore
ugustus
Aberdeen
Braemar
Dee
A93
A90
OTLAND
itlochry
A926
Montrose
Forfar
A92
Arbroath
Perth
Dundee
A85
St Andrews
Stirling
A985
A91 A915
Kirkcaldy
Dunfermline
A80 M9
lasgow
M8
EDINBURGH
A1
Berwick-upon-Tweed
East Kilbride
A702
Peebles
Galashiels
A72
Hawick
Jedburgh
Alnwick
A76
Dumfries
Hexham
Newcastle Upon Tyne
Castle ouglas
Carlisle
ENGLAND
Sunderland
Cockermouth
M6
Penrith
Whitehaven
Keswick
A66
A685
Kendal
Barrow-in-Furness
Heysham
Lancaster
M6

NORTH SEA

Stavanger bergen

KEY TO MAP

═══ Motorway (highway)
▬▬▬ Major road
‒ ‒ ‒ Ferry route
〰〰 National border

0 kilometres 100
0 miles 100

MILEAGE CHART

LONDON

10 = Distance in miles
10 = Distance in kilometres

LONDON							
111 **179**	BIRMINGHAM						
150 **241**	102 **164**	CARDIFF					
74 **119**	185 **298**	228 **367**	DOVER				
372 **599**	290 **467**	373 **600**	442 **711**	EDINBURGH			
389 **626**	292 **470**	374 **602**	466 **750**	45 **72**	GLASGOW		
529 **851**	448 **721**	530 **853**	600 **965**	158 **254**	167 **269**	INVERNESS	
184 **296**	81 **130**	173 **278**	257 **414**	213 **343**	214 **344**	371 **597**	MANCHESTER

A PORTRAIT OF SCOTLAND

W*ITH SUCH A DISTINCTIVE national dress, drink, bagpipe music, landscape and folklore, Scotland has shaped an identity recognizable the world over. It is a land of astonishing contrasts and possesses a magical quality, whether seen shrouded in mist or rising majestic above the mirror of a loch.*

In a straight line from the far south to the far north, the Scottish mainland reaches about 440 km (275 miles), yet its coastline stretches nearly 10,000 km (6,200 miles). There are 787 major islands, almost all lying off the northern or western coasts. The topography is generally extremely mountainous with wild heather moorlands in the north and west, pine forests mixed with quality pasture in the middle, fertile farmland in the east and, in the south, the rounded, grass-covered hills of the Lowlands. Picturesque lochs and rivers are scattered throughout. Most of Scotland's five million people live in the country's Central Belt.

Red deer in the Highlands

The Scots cherish the differences that set them apart from the English, and cling tenaciously to the distinctions that differentiate them region by region – their customs, dialects and the Gaelic language. It is perhaps more by their differences than similarities that the Scots can be defined but, for all that, they are immensely proud of their nation and its separate institutions, such as education and law. The Scots can be dour but equally they can flash with inspiration. They delight in self-deprecating humour and continue to honour their tradition of hospitality.

A view from Edinburgh Castle over the rooftops of the capital to Calton Hill

◁ Isolated dwellings set among the lofty mountains on Skye, the largest island of the Inner Hebrides

POLITICS AND THE ECONOMY

Ever since the Treaty of Union in 1707, which combined the parliaments of Scotland and England into one governing body convening in Westminster (London), Scotland has felt estranged from the mechanisms of government, and short-changed by the small allocation of time given to Scottish affairs. Today, all the major political parties of the UK find support in Scotland. The Scottish National Party, which campaigns for complete independence, has gained in popularity. In 1997 the Scots voted for the re-establishment of a Scottish parliament, to begin in 1999. This parliament has a wide-ranging administrative role, though major financial controls and decisions of national interest are retained by Westminster.

A hammer-thrower at the Braemar Games

Scotland's economy has fluctuated in the last 100 years. It has had to fight back from the demise of its heavy industries – shipbuilding, coal mining and steel production. Today, the major contributors to the economy are North Sea oil, tourism and services, aided by a wide spectrum of light industries. Chief among these is the manufacture of electronic components and microchips, contributing to the sobriquet of a "Silicon Glen", but this industry, which employs many people, has become shaky in response to the global market.

Whisky production is a leading revenue earner for the Exchequer (treasury department), although it employs few people. Agriculture retains its importance but has become beleaguered by disastrous markets. Fishing also remains an important industry, yet there is increasing competition for dwindling stocks. Scotland's level of unemployment is on a par with the UK, though there are worse-off areas, such as the Western Isles where it reaches 15 per cent.

SOCIETY

The Scots are a gregarious people and enjoy company, whether this be in a small group at a Highland *ceilidh* (literally, a "visit"), a crowded bar, or as part of the colourful, and usually peaceful, Saturday armies of football (soccer) fans. Sometimes they have to travel far to find company; the Highland region has a population density of eight people per square kilometre (20 per sq mile), and the lack of public transport means a car is vital.

Edinburgh bagpiper

Church attendance is in decline in all but the Gaelic-speaking areas, where Sundays are observed as days of rest. In most towns, and all cities, a full range of leisure activities and entertainment runs into the wee hours, but in rural areas opening hours are shorter, and restaurants may stop serving early.

Scotland is renowned as the home of golf, but football is without doubt the national passion, and England the favourite opponent. Other popular sports include hill-walking, skiing, rugby, shinty and curling. There are also annual Highland Games – great gatherings of whisky, music, craft stalls and tests of stamina and strength (*see p29*).

The Viking fire festival, *Up Helly Aa*, in Shetland

Small-scale farming in the Western Isles

many smaller festivals. The Scottish film industry is booming, following the success of *Trainspotting* (1993). The musical scene has also been enjoying a time of vibrancy, ranging from opera, Gaelic song, *pibroch* (the classical music of the bagpipes) to such varied international bands as Simple Minds, Runrig, Texas and Wet Wet Wet. Traditional music has experienced a renaissance over the last decade using rhythms and instruments from around the world. With an estimated four Scots living abroad for every one living in the homeland, this influence is not surprising. Bands like Macumba combine bagpipes and Brazilian percussion to wonderful effect. In dance, on offer are the varied delights of Scottish country, Highland and *ceilidh* dancing and step dancing, a tradition reintroduced from Cape Breton.

Yet for all their love of sports, the Scots are an unhealthy race. Their appetite for red meat and greasy fish and chips contributes to a high incidence of heart problems, and they have the highest consumption of alcohol and tobacco in the UK.

CULTURE AND THE ARTS

Scotland offers an excellent programme of the performing arts, subsidized generously by the Scottish Arts Council. The Edinburgh Festival and Fringe *(see pp 78–9)* is the largest celebration of its kind in the world, and there are

Edinburgh's Festival Fringe Office detail

Although only about 50,000 people speak Gaelic, the language has been boosted by increased funding for Gaelic radio and television programmes. Literature has a strong following, too, with no shortage of respected Scottish authors and poets *(see pp 24–5)*.

The blue waters of Loch Achray in the heart of the Trossachs, north of Glasgow

The Geology of Scotland

SCOTLAND IS A GEOLOGIST'S PLAYGROUND, with rocks displaying three billion years of geological time. Starting with the hard granitic gneiss in the Western Isles, which was formed before life developed on earth, the rocks tell a story of lava flows, eras of mountain-building, numerous ice ages and even a time when the land was separated from England by the ancient Iapetus Ocean. Four major fault and thrust lines, running across Scotland from north-east to southwest, define the main geological zones.

FAULT AND THRUST LINES

– – Moine Thrust

– – Great Glen Fault *(see pp148–9)*

– – Highland Boundary Fault

– – Southern Uplands Fault

The gabbro (dark rock) of the Cuillin Hills on Skye was created by subterranean magma in the Tertiary period, a time when the dinosaurs had died out and mammals were flourishing.

CHANGING EARTH

Scotland
Equator
Iapetus Ocean
England

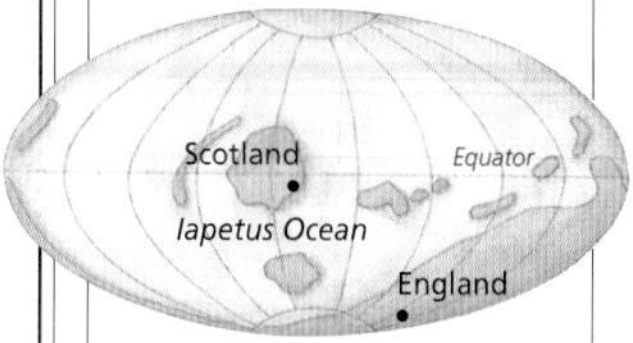

☐ Ancient landmass

About 500 million years ago
Scotland was part of a landmass that included North America, while England was part of Gondwana. After 75 million years of continental breakup and drift, the two countries "collided", not far from the modern political boundary.

Scandinavia

Scotland

☐ Glaciation in the last Ice Age

··· Present-day national boundaries

The last Ice Age, which ended 10,000 years ago, was the most recent chapter in Scotland's geological history when, like Scandinavia, it became glaciated.

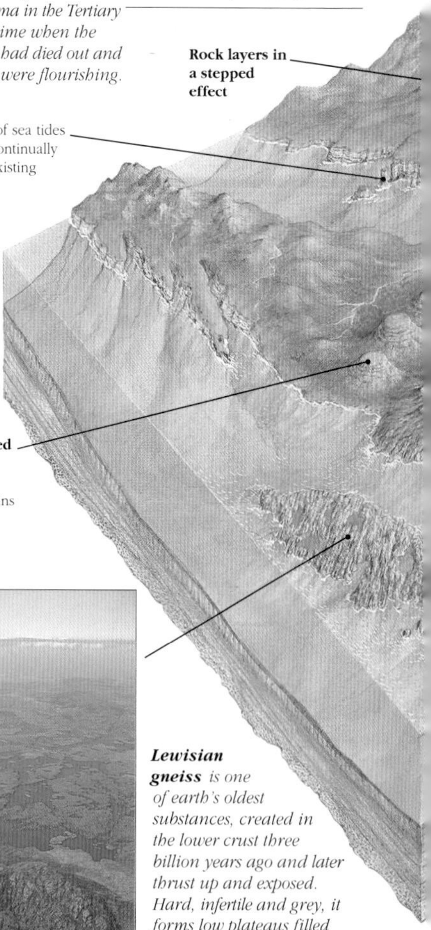

The action of sea tides and waves continually erodes the existing coastline.

Rock layers in a stepped effect

Plateau-topped hills on the island are the exposed remains of a basalt lava flow.

Lewisian gneiss is one of earth's oldest substances, created in the lower crust three billion years ago and later thrust up and exposed. Hard, infertile and grey, it forms low plateaus filled with thousands of small lochs in the Western Isles.

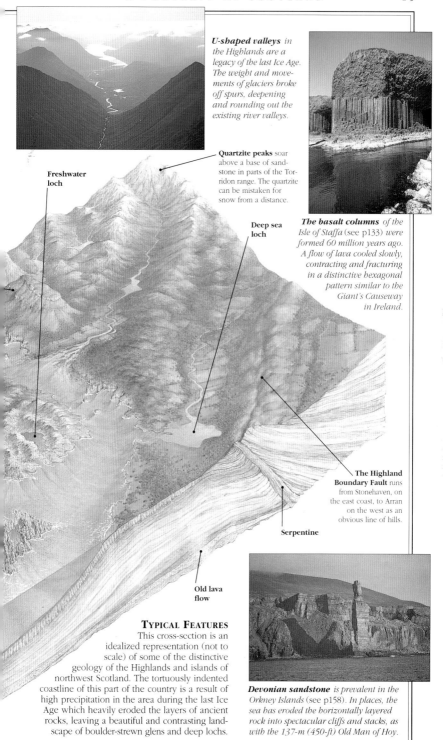

U-shaped valleys *in the Highlands are a legacy of the last Ice Age. The weight and movements of glaciers broke off spurs, deepening and rounding out the existing river valleys.*

Quartzite peaks soar above a base of sandstone in parts of the Torridon range. The quartzite can be mistaken for snow from a distance.

Freshwater loch

Deep sea loch

The basalt columns *of the Isle of Staffa (see p133) were formed 60 million years ago. A flow of lava cooled slowly, contracting and fracturing in a distinctive hexagonal pattern similar to the Giant's Causeway in Ireland.*

The Highland Boundary Fault runs from Stonehaven, on the east coast, to Arran on the west as an obvious line of hills.

Serpentine

Old lava flow

TYPICAL FEATURES

This cross-section is an idealized representation (not to scale) of some of the distinctive geology of the Highlands and islands of northwest Scotland. The tortuously indented coastline of this part of the country is a result of high precipitation in the area during the last Ice Age which heavily eroded the layers of ancient rocks, leaving a beautiful and contrasting landscape of boulder-strewn glens and deep lochs.

Devonian sandstone *is prevalent in the Orkney Islands (see p158). In places, the sea has eroded the horizontally layered rock into spectacular cliffs and stacks, as with the 137-m (450-ft) Old Man of Hoy.*

The Landscape and Wildlife of Scotland

SCOTLAND IS A LAND OF CONTRASTS, from the austere majesty of the mountains to the subtle undulations of the Lowland valleys, and from dramatic coastal cliffs to dense forests. It is in the wilds of the Highlands and islands that you are most likely to encounter Scotland's wealth of wildlife. Many once prolific species are slowly dying out; preserving them and their habitats is now paramount.

A tiny goldcrest

NATIVE ANIMALS

There are no large or dangerous wild animals in Scotland, but there are a few which are rarely found living wild elsewhere in the British Isles. Shetland ponies and Highland cattle, by their names alone, are instantly associated with Scotland, and you are unlikely to see a golden eagle or red deer outside of the Scottish Highlands.

COASTAL

The immense, windswept coastline of Scotland provides some of the best chances to view the country's wildlife. Islands such as Skye *(see pp152–3)*, pictured above, sustain myriad nesting seabirds, including puffins, guillemots and kittiwakes, while the Bass Rock, off the east coast near North Berwick, has a breeding colony of gannets. The Scottish coast is also home to seals, whales and dolphins.

Puffin

Grey seals *have long inhabited the rocky Scottish coasts, such as in Shetland or in North Rona, and are easily spotted.*

Kittiwakes, *with their white and grey plumage, are widespread along the Scottish cliffs, from St Abb's Head on the east coast to Handa Island off the northwest coast (see p157).*

LOCHS AND RIVERS

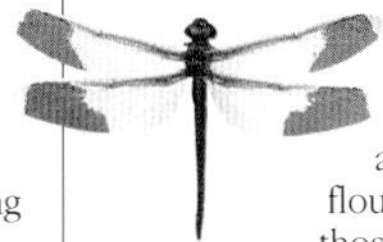

Scotland has an abundance of sea lochs, fresh water lochs and rivers, enabling a wide range of animal and insect life to flourish. Sea lochs, such as those shown above on the western isle of North Uist, may contain wild salmon and otters, although the latter are more likely to be spotted at a manmade sanctuary, such as the one at Kylerhea on Skye. Many Scottish rivers, the Tay being just one example, provide a wonderful opportunity for fishermen to catch salmon and trout.

Dragonfly

Wild otters *breed along many parts of Scotland's coast and in its sea lochs. Unlike their Asian cousins, they have webbed feet with which they catch and eat their prey.*

Salmon *swim into Scotland's lochs and rivers every year to breed. They travel miles upstream and up steep waterfalls in order to spawn.*

Shetland ponies are indigenous to the windswept, northerly isles of the same name, but can also be found on the mainland. The ponies are small, with thick, wiry coats.

Highland cattle, bred in Scotland since the 1500s, are recognizable by their long horns and shaggy coats.

The golden eagle is one of Scotland's most enduring emblems. Found at high altitudes, this majestic bird takes its prey in one silent swoop.

MOUNTAIN AND MOORLAND

The hills and mountains of Scotland are a refuge for rare arctic and alpine plants, while heather and grasses flourish on the moorlands and Lowlands. This contrast of landscapes can be seen right across the Scottish Highlands and islands, as shown here on Mull. Birds of prey, such as eagles and kestrels, favour this terrain; red deer graze on the bleak moorland.

Kestrel

WOODLAND AND FOREST

Some of Scotland's forests form part of a protected Forest Park. Woodland refuges, such as the one in the Borders shown above, are home to red squirrels and goldcrests, while pine martens and wildcats favour the rockier terrain of the Highland forests. Birch and oak woods are dotted around the country.

Pine marten

Sheep roam freely on the moorland and hills of Scotland, but they are usally marked so they can be identified by the farmer.

Red deer are the most common deer in Europe and can often be sighted in the Highlands of Scotland. Their signature coats are at their most vibrant in summer. The stags shed their antlers in spring.

Wildcats can still be found in forest areas, but their numbers are dwindling. A stocky body, thick fur and short, blunt tail distinguish them from a domestic cat.

Red squirrels are far rarer than their grey counterparts, but they share the same bushy tail for agility and communication, and sharp, hooked claws for a sure grip on trees.

Evolution of the Scottish Castle

Few sights can match the romance of a Scottish castle set upon a small island in the middle of a quiet loch. These formidable retreats, often in remote settings, were built all over the Highlands, where incursions and strife between the clans were common. From the earliest Pictish *brochs* (Iron Age stone towers) and Norman-influenced motte and bailey castles, the distinctively Scottish tower-house evolved, first appearing in the 14th century. By the mid-17th century fashion had become more important than defence, and there followed a period in which numerous huge Scottish palaces were built.

Detail of the Baroque façade, Drumlanrig

MOTTE AND BAILEY

These castles first appeared in the 12th century. They stood atop two adjacent mounds enclosed by a wall, or palisade, and defensive ditches. The higher mound, or motte, was the most strongly defended as it held the keep and chief's house. The lower bailey was where the common people lived.

The keep contained the chief's house, lookout and main defence.

Duffus Castle, Morayshire

Duffus Castle
(c.1150) was atypically made of stone rather than wood. Its fine defensive position dominates the surrounding flatlands north of Elgin.

The Motte of earth or rock was sometimes partially man-made.

The Bailey enclosed dwellings and storehouses.

EARLY TOWER-HOUSE

Designed to deter local attacks rather than a major assault, the first tower-houses appeared in the 13th century, and their design lived on for 400 years. They were built initially on a rectangular plan, with a single tower divided into three or four floors. The walls were unadorned, with few windows. Defensive structures were on top, and extra space was made by building adjoining towers. Extensions were vertical, to minimize the area open to attack.

Crenellated parapet for sentries

Claypotts Castle (c.1570), with uniquely projecting garrets above its towers

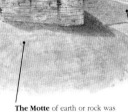

Braemar Castle (c.1630), a con-glomeration of extended towers

Neidpath Castle, standing upon a steep rocky crag above the River Tweed, is an L-shaped tower-house dating from the late 14th century. Once a stronghold for Charles II, its walls still bear damage from a siege conducted by Oliver Cromwell.

Featureless, straight walls contain arrow slits for windows.

LATER TOWER-HOUSE

Though the requirements of defence were being replaced by those of comfort, the style of the early tower-house remained popular. By the 17th century wings for accommodation were being added around the original tower (often creating a courtyard). The battlements and turrets were kept more for decorative than defensive reasons.

Drum Castle, near Aberdeen, a 13th-century keep with a mansion house extension from 1619

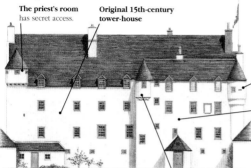

The priest's room has secret access.

Original 15th-century tower-house

This round angle tower contains a stairway.

Sixteenth-century horizontal extension

Traquair House (see p87), *by the Tweed, is reputedly the oldest continuously inhabited house in Scotland. The largely unadorned, roughcast exterior dates from the 16th century, when a series of extensions were built around the original 15th-century tower-house.*

Decorative, corbelled turret

Blair Castle *(see p139),* **incorporating a medieval tower**

CLASSICAL PALACE

By the 18th century the defensive imperative had passed and castles were built in the manner of country houses, rejecting the vertical tower-house in favour of a horizontal plan (though the building of imitation fortified buildings continued into the 19th century with the mock-Baronial trend). Outside influences came from all over Europe, including Renaissance and Gothic revivals, and echoes of French châteaux.

Dunrobin Castle (c.1840), Perthshire

Larger windows are due to a lesser need for defence.

Balustrades replace defensive battlements.

Decorative cupola

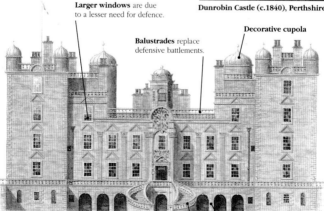

Drumlanrig Castle (see p88) *was built in the 17th century and has traditional Scots aspects as well as Renaissance features, such as the decorated stairway and façade.*

Renaissance-style colonnade

Baroque horseshoe stairway

Scottish Gardens

SCOTLAND HAS A GREAT number of diverse
and beautiful gardens. Some are renowned
for their layout, such as Pitmedden, or for
particular plants. Rhododendrons flourish in
Scotland's acidic, peaty soil, and the Royal
Botanic Garden in Edinburgh is famous for its
spectacular, colourful display. Some gardens
have a striking backdrop of lakes or mountains,
while others form the grounds of a stately
home. Gulf Stream gardens like Inverewe offer
visitors a rare chance to view exotic, subtropical
flora at a northern
latitude. The gardens
shown here are some
of Scotland's finest.

Inverewe Gardens (see p156) *are
renowned for their lush, exotic,
subtropical flora. Ferns, lilies,
giant forget-me-nots and rare
palms are just some of the
2,500 species that thrive
in the mild climate.*

Crarae Gardens (see p130)
*are sited on a slope overlook-
ing Loch Fyne, surrounded
by mature woodland. There
are many walks, all designed
to cross a picturesque burn at
the centre. The gardens are
riotous with spectacular rhododendrons in spring and ablaze
with golden and russet leaves
during the autumn.*

*The Botanic Gardens,
Glasgow* (see p103)*, have a
wonderful collection of orchids,
begonias and cacti. Kibble
Palace, a domed, iron conservatory, houses tropical tree ferns
from around the world.*

*Logan Botanic Garden is an
outpost of the Royal Botanic
Garden in Edinburgh. The
garden is divided into two main
areas – a walled garden with
cabbage palms, and a woodland
area. The Gulf Stream enables
subtropical plants to grow here.*

Inverewe
Gardens

Angus'
Garden

Crarae
Gardens

Arduaine
Garden

Botanic
Gardens,
Glasgow

Younger
Botanic
Garden

Logan
Botanic
Garden

THE RHODODENDRON

These examples illustrate three of
the 900 rhododendron varieties. The
first is tropical, grown under glass
in Scotland; the second is evergreen;
the third is an azalea, which used
to be considered a separate species.
Rhododendrons also fall into scaly-
leaved and non-scaly groups.

Macgregoriae

Augustini

Medway

Drummond Castle Gardens *are laid out as a large boxwood parterre in the shape of a St Andrew's Cross. Yellow and red roses and antirrhinums provide the colour, and a sundial forms the centrepiece.*

THE GULF STREAM

The west coast of Scotland is the surprising location for a number of gardens where tropical and subtropical plants bloom. Although on the same latitude as Siberia, this area of Scotland lies in the path of a warm water current from the Atlantic. Inverewe is the most famous of the Gulf Stream gardens, with plants from South America, South Africa and the South Pacific. Other gardens include Achamore on the Isle of Gigha and Logan Botanic Garden near Stranraer.

Eucalyptus tree ferns warmed by the Gulf Stream, Logan Botanic Garden

Pitmedden Garden •

Crathes Gardens •

Pitmedden Garden *was created in 1675 and later restored to its full glory as a formal garden by the National Trust for Scotland. Split into two levels, it has four parterres, two gazebos, box hedges and a splendid fountain at its centre.*

Drummond
Castle
Gardens
•

• Royal Botanic
Garden, Edinburgh

Kailzie Gardens
•

Dawyck   Priorwood
Botanic   Gardens
Garden

0 kilometres   50

0 miles   50

Crathes Gardens' *topiary and scented borders are centred around the beautiful tower house, Crathes Castle (see p145). There are eight different themed gardens, such as the Golden Garden designed in the style of Gertrude Jeckyll.*

Dawyck Botanic Garden *is another branch of Edinburgh's Botanic Garden, and specializes in rare trees, such as the Dawyck Beech, flowering shrubs and blankets of narcissi. The garden's chapel was designed by William Burn.*

The Royal Botanic Garden, Edinburgh *(see p68), is internationally renowned as a base for scientific research, as well as having a marvellous range of plants. Enhanced by beautifully maintained lawns, it nurtures almost 17,000 species. Exotic plants are found in the many glasshouses.*

Great Scottish Inventions

Marmalade

DESPITE ITS RELATIVELY small size and population, Scotland has produced a remarkable number of inventors over the centuries. The late 1700s and 1800s were years of such intense creativity that they became known as the Period of Scottish Enlightenment. Many technological, medicinal and mechanical breakthroughs were made at this time, including the invention of the steam engine, the bicycle, antiseptic and the telephone. Out of the country's factories, universities and laboratories came a breed of men who were intrepid and forward-thinking. Their revolutionary ideas and experiments produced inventions that have shaped our modern, progressive society.

Logarithm tables (1594) were devised by John Napier as a practical way of multiplying and dividing large numbers. Though easy to use, the tables took 20 years to create.

Continous electric light (1834) was invented by James Bowman Lindsay using galvanic cells in a revolutionary design.

The pneumatic tyre/tire (John Dunlop, 1887), was originally patented by RW Thomson and then developed by Dunlop for use on bicycles and, later, cars.

Parallel motion operated all the valves in time.

Piston rod

A flywheel stored energy so that the engine ran smoothly.

Golf clubs were originally wooden and hand-crafted by carpenters such as Old Tom Morris. By 1890, aluminium-headed clubs had been introduced.

The rotative steam engine (James Watt, 1782) was a refinement of the existing steam engine. This new model soon became the driving force behind the Industrial Revolution in Britain, powering all manner of machinery. Watt's success led to his name being given to the modern unit of power.

The bicycle (Kirkpatrick Macmillan, 1839) was originally known as a velocipede, and it was not until the 1860s that bicycles began to be manufactured and sold in significantly large quantities.

Colour photography (1861) was developed by the Scottish physicist, James C Maxwell. The first to experiment with three-colour photography, he photographed this tartan ribbon using coloured water as a filter.

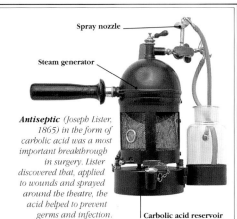

Spray nozzle

Steam generator

Antiseptic (Joseph Lister, 1865) in the form of carbolic acid was a most important breakthrough in surgery. Lister discovered that, applied to wounds and sprayed around the theatre, the acid helped to prevent germs and infection.

Carbolic acid reservoir

The thermos flask (Sir James Dewar, 1892) was first designed as a vacuum for storing low-temperature gases. The flask was later mass produced as the thermos, for maintaining the temperature of hot and cold drinks.

The telephone (Alexander Graham Bell, 1876) was the scientific breakthrough that revolutionized the way the world communicated, introducing the transmission of sound by electricity.

Penicillin (Alexander Fleming, 1928) is a discovery that has changed the face of medicine. Fleming's brainchild was the first antibiotic drug to treat diseases, and by 1940 it was being used to save the lives of wounded soldiers.

The radar receiver (Robert Watson-Watt, 1935) was in use long before World War II, since Watson-Watt's team had built the first working radar defence system by 1935. Radar is an acronym for "radio detection and ranging".

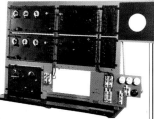

The first television (John Logie Baird, 1926), or "televisor", was black and white, and unable to produce sound and pictures together, but it was nevertheless hailed as a monumental invention. In 1928, Baird demonstrated the possibilities of creating colour images.

Dolly the cloned sheep was developed in 1996 by a team of scientists at Edinburgh's Roslin Institute. Dolly, the first successful clone of an adult animal in the world, gave birth in 1998.

Writers and Intellectuals

FROM MEDIEVAL POETS through Robert Burns to Irvine Welsh, writers in the three literary languages of Scotland – Scots, English and Gaelic – have created a body of literature expressing both their place in the European mainstream and the diversity within Scotland. Three centuries after the dissolution of its parliament, Scotland stands on the threshold of a new one. Political devolution follows three decades of ferment in which literature has reached new heights of success.

THE GOLDEN AGE BEFORE ENLIGHTENMENT

OFTEN REGARDED as the golden age of Scottish literature, the century leading up to the Reformation of 1560 showed strong links with the Continent and a rich tradition of poetry, culminating in the achievements of William Dunbar and Robert Henryson. John Barbour established the mythic heroism of the national hero in *The Bruce* (c.1375). Other early works were James I's *Kingis Quair* (c.1424) and Blind Harry's *Wallace* (c.1478).

Dunbar rose to pre-eminence for his polished art, from *Lament for the Makars* (1508), an elegy to poets, to his insult poetry known as "flyting". Henryson's work has insight, as in *The Testament of Cresseid* (c.1480), which tells the legend from the woman's point of view. Gavin Douglas translated Virgil's *Aeneid* into Scots in 1513. The golden age ended with Sir David Lindsay's much revived play, *A Satire of the Three Estates*, in 1540. The ballad tradition continues to influence Scottish literature.

Philosopher David Hume

ENLIGHTENMENT AND ROMANTICISM

THE INTELLECTUAL TRIUMPHS of the Enlightenment in Scotland were fuelled by the expanding educational system. Among the great thinkers of the time were Adam Smith (1723–90), who theorized on political economy, and Adam Ferguson (1723–1816), who founded modern sociology. Other prominent figures were William Robertson (1721–93) and David Hume (1711–76), both of whom helped to define modern history. Hume's greatest legacy was in philosophy – his rigorous empiricism offended Christian orthodoxy and foretold crises of faith versus scientific knowledge. James Macpherson published the *Ossian Chronicles* in 1760, supposedly the documentation of his discovery of an old Celtic tradition in the Hebrides. This fictional work tapped a nostalgia for ancient civilizations and, allied to fears about progress, Romanticism was born. Allan Ramsay wrote poems in Scots, as did the tragic Robert Fergusson, who died in poverty aged 25.

The country's most fêted literary figure, Robert Burns (1759–96), was a man of his time. His "heaven-taught ploughman" persona fitted fashion but belied a sound education. His works ranged from love lyrics to savage satire (*Holy Willie's Prayer*), nationalism to radical ideals (*A Man's a Man for a' That*).

Robert Burns encircled by images of his literary creations

THE 19TH CENTURY

DESPITE THE importance of Edinburgh in British culture, it was the pattern of leaving Scotland to achieve fame in London, initiated in the mid-18th century by James Boswell and Tobias Smollett, that would predominate in the Victorian decades.

The poetry of Walter Scott (1771–1832) enjoyed phenomenal success. His novels, especially *Waverley* (1814), rose to greater glory. Francis Jeffrey's Whig-orientated *Edinburgh Review* led opinion, challenged by *Blackwood's* Tory alternative. James Hogg published by the latter work before writing his startling,

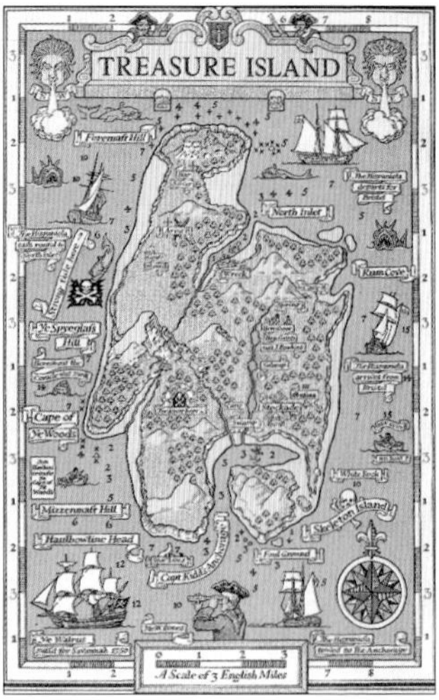

Map of Robert Louis Stevenson's Treasure Island, based on an island in the Firth of Forth

gothic *Private Memoirs and Confessions of a Justified Sinner* (1824). Following Susan Ferrier and John Galt, standards were modest, despite the prodigious career of Margaret Oliphant. Thomas Carlyle noted the provinciality of Edinburgh in the 1830s.

A later response to anxieties of the age came from Robert Louis Stevenson (1850–94) in *Dr Jekyll and Mr Hyde*. This contrasted with the sentimentality of home-spun or so-called kailyard (literally "cabbage patch") fiction, led by JM Barrie and SR Crockett. Barrie's dramas often catered for bourgeois tastes, as did the *Sherlock Holmes* stories of Arthur Conan Doyle (1859–1930), which endure today.

Arthur Conan Doyle's sleuth, Sherlock Holmes, in *The Graphic* (1901)

***Rob Roy* film poster (1995), from Walter Scott's novel of 1817**

EARLY 20TH-CENTURY RENAISSANCE

GEORGE DOUGLAS BROWN'S fierce anti-kailyard novel, *The House with the Green Shutters* (1901), opened the century and serious art was reborn. Hugh MacDiarmid's poetry in the 1920s carried literature into the stream of modernism. *A Drunk Man Looks at the Thistle* (1926) combines disparate Scottish dialects with political and social commentary in one of the century's great symbolist works. Edwin Muir also won international acclaim. Successors included Sidney Goodsir Smith and William Soutar. Fiction reached epic and innovative proportions with Neil Gunn (*Butcher's Broom*, 1933) and Lewis Grassic Gibbon (*A Scots Quair*, 1932–4). Others included Willa Muir, Nan Shepherd and Fionn MacColla. John Buchan attempted serious work and popular thrillers. Nationalist impetus was dissipated by the rise of fascism, and new directions were sought after World War II.

POST-1945

SORLEY MACLEAN wrote in his native Gaelic of the ancient Highland culture's plight. Norman MacCaig began a career characterized by metaphysical whimsy, and George Bruce and Robert Garioch evoked the strictures of nature and social class. Edwin Morgan has celebrated art and modernity (*Sonnets from Scotland*, 1984), Liz Lochhead continues to produce fresh drama and poetry and, among the newest generation, Jackie Kay explores the experience of being a black Scottish citizen in prose and poetry. While James Bridie, Bill Bryden and John Byrne made an impact in the theatre, Muriel Spark rose to international acclaim for her blackly comic novels (*The Prime of Miss Jean Brodie*, 1961). Urban realism developed quietly before William MacIlvanney's breakthrough with *The Big Man* (1985).

Following Alasdair Gray's bizarre *Lanark* (1981), a powerful wave propelled fiction into the highly productive present, in which Iain Banks remains a bestseller (*The Crow Road*, 1992). Tom Leonard's poems initiated a tradition using urban demotic speech. James Kelman elevated this to new levels: the Booker Prize-winning *How Late it Was, How Late* (1994) affirms ordinary life within a Kafkaesque vision of sinister bureaucracy. Irvine Welsh's portrayal of drug culture is now world famous, though the energy and profundity of *Trainspotting* (1993) is absent from its successors. The private dramas articulated in AL Kennedy's stories are poignant and mysterious (*So I am Glad*, 1995).

"Trainspotting is the best British film of the decade" ★★★★★ EMPIRE

Poster for the film version of Irvine Welsh's novel

Clans and Tartans

THE CLAN SYSTEM, by which Highland society was divided into tribal groups led by autocratic chiefs, can be traced to the 12th century, when clans were already known to wear the chequered wool cloth later called tartan. All members of the clan bore the name of their chief, but not all were related by blood. Though they had noble codes of hospitality, the clansmen had to be warriors to protect their herds, as can be seen from their mottoes. After the Battle of Culloden *(see p146)*, all the clan lands were forfeited to the Crown, and the wearing of tartan was banned for nearly 100 years.

The Mackays, also known as the Clan Morgan, won lasting renown during the Thirty Years War.

The MacLeods are of Norse heritage. The clan chief still lives in Dunvegan Castle, Skye.

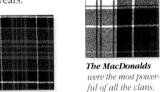

The MacDonalds were the most powerful of all the clans, holding the title of Lords of the Isles.

The Mackenzies received much of the lands of Kintail (see p151) from David II in 1362.

CLAN CHIEF

The chief was the clan's patriarch, judge and leader in war, commanding absolute loyalty from his clansmen who gave military service in return for his protection. The chief summoned his clan to do battle by sending a runner across his land bearing a burning cross.

Bonnet with eagle feathers, clan crest and plant badge.

Dirk

Sporran, or pouch, made of badger's skin.

Feileadh-mor, or "great plaid" (the early kilt), wrapped around waist and shoulder.

Basket-hilted sword

The Campbells were a widely feared clan who fought the Jacobites in 1746 (see p147).

The Black Watch, raised in 1729 to keep peace in the Highlands, was one of the Highland regiments in which the wearing of tartan survived. After 1746, civilians were punished by exile for up to seven years for wearing tartan.

The Sinclairs came from France in the 11th century and became Earls of Caithness in 1455.

George IV, dressed as a Highlander, visited Edinburgh in 1822, the year of the tartan revival. Many tartan "sets" (patterns) date from this time, as the original ones were lost.

PLANT BADGES

Each clan had a plant associated with its territory. It was worn on the bonnet, especially on the day of battle.

Scots pine was worn by the MacGregors of Argyll.

The Frasers came over to Britain from France with William the Conqueror and his followers in 1066.

Rowan berries were worn by the Clan Malcolm.

The Gordons were famously good soldiers; the clan motto was "by courage, not by craft".

Ivy was worn by the Clan Gordon of Aberdeenshire.

The Stuarts were Scotland's royal dynasty. Their motto was "no one harms me with impunity".

Spear thistle, now a national symbol, was a Stuart badge.

CLAN TERRITORIES

The territories of 10 major clans are marked here with their clan crests and tartan. The patterns shown are modern versions of original tartan designs.

The Douglas clan was prominent in Scottish history, though its origin is unknown.

Cotton grass was worn by the Clan Henderson.

HIGHLAND CLANS TODAY

Once the daily dress of the clansmen, the kilt is now largely reserved for formal occasions. The one-piece *feileadh-mor* has been replaced by the *feileadh-beag*, or "small plaid", made from approximately 7 m (23 ft) of material with a double apron fastened at the front with a silver pin. Though they exist now only in name, the clans are still a strong source of pride to Scots, and many still live in areas traditionally belonging to their clans. Many visitors to Britain can trace their Scots ancestry back to the Highlands.

Modern Highland formal dress

Highland Music and Games

THE HIGHLANDS AND ISLANDS of Scotland have been the focus of Gaelic culture for hundreds of years. Although the language itself is little spoken today, the legacy of the Gaelic lifestyle lives on in the music and activities of the people. The bagpipes, a traditional Highland instrument, are an important part of Scotland's identity around the world, and the Highland Games are an amalgamation of the Gaelic customs of music, dancing and contests of strength.

The blow-pipe is used to inflate the bag by blowing air, as continuously as possible, into the pipe's mouthpiece.

A piper's hat is made traditionally from ostrich feathers.

Pibroch is the classical music of the piping world. Played by solo pipers, these slow, melancholy tunes produce a haunting sound that is easier on the ear than the almost discordant sound a group of bagpipers makes.

The chanter is a pipe with six finger-holes, used to play the melody.

The drones, or "borduns", are the three pipes that give the pitch. They are pitched on a fixed note, one bass and the other two higher, each at intervals of a fifth.

The bag, made from animal hide, is inflated by air from the blow-pipe; the air is then expelled under pressure applied by the piper's elbow.

THE BAGPIPES

Bagpipes have been the traditional sound of the Highlands for many centuries and are thought to have been introduced to Britain by the Romans. After the Battle of Culloden in 1746 they were banned for 11 years, along with Highland dress, for inspiring the Highlanders to rebel against English rule. The pipes have now become one of the most recognized emblems of Scotland.

TRADITIONAL GAELIC MUSIC

Music has always featured strongly in the Highlands' Gaelic communities. Solo instruments include the harp and accordion, and *ceilidh* bands are still common.

Accordions have accompanied ceilidhs ever since the dances began in the crofting communities of the Scottish Highlands and islands.

The harp *is Irish in origin but was introduced to Scotland in the 1800s. The "clarsach", as it is known, has enjoyed a revival in recent years.*

Ceilidh bands *are an alternative to the solo accordion as accompaniment for the modern* ceilidh *(a Gaelic word for "visit"). The band's instruments usually include fiddles, accordions and penny whistles.*

HIGHLAND GAMES AND ACTIVITIES

As well as music, the Highlands of Scotland are famous for their Games. The first Games took place many hundreds of years ago, and may have served a military purpose by allowing clan chiefs to choose the strongest men from those competing in contests of strength. Highland Games are held annually at Braemar *(see p38)*, as well as at Oban and Dunoon, among others. Another activity in the Highlands is the re-enactment of past battles and rebellions.

Re-enacting Highland battles *is popular with modern-day clansmen to commemorate their forefathers' fight for freedom. The above occasion was the 250th anniversary of the Battle of Culloden, where over 2,000 Highland warriors died.*

The Highland Games (or Gatherings) *as they are played today date from the 1820s. The most common contests and events are tossing the caber, weight shifting, piping, singing, dancing and throwing the hammer. The result is a cacophany of sound and activity, which can be overwhelming to a first-time spectator.*

Throwing the hammer *involves revolving on the spot to gather speed, while swinging the hammer (a weight on the end of a long pole) around the head, before launching it across the field. The winner is the contestant whose hammer reaches the furthest distance.*

Tossing the caber is *one of the most famous Highland sports, and requires strength and skill. The athlete must run with the tree trunk and toss it so that it flips over 180° and lands vertically, straight ahead.*

Highland dancing *is an important part of the Games, and the dances often have symbolic meanings – for instance the circle in a reel represents the circle of life. In the sword dance, the feet skip nimbly over the swords without touching them.*

Weight shifting *is a severe test of strength and stamina. Here, the man stands with his back to a bar, over which he must throw the huge weight. The bar is raised after each successful attempt, until only one person is left in the competition.*

Scotch Whisky

WHISKY IS TO THE SCOTS what champagne is to the French, and a visit to Scotland would not be complete without sampling this fiery, heart-warming spirit. All malt whiskies are produced using much the same process, but the environment, maturity and storage of the whisky have such a strong bearing on its character that every one is a different experience. There is no "best" malt whisky – some are suited to drinking at bedtime, others as an aperitif. All the distilleries named below produce highly rated Single Malt Scotch Whiskies, a title that is revered by true whisky connoisseurs.

A 1920s steam wagon transporting The Glenlivet to the nearby railways

Talisker is an individualistic malt with an extremely hot, peppery, powerful flavour that is guaranteed to warm the toes.

Glenmorangie is the biggest selling single malt in Scotland, with a light, flowery taste and strong perfume.

Lochnagar is reputed to have been a favourite with Queen Victoria, who visited this distillery located near Balmoral. This is a sweet whisky with overtones of sherry.

Lagavulin is a classic Islay whisky with a dry, smoky palate. Islay is thought to be the best of the whisky-producing islands.

Edradour is the smallest distillery in Scotland but it succeeds in producing a deliciously minty, creamy whisky.

SPEYSIDE WHISKIES

The region of Speyside *(see p144)*, where barley is widely grown, is the setting for over half of Scotland's malt whisky distilleries.

Highland Park
Pulteney
Glen Ord
Glen Albyn
Glenmorangie
See inset SPEYSIDE
Balmenach
Talisker
CENTRAL HIGHLANDS
Lochnager
Glenury
Dalwhinnie
Edradour
Blair Athol
Fettercairn
Aberfeldy
North Point
Tobermory
Glenturret
Tullibardine
Littlemill
Rosebank
Auchentoshan
Glenkinchie
Lagavulin
Springbank
Glen Scotia
LOWLANDS
Bladnoch

NORTHERN HIGHLANDS
EASTERN HIGHLANDS
WESTERN HIGHLANDS
ISLAY

Glen Moray
Linkwood
Dallas Dhu
Glenlossie
Glen Eilgin
Glen Rothes
Speyburn
Macallan
Glenfiddich
Glenfarclas
Cragganmore
Mortlach
The Glenlivet
Tamnavulin

The Macallan is widely acknowledged as being the "Rolls Royce of Single Malts". Aged in sherry casks, it has a full flavour.

The Glenlivet is the most famous of the Speyside malts, distilled since 1880.

MALT REGIONS

Single malts vary according to regional differences in the peat and stream water used. This map illustrates the divisions of the traditional whisky distilling regions in Scotland. Each whisky has subtle but recognizable regional flavour characteristics.

KEY

• Single malt distilleries

How Whisky is Made

Traditionally made from just barley, yeast and stream water, Scottish whisky (from the Gaelic *usquebaugh*, or the "water of life") takes a little over three weeks to produce, though it must be given at least three years to mature. Maturation usually takes place in oak casks, often in barrels previously used for sherry. The art of blending was pioneered in Edinburgh in the 1860s.

Barley grass

1 Malting is the first stage. Barley grain is soaked in water and spread on the malting floor. With regular turning the grain germinates, producing a "green malt". Germination stimulates the production of enzymes which turn the starches into fermentable sugars.

2 Drying of the barley halts germination after 12 days of malting. This is done over a peat fire in a pagoda-shaped malt-kiln. The peat-smoke gives flavour to the malt and eventually to the mature whisky. The malt is gleaned of germinated roots and then milled.

3 Mashing of the ground malt, or "grist", occurs in a large vat or "mash tun", which holds a vast quantity of hot water. The malt is soaked and begins to dissolve, producing a sugary solution called "wort", which is then extracted for fermentation.

4 Fermentation occurs when yeast is added to the cooled wort in wooden vats, or "washbacks". The mixture is stirred for hours as the yeast turns the sugar into alcohol, producing a clear liquid called "wash".

5 Distillation involves boiling the wash twice so that the alcohol vaporizes and condenses. In copper "pot stills", the wash is distilled – first in the "wash still", then in the "spirit still". Now purified, with an alcohol content of 57 per cent, the result is young whisky.

6 Maturation is the final process. The whisky mellows in oak casks for a legal minimum of three years. Premium brands give the whisky a 10- to 15-year maturation, though some are given up to 50 years.

Traditional drinking vessels, or *quaichs*, made of silver

Blended whiskies are made from a mixture of up to 50 different single malts.

Single malts are made in one distillery, from pure barly malt that is never blended.

Scottish Food and Drink

T HE SCOTTISH LARDER is generous in meat and fish, which are usually served simply, without heavy sauces. Grouse, venison, Aberdeen Angus beef, salmon, trout and Scotland's many cheeses are all highly regarded. The country's cold, wet climate and shallow soil have proved better suited to growing oats than wheat. Oats are still present in traditional Scottish foods such as porridge and oatcakes (as opposed to wheat-based bread) and, of course, the haggis.

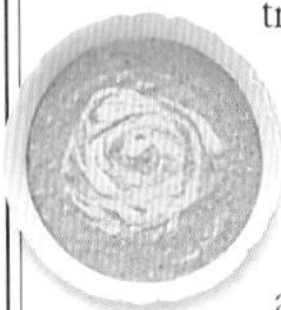

Porridge

Kippers *are in fact fresh herring, split down the back, then salted and cured by smoking over a fire. They are eaten at breakfast with toast.*

Toasted bread

Roast grouse with crispy bacon on top

Fried bread-crumbs

Green beans

Rowan jelly

Bread sauce

Game chips

Grouse *is one of the best known game birds, and a young bird is delicious when roasted. The meat should be served with game chips (thinly sliced, deep-fried potatoes), home-made bread sauce and vegetables.*

Scotch broth *is a light, thin soup based on neck or shoulder of mutton or beef, to which pearl barley and vegetables, such as carrots and leeks, are added.*

Cock-a-leekie soup *is a famous Scottish dish, consisting of pieces of chicken, leeks, rice and prunes, simmered together in the stock from the cooked chicken.*

Cullen skink *is a delicious soup made from smoked, or "finnan", haddock, milk and mashed potato. It originates from the village of Cullen, on the Moray Firth.*

THE HAGGIS

Haggis is undoubtedly the most famous of all Scottish dishes. It can be counted alongside the tartan kilt and the bagpipes as one of the most recognized symbols of Scotland. It is on Burns Night, 25 January, that the haggis is particularly celebrated. The poet Robert Burns *(see p89)* wrote an address to this extraordinary pudding and it is now the custom to read the poem aloud, while plunging a knife into the haggis at the appropriate moment. Haggis contains spiced sheep's innards and oatmeal and is eaten with "neeps" (turnips) and potato.

Aberdeen Angus steak *is a favourite with all meat-eating Scots and is best served medium-rare with a mushroom and wine sauce, chunky chips (French fries) and mixed vegetables.*

Venison *should be hung for ten days before being seasoned with mixed spices, wine and vinegar, then roasted and cut into collops (slices).*

Stovies, *a mixture of onions and potatoes, were traditionally cooked with dripping (fat) from the Sunday joint.*

Skirlie *is a mixture of oatmeal and onions; it is usually flavoured with thyme, a herb that grows wild in Scotland.*

Poached salmon *tastes best when cooked whole in a bouillon of water, wine and vegetables, during which its deep red flesh turns a delicate pink. Salmon is caught in Scotland's east coast rivers.*

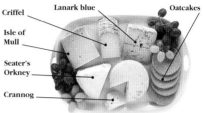

Criffel
Lanark blue
Oatcakes
Isle of Mull
Seater's Orkney
Crannog

Scottish cheeses *are among the finest in Europe. The many varieties range from hard, cheddar-like varieties to soft and creamy cheeses, or those flavoured with herbs and garlic. Eat them with traditional oatcake crackers.*

Scotch pancakes *are a wonderful teatime treat. They are best served warm, with plenty of butter and a homemade fruit jam, honey or golden syrup.*

Butterscotch tart, *a delicious pastry-based dessert, has a rich butterscotch filling and a topping of fluffy meringue. This is for the sweet-toothed only.*

Orange marmalade

Grapefruit and ginger marmalade

Marmalade *was created in Dundee in the 1700s when grocer James Keiller was landed with a large cargo of unsaleable, bitter Seville oranges. His wife, Janet, made them part of a preserve that now appears on breakfast tables worldwide.*

Dundee cake

Dundee cake and shortbread *are two classic Scottish delicacies. The cake is rich and sweet, made with dried fruits and spices and topped with almonds. Shortbread tastes great with fruit yogurt.*

Crabbie's ginger wine

Glayva liqueur

A pint of stout

A pint of bitter

Irn-bru soda drink

Drinks *available in Scotland cover the usual gamut of wines, beers, spirits, liqueurs and soft drinks. A pint of bitter, or "heavy", is a popular drink in Scottish bars, and there are many whisky-based liqueurs, such as Glayva. Irn-bru is refreshing and non-alcoholic.*

Touring Scotland by Car

T HE TEN ROUTES marked on this map are
excellent examples of the options open
to motorists touring Scotland. Some routes are
circular, using a major city as a base; some
can be combined into longer itineraries. Main
roads are few and far between in the Highlands, but driving conditions are generally
good, and traffic is light outside the peak July
and August holiday period. The driving times
given in the key assume normal conditions
without lengthy stops. Further information
about road travel is on pages 214–15.

The far northwest can be visited in a
circular tour starting at Braemore
Junction, near Ullapool, heading
west on a series of single-track
roads past tiny crofting settlements and some of the oldest
rocks in Britain. The route
rejoins the two-lane road
near Unapool.

From Kyle of Lochalsh, this route
along the west coast encompasses
the magnificent mountains and
coastline of Wester Ross, taking in
Loch Carron, Torridon, Loch Maree,
Gairloch and Inverewe Gardens.

The Road to the Isles (see
pp136–7) begins in Crianlarich,
then crosses desolate Rannoch
Moor to Glencoe (see p134)
and past Fort William. The
rugged scenery shown here is
near the end of the tour route.

KEY TO TOURING ROUTES

▬▬	The Border Abbeys & Scott's View *195 km (120 miles), 3–4 hours*
▬▬	Walter Scott's Country *185 km (115 miles), 3–4 hours*
▬▬	Fife Fishing Villages & St Andrews *195 km (120 miles), 3–4 hours*
▬▬	Eastern Grampians & Royal Deeside *180 km (110 miles), 4 hours*
▬▬	High Mountains of Breadalbane *180 km (110 miles), 4 hours*
▬▬	Loch Lomond & the Trossachs *225 km (140 miles), 5 hours*
▬▬	Inveraray & the Mountains of Lorne *225 km (140 miles), 4 hours*
▬▬	Glencoe & the Road to the Isles *160 km (100 miles), 3 hours*
▬▬	Sea Lochs of the West Coast *195 km (120 miles), 4 hours*
▬▬	The Far Northwest *160 km (100 miles), 3–4 hours*

Loch Lomond is the first point of
interest on a tour of Inveraray and
the Mountains of Lorne. After Tarbet
is a pass known as "The Rest and
Be Thankful", then a drive to the
18th-century town of Inveraray (see
p130), and on past Kilchurn Castle.

Unapool
Lochinver
Ullapool
Poolewe
Gairloch
Braemo
Torridon
Shieldaig
Achnasheen
Kyle of
Lochalsh
Mallaig
Fort
William
Crianlarich
Inveraray
Tarbet

0 kilometres   50

0 miles   50

TIPS FOR DRIVERS

Hazards Watch out for sharp
bends and animals on the roads
in the Highlands. The sudden
noise of jets above the glens can
also startle drivers. Minor roads
are often single track. Snowfall
may result in road closures.
Fuel Fill up your car with fuel in
towns, as there are few filling
stations in rural areas.

Passing through Royal Deeside
*in the eastern Grampians, this route
links Perth with Aberdeen, crossing a
700-m (2,000-ft) pass before descend-
ing to Balmoral Castle. The stretch
from Braemar is on pages 144–5.*

St Andrews (see p123) *and the historic
fishing villages of East Fife can be reached
from Edinburgh over the Forth Bridge,
and back via the hunting palace of the
Stuart kings at Falkland (see p124).*

**A tour of
Walter Scott's
Country** takes
in the River
Tweed Valley,
with its attractive
hills, market
towns and an
arboretum at
Dawyck.

Melrose Abbey *is one of the highlights of a
tour taking in attractive Border towns, the
famous Border Abbeys and Scott's View – one
of the finest viewpoints in southern Scotland.
More details of part of this tour are on page 85.*

From Glasgow, this route
includes Loch Lomond,
Lochearnhead and
Balquhidder. Just north of
Callander, it turns west into
the Trossachs. Heading
back via Drymen, there is
access to Loch Lomond.

Stirling, *with its castle,
is the base from which
to explore the high
mountains of Breadal-
bane. The route passes
through Callander, past
Rob Roy's grave and
Loch Earn. It then
climbs over a mountain
pass down to Glen
Lyon, one of the most
beautiful glens, and
on through Crieff.*

Scotland Through the Year

Poster for the Edinburgh Fringe

MOST VISITORS come to Scotland between May and August when they enjoy the best weather, long hours of daylight and the chance to sample world-class events such as the Edinburgh International Festival or the Glasgow International Jazz Festival. The countryside lures tourists and Scots alike, and at the height of summer it gets very busy in areas such as Loch Ness (monster spotting) or Royal Deeside (site of Balmoral Castle, the British Royal Family's Scottish residence). Out of season, a good winter snowfall in the Highlands provides an opportunity for snowboarding or skiing. The recent publicity about New Year – known locally as Hogmanay – has seen an increase in visitor numbers in late December. During most weeks of the year, but especially during the summer, a festival is held somewhere across the country.

Full colours of gorse in springtime

SPRING

THE SNOW clears off the mountains after April, the salmon swim up the rivers and the country prepares for visitors. There are some excellent festivals and a series of important sporting events. British Summer Time, when the clocks go forward one hour, starts at the end of March.

MARCH

Cairngorm Snow Festival *(third weekend)*, Aviemore. Daytime events at the Cairngorm ski area and evening street parades in Aviemore.

APRIL

Shoots & Roots I *(Easter weekend)*, Teviot House, Edinburgh. Contemporary folk music festival. (More traditional one in November.)
International Science Festival *(two weeks, early Apr)*, Edinburgh. World's largest science festival, hosted in various venues.
Scottish Grand National *(mid-Apr)*, Ayr Racecourse. Scotland's top steeplechase event.
The Melrose Sevens *(mid-Apr or early May)*, Melrose, Borders. International seven-a-side rugby union event.
Glasgow Art Fair *(late Apr)*. Commercial art show in various galleries; the main pavilion is in George Square.
Royal Scottish Academy Annual Exhibition *(late Apr)*, RSA, Edinburgh.
Shetland Folk Festival *(late Apr)*. Traditional Scottish music in an island setting.
Beltane *(30 Apr)*, Calton Hill, Edinburgh. Pagan celebration to welcome start of summer.

MAY

Scottish Rugby Union Cup Final *(mid-May)*, Murrayfield Stadium, Edinburgh. Scotland's showpiece club rugby event.
Scottish Cup Final *(mid-May)*, Hampden Park, Glasgow. Scottish football's showpiece club event.
International Children's Festival *(third week)*, Edinburgh. Performing arts event.
Traquair Beer Festival *(last weekend)*, Traquair House, Innerleithen, Borders.

An inter-Scotland rugby match at Murrayfield Stadium, Edinburgh

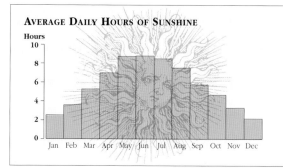

AVERAGE DAILY HOURS OF SUNSHINE

Hours

Sunshine Chart
Although Scotland is not in any way synonymous with sunshine, its summers are marked by very long hours of daylight, due to the country's northerly latitude. Thus there is a relatively high proportion of hours of sunshine between the months of May and July.

SUMMER

THIS IS THE BUSIEST TIME of year. Almost every town and village stages its own version of the Highland Games, at varying scales. Days are long – in Shetland there is no proper night at midsummer, while even the south sees sunrise around 4:30am, sunset around 10pm.

The traditional event of tossing the caber at the Highland Games

JUNE

Hawick Common Riding *(early Jun)*. Patrolling district boundaries on horseback.
RSAC Scottish Rally *(mid-Jun)*, Dumfries & Galloway. Major motor sport event.
Eyemouth Seafood Festival *(mid-Jun)*, Berwickshire. Music, crafts and seafood.
St Magnus Festival *(third week)*, Orkney. Arts event.
The Longest Day *(late Jun)*. No formal celebration, but many people see in the longest day on hilltops such as Arthur's Seat in Edinburgh.

Royal Highland Show *(late Jun)*, Ingliston, Edinburgh. Agricultural and food fair.
Traditional Boats Festival *(last weekend)*, Portsoy harbour, Banffshire. Scotland's fisheries heritage on display.

JULY

Game Conservancy Scottish Fair *(first weekend)*, Scone Palace, Perth. Major shooting and fishing event.
Glasgow International Jazz Festival *(first weekend)*. Various venues across the city.
T in the Park *(second weekend)*, Balado, Fife. Scotland's biggest rock festival.
Loch Lomond Golf Tournament *(mid-Jul)*, Alexandria. Fixture on European golf tour.

AUGUST

Traquair Fair *(first weekend)*, Innerleithen, Borders. Folk music, theatre and market stalls at a country house.
Edinburgh Festival *(various dates in Aug)*. "The

Grouse shooting on the "Glorious Twelfth" of August

Festival" comprises an international arts festival, an extensive fringe festival and other events dedicated to film, television, books, jazz and blues music *(see pp78–9)*.
Edinburgh Military Tattoo *(throughout Aug)*. Martial music and displays on Edinburgh Castle Esplanade.
Glorious Twelfth *(12 Aug)*. Grouse shooting season opens.
World Pipe Band Championships *(mid Aug)*, Glasgow Green. Bagpipe music competition with some Highland Games events.
Great Scottish Run *(third Sun)*, Glasgow. A half-marathon for all to enter.

Drums and marching at the Edinburgh Military Tattoo in August

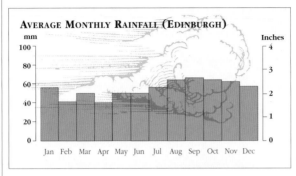

AVERAGE MONTHLY RAINFALL (EDINBURGH)

Rainfall Chart
The east coast has a consistently lower rainfall in comparison with the rest of the country. The Northern Isles, Inner and Outer Hebrides (Western Isles) and Western Highlands are likely to have three times as much precipitation as Edinburgh, Fife or Tayside.

The soft colours of autumn in Tayside

AUTUMN

CATCH A FINE DAY in the countryside and the autumn colours can be spectacular. Scotland may be beginnning to wind down after the summer, but there are still some attractions to be found for the attentive visitor. Schools have a week's holiday in October, which was traditionally a break to allow the children to work on the potato harvest.

Shot-putting at Braemar

SEPTEMBER

Ben Nevis Hill Race *(first Sat)*, Fort William. Annual race up and down the highest mountain in Britain.
Braemar Gathering *(first weekend)*, Braemar, Aberdeenshire. One of the country's leading Highland Games *(see p29)* with members of the Royal Family usually in attendance.
Leuchars Air Show *(mid-Sep)*, RAF Leuchars, Fife. Airshow with flying displays and other attractions.
Ayr Gold Cup *(mid-Sep)*, Ayr Racecourse. Prestigious flat-race for horses.
Open Doors Day *(last Sat)*, Edinburgh. Organized by the Cockburn Association, a number of the city's finest private buildings are opened to the public. Contact the Association for details (0131 557 8686).

OCTOBER

Royal National Mod *(second week)*, venue changes yearly. Performing arts competition promoting Gaelic language and Gaelic culture in general.

Aberdeen Alternative Festival *(third week)*, Aberdeen. Music, comedy, drama and children's events in Scotland's third city.
World Piping Championships *(last Sat)*, Blair Castle, Blair Atholl. Annual competition for top-class bagpipers.

NOVEMBER

Shoots & Roots II *(third weekend)*, Edinburgh. Traditional folk music festival staged in venues across the city. (A contemporary version is held at Easter.)
St Andrew's Night *(30 Nov)*. National day of Scotland's patron saint. No formal celebration but many private and society dinners.

PUBLIC HOLIDAYS

These public holidays are observed throughout Scotland. Some local authorities declare extra holidays that apply only to their own areas.

New Year *(1–2 Jan)*. Two days in Scotland, compared with just the one day in England.
Good Friday *(late Mar or early Apr)*. Easter Monday is not an official holiday in Scotland.
May Day *(first Monday in May)*.
Spring Bank Holiday *(last Monday in May)*.
Summer Bank Holiday *(first Monday in August)*.
Christmas Day *(25 Dec)*
Boxing Day *(26 Dec)*.

AVERAGE MONTHLY TEMPERATURE (EDINBURGH)

Temperature Chart

This bar chart illustrates the average minimum and maximum monthly temperatures recorded in Edinburgh. The west of Scotland tends to be warmer than the east, while the Highlands can be arctic-like, with heavy snowfalls during the winter.

WINTER

THIS IS A SEASON of short days and cold weather, but Christmas and New Year celebrations provide a welcome antidote. Haggis sales peak in late January with Burns Night parties. This quiet period is probably the best time of year to visit Scotland's museums and galleries.

DECEMBER

Edinburgh's Hogmanay *(late Dec into early Jan).* World's biggest New Year celebration. Several days of events, including processions and street theatre, in the capital. The centrepiece is a vast street party on 31 December.

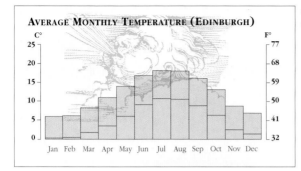

Edinburgh's Royal Mile overflowing with Hogmanay revellers

JANUARY

The Ba' Game *(1 Jan),* Kirkwall, Orkney Isles. A centuries-old tradition to welcome the New Year involving the young men of Kirkwall playing a ball game on the town's streets.

Celtic Connections *(second half of month),* Glasgow. Two weeks of music and *ceilidhs* on a Celtic theme, held in various venues.

Burns Night *(25 Jan).* Scotland celebrates the birth of its national poet with readings and "Burns Suppers". Haggis, potatoes, turnips and whisky are on the menu.

Up Helly Aa *(last Tue),* Lerwick, Shetland Isles. Midwinter fire festival.

FEBRUARY

Inverness Music Festival *(last week),* Inverness. A week of classical and traditional music and dance.

Walker surveying the winter landscape in the Mamores in the Scottish Highlands

THE HISTORY OF SCOTLAND

SCOTLAND HAS BEEN TORN APART *by religion and internal politics, coveted by a richer and more powerful neighbour and wooed and punished for 400 years as the vital partner in the power struggles between England, France and Spain. She has risen and fallen through the ages, acquiring romance from tragedy, producing genius out of poverty and demonstrating an irrepressible spirit.*

"They spend all their time in wars, and when there is no war, they fight one another" is a description of the Scots written in about 1500. For the visitor, the chief delight in this turbulent history is that so much is still tangible and visible.

The earliest settlers in the country are believed to have been Celtic-Iberians, who worked their way north along the coast from the Mediterranean, and arrived in Scotland about 8,000 years ago. Around 2000 BC their descendants erected majestic standing stones, which are found all over the country. The layout of those at Callanish in the Western Isles shows an advanced knowledge of astronomy. These people also built underground round-houses and an abundance of forts, indicating that they were no strangers to invasion and warfare.

In AD 82 the Romans penetrated deep into " Caledonia", as they called the country, and Tacitus recorded victories against the Picts (the "painted people") and other tribes. Yet the

An elaborately carved Pictish stone at Aberlemno, Angus

Romans never conquered Caledonia because their resources were stretched too thin. Instead, they built Hadrian's Wall from Wallsend on the east coast to Bowness-on-Solway in the west, and later the Antonine Wall, a shorter wall further north, thereby endeavouring to shut out the Caledonians. Despite the country's relative isolation from the rest of Britain, however, it is believed that the original form of the Scottish kilt derived from the Roman tunic, or toga.

By AD 400 the Romans had abandoned their northern outposts, and Scotland was divided between four races, each with its own king. These were the predominant Picts, the Britons and Angles in the south, and the smallest group – the Scots – who originally came from Ireland and occupied the southwest of the country.

In the late 4th century AD a Scot, St Ninian, travelled to Rome and, upon his return, built a church at Whithorn, thereby introducing Christianity to "Dalriada", the Kingdom of the Scots.

TIMELINE

Skara Brae

4000 BC	2500 BC	1000 BC	AD 500

300 BC Iron Age begins; weapons are improved

AD 82–4 Romans invade but do not conquer "Caledonia"

AD 121 Hadrian's Wall built

3100 BC Skara Brae settlement on Orkney buried by a storm

2900–2600 BC Callanish standing stones and others erected, showing advanced astronomical knowledge

Roman coin

AD 400 Romans abandon Caledonian outposts. Picts, Scots, Britons and Angles have separate kingdoms

◁ *Return of Mary, Queen of Scots to Edinburgh* in 1561, by James Drummond (1816–77)

CHRISTIANITY AND UNIFICATION

Christianity remained in an isolated pocket until the great warrior-missionary, St Columba, arrived from Ireland and established his monastery on the small Hebridean island of Iona in 563. Fired by his zeal, the new religion spread rapidly. By 800, Iona – the "Cradle of Christianity" as historians refer to it – had achieved widespread influence, and Columban missionaries worked all over Europe. The Celtic Church developed along monastic lines and remained predominantly reclusive by nature, dedicating itself to worship and scholarship. Among its surviving works of art is the famous *Book of Kells*. This lavish, illuminated 8th- to 9th-century manuscript is thought to have been started on Iona, and later moved to Ireland for safe-keeping.

An illustrated page from the ornate *Book of Kells*, now kept in Trinity College, Dublin

The consolidation of a common religion helped to ease the merging of tribes. In 843 the Picts and Scots united under Kenneth MacAlpin. Curiously, the once-mighty Picts were the ones to lose their identity. They remain a mystery, except for their exquisite stone carvings depicting interwoven patterns, warriors and a wondrous mythology.

A long era of terrible Viking raids began in 890, resulting in the Norse occupation of the Western Isles for 370 years, and Shetland and Orkney for almost 600 years. The Norse threat possibly encouraged the Britons to join "Scotia", and in 1018 the Angles were defeated. Scotland became one united kingdom for the first time.

Viking axe

FEUDALISM AND THE CLANS

Under the powerful influence of Margaret, the English wife of Malcolm III (1057–93), a radical shift occurred during the king's reign away from the Gaelic-speaking culture of most of Scotland to the English-speaking culture of the south. This divide was widened under "good king" David I (1124–53). Under his reign Royal Burghs were created – towns built on the king's land and given special trading privileges in exchange for annual payments to him. He also introduced a national system of justice and weights and measures and, in the Lowlands, a feudal system based on Anglo-Norman lines.

Power devolved through an introduced aristocracy, largely French-speaking, and a structure bonded through land tenure. David I tried to impose this system in the north, but the region remained out of his control and, indeed, had its own "kings" –

TIMELINE

St Martin's cross, Iona

563 Columba founds a monastery on Iona and spreads Christianity, easing the merging of tribes

1018 King Malcolm of Scotia defeats the Angles. His grandson, Duncan, unites the country of Scotia, excluding the Norse-held islands

600	700	800	900	1000

685 The Pictish King Bruide defeats the Angles of Northumbria at Forfar in Angus

843 Picts and Scots are united under Kenneth MacAlpin. Picts subsequently become lost to obscurity

890 Northern and Western Isles occupied by the Norsemen

the Lords of the Isles. In the Highlands a different social structure based on kinship – that of families, or clans – had evolved. The chief was a patriarch who held land, not privately, but on behalf of his people. It was an inheritable position, but the chief remained accountable to the clan and could be removed by common consent, unlike the feudal landlords whose power was vested through legal title to the land. This subtle but fundamental difference was mirrored on a national level – in England, the monarch was the King of England; in Scotland, he was known as the King of Scots.

The lion of Scotland, dating from 1222

THE WARS OF INDEPENDENCE AND THE BATTLE OF BANNOCKBURN

In 1222 the lion of Scotland's coat of arms first appeared on the great seal of Alexander II. This was during a relatively peaceful interlude among frequent periods of turmoil when it seemed that Scotland was in danger of breaking apart.

When Alexander III's infant daughter died in 1290, there was no heir to the throne. Edward I of England installed a puppet king and, in 1296, led a devastating invasion that carried off the Stone of Destiny – the Scots' coronation throne – and earned him the title "Hammer of the Scots". Scotland was crushed and, but for one man, lost. William Wallace rose and led a revolt that rekindled

hope until his capture and execution six years later. His cause was taken up by Robert the Bruce who, against all odds, won support and raised an army that changed the course of history by winning a decisive victory over the English at the Battle of Bannockburn, near Stirling, on 23 June 1314.

Confronted by the largest English army to cross the border, the Scots were outnumbered three to one, and their arms were inferior. Yet Bruce had chosen his ground and his strategy carefully and, despite the enemy's skilful bowmen and heavy cavalry, the Scots soon gained the victory they needed so badly. Scotland had won back her independence, but it was not until 1329 that her sovereign status was recognized and secured by a Papal bull (six days after Bruce had died). Even so, the wars with England would continue for another 300 years.

Robert the Bruce in combat at the Battle of Bannockburn (1314)

1124–53 David I imposes Norman feudal system. A clan system prevails in Highlands

1296 Edward I takes Stone of Destiny from Scone Abbey to Westminster

1320 Declaration of Arbroath sent to the Pope – an eloquent appeal for recognition of Scottish independence and sovereignty

| 1100 | 1200 | 1300 | 1400 |

1154 Loss of "southern counties" to England

Edward I (1239–1307)

1263 Western Isles won back from Norse

1314 Robert the Bruce defeats the English at Bannockburn

1328–9 Independence and sovereignty affirmed by Treaty with England and Papal bull

1326 Meeting of first Scottish Parliament

THE STUARTS

In 1371 began the long dynasty of the House of Stuart, a family distinguished by intelligence and flair but prone to tragedy. James I introduced wide legal reforms and approved the first university. James III won Orkney and Shetland from King Christian of Norway through marriage to his daughter. James IV ended his illustrious reign with uncharacteristic misjudgement at the Battle of Flodden, in which 10,000 Scots were slaughtered. But the most famous of the Stuarts was Mary, Queen of Scots (1542–87) who acceded to the throne as an infant.

Raised in France, Mary was beautiful, clever, gentle and spirited, but her reign was destined to be difficult. She was a Catholic in a country changing to Protestantism, and a threat to her cousin, Elizabeth I, whose claim to the English throne was precarious. Had Mary married wisely she might have ruled successfully, but her husbands alienated her potential supporters.

Mary returned to Scotland aged 18, already the widow of the heir to the French throne, and spent just six turbulent years as Scotland's queen. She married again, but was soon implicated in her second husband's murder. She was then the subject of public scandals over both her friendship with her secretary and her third choice of husband. The Church reformers were ruthless in exploiting such indiscretions.

She was deposed and held captive, making a daring escape from an island castle to England, only to be imprisoned there for 18 years and then finally executed on the orders of her cousin, Elizabeth.

Woodcut of Protestant martyr George Wishart being burned at the stake in 1546

THE REFORMATION

Until Mary's reign, Scotland's national religion, like the rest of Europe, was the Church of Rome. It had become extremely rich and powerful and, in many ways, self-serving and divorced from the people. When Martin Luther sparked the Reformation in Germany in 1517, the ripples of Protestanism spread. In Scotland the most vociferous leader was the firebrand preacher John Knox *(see p58)*, who fearlessly denounced Mary.

There followed a long period of religious tension and strife. At first the main contentions were between Roman Catholics and Protestants. As Catholicism was purged, albeit with revivals and impregnable strongholds in the Highlands and islands, the conflicts shifted to Presbyterians versus Episcopalians. The differences lay in the structures of the churches and in their forms of worship. The feuds blazed and spluttered for 150 years.

Mary, Queen of Scots, of the House of Stuart

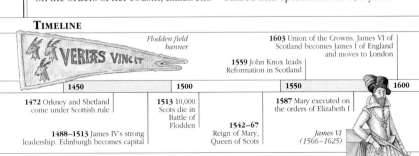

UNION WITH ENGLAND

Mary's son, James VI, had reigned for 36 years when he became heir to the English throne. In 1603 he moved his court to London (taking his golf clubs), thus removing the monarchy from a permanent presence in Scotland for good. Scotland still retained its own parliament but found it increasingly difficult to trade in the face of restrictive English laws. In 1698 it tried to break the English monopoly on foreign trade by starting its own colony in Panama, a scheme that failed and brought financial ruin.

Articles of Union between England and Scotland, signed 22 July 1706 and accepted in 1707

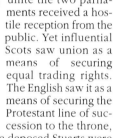

Protestant preacher John Knox

The first proposal to unite the two parliaments received a hostile reception from the public. Yet influential Scots saw union as a means of securing equal trading rights. The English saw it as a means of securing the Protestant line of succession to the throne, for by now the deposed Stuarts were threatening to reinstate the Catholic line. James VII was deposed in 1689 and fled to France. In 1707 the Act of Union was passed and the Scottish Parliament was dissolved.

BONNIE PRINCE CHARLIE
AND THE JACOBITES

In 1745 James VII's grandson, Prince Charles Edward Stuart, secretly entered Scotland, landing on the west Highland coast with seven men and a promise of French military support, which never materialized. His call to arms to overthrow the Hanoverian usurper, George II, drew a poor response and only a few Highland chiefs offered support. From this dismal start his campaign achieved remarkable success, but indecisive leadership weakened the side.

The rebel army came within 200 km (125 miles) of London, throwing the city into panic, before losing heart and retreating. At Culloden, near Inverness, the Hanoverian army (which included many Scots, for this was not an issue of nationalism) defeated the Jacobites on a snowy 16 April 1746. The cause was lost. Bonnie Prince Charlie became a fugitive hotly pursued for six months, but despite a £30,000 reward on his head he was never betrayed.

Feather-capped Scottish Jacobites being attacked by Royalists at Glen Shiel in the Highlands, 1719

MacDonald shield

1642 Civil war in England	**1692** Massacre of Glencoe – a Campbell-led force murders its hosts, the MacDonalds, as an official punitive example	**1745–6** Jacobite rising. Bonnie Prince Charlie tries to recover throne, but loses the Battle of Culloden and flees
1650	**1700**	**1750**
		1746 Abolition of Feudal Jurisdictions
1689 James VII loses throne as he tries to restore Catholicism		**1726** Roadbuilding under General Wade
1698 First Darien (Panama) Expedition to found a trading colony. Bank of Scotland established	**1706–7** Union of Parliaments. Scottish Parliament dissolved	

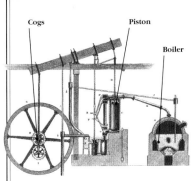

Cogs   Piston

Boiler

James Watt's steam engine, which shifted the
source of industrial power from water to steam

THE AFTERMATH OF CULLODEN
AND THE CLEARANCES

Culloden was the turning point in
Highland history, such was the severity
of the oppressive measures following
the battle. An Act was passed banning
the wearing of tartan, the playing of
pipes and the carrying of arms. The
ties of kinship between chief and
people were severed, and a way of life
was extinguished. From then on chiefs
assumed the roles of feudal landlords,
and the land, once held for the people,
became their private prop-
erty. When sheep were
found to thrive profitably
on the land, the people
became a hindrance and,
as a result, were removed.

The evictions, or so-
called Clearances, began
in the 1760s. Some were
achieved quite peacefully
through financial incen-
tives, but increasingly they
were enforced through
violence and burning, the
most notorious taking
place on the Duke of
Sutherland's estate in 1814.

In the 1860s, by which time Queen
Victoria had made the Highlands
popular and sporting estates all the
rage for hunting deer, the inland glens
were as empty as they are today.

INDUSTRIALIZATION AND THE
SCOTTISH ENLIGHTENMENT

While the Highlands were emptying,
parts of southern Scotland were
booming. For a large part of the 18th
century Glasgow's tobacco lords
operated a lucrative stranglehold on
the European market, and linen,
cotton and coal in their turn became
important national industries.

The Industrial Revolution, made
possible by Scotsman James Watt's
revolutionary contribution to the
steam engine, brought wealth to the
nation (yet at the expense of health
and social conditions) and turned
Glasgow into the "Workshop of the
Empire" – a reputation it retained until
the demise of its famous shipbuilding
industry in the 20th century.

A flowering of original thinkers also
emerged in Scotland in the 18th
century *(see pp24–5)*, most notably

Shipbuilding factory in Clydeside, now closed

TIMELINE

1769 James Watt patents his steam engine	**1832** Sir Walter Scott buried at Dryburgh Abbey	*Early telephone*
	1814 "The Year of Burning" of the Sutherland Clearances	**1886** Crofters Act provides secure tenure and fair rents

1775	1800	1825	1875

1786 Robert
Burns publishes
*Poems, Chiefly
in the Scots
Dialect*

1840 Glasgow's population reaches
200,000 as its shipbuilding and
cotton industries flourish

1848 Queen Victoria uses Balmoral as a retreat, and
Scottish culture becomes fashionable with the English

1876 Alexander
Graham Bell
patents the first
working telephone

the philosopher David Hume, economist Adam Smith and the "Bard of Humanity", Robert Burns.

In the 19th century, Scotland's architecture led the way in Europe, as epitomized by the development of Edinburgh's New Town *(see pp64–5)*. This bold plan to create a residential centre away from the congested Old Town was begun in 1770, and the design was greatly expanded in 1822 to produce a model of elegance that is outstanding to this day. Among the more famous of those who have occupied these classic Georgian houses was Sir Walter Scott, one of the world's earliest best-selling novelists.

In this same period, known as the Scottish Enlightenment, Thomas Telford excelled in engineering and, ever increasingly, Scots were finding fame and fortune abroad by exploring and developing foreign lands.

A North Sea oil rig, providing prosperity in the late 20th century

The Scottish National Party, founded in 1934, is seen by many as too extremist, and its popularity has fluctuated. The exploration of North Sea oil since the late 1960s boosted Scotland's economy and its ability to self govern. In 1997 the Labour government held a referendum in which, by a large majority, the Scots voted for the re-establishment of a Scottish Parliament in 1999.

Although its tax-raising powers are restrained, the new Scottish Parliament has devolved authority over health, education, local government, social work, housing, economic development, transport, law, home affairs, environment, agriculture, forestry, fishing, sport and the arts. For many Scots it is seen as heralding a new beginning with a renewed pride and strength in their culture, identity and heritage.

THE PROCESS OF DEVOLUTION

For a long time, following the Act of Union, it was clear that England and Scotland were never intended to be equal. The political centre moved to Westminster and accordingly forced any Scot with a talent or aptitude for politics to leave Scotland. This, and an imbalance in the system weighted in favour of English affairs, caused a general feeling of apathy and impotence to take root in the Scottish psyche. Various reforms adjusted the imbalance, but the sense of political estrangement continued to fester.

SNP demonstrations in 1997, encouraging voters to say "Yes" to Scottish devolution

			1945 Alexander Fleming wins Nobel Prize		1996 Stone of	1999 Scottish
1888 Scottish Labour Party founded by James Keir Hardie	1920s Hugh MacDiarmid reinstates Scots as literary language		1967 North Sea oil exploration begins		Destiny *(see p60)* returns to Scotland	Parliament re-established
1900	**1925**	**1950**		**1975**	**2000**	
1914–18 74,000 Scots die in World War I	1934 Scottish National Party founded					
	1931 Economic slump – 65 per cent unemployment in Clyde shipyards					

Stone of Destiny

SCOTLAND REGION BY REGION

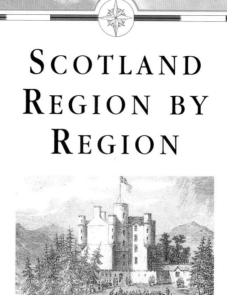

Scotland at a Glance

STRETCHING FROM the rich farmlands of the
Borders to a chain of isles only a few degrees
south of the Arctic Circle, the Scottish landscape
has a diversity without parallel in Britain. The cities
of Glasgow and Edinburgh bustle with people and
offer numerous attractions. The northeast is an
area rich in wildlife, and as you travel northwest, the land becomes more mountainous
and its archaeological treasures more numerous. In the far northwest, in the Western
Isles, Scotland's earliest relics stand upon
some of the oldest rock on earth.

Western Isles

*__The Isle of Skye__
(see pp152–3),
renowned for its
dramatic scenery,
has one of Scotland's
most striking coast-
lines. On the east
coast, a stream
plunges over Kilt
Rock, a cliff of
hexagonal basalt
columns named
after its likeness to
an item of Scottish
national dress.*

**THE HIGHLANDS
AND ISLANDS**
(see pp126–61)

*__The Trossachs__ (see pp116–17) are a beautiful range
of hills straddling the border between the Highlands
and the Lowlands. At their heart, the forested slopes of
Ben Venue rise above the still
waters of Loch Achray.*

Strathclyde

GLASGO
(see pp94–10

*__Culzean Castle__ (see pp92–3)
stands on a cliff's edge on the
Firth of Clyde, amid an extensive
country park. One of the jewels of
southern Scotland, Culzean is a
magnificent showcase of work by
the Scottish-born architect,
Robert Adam (1728–92).*

◁ **Loch Lomond in the Highlands**

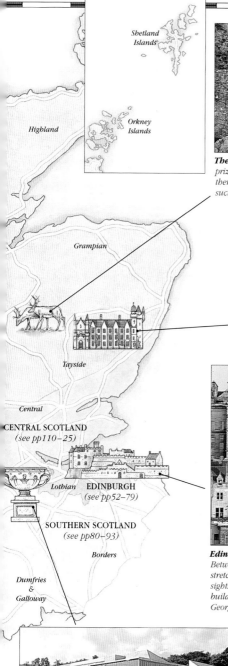

Shetland Islands

Orkney Islands

Highland

Grampian

Tayside

Central

CENTRAL SCOTLAND
(see pp110–25)

Lothian　**EDINBURGH**
(see pp52–79)

SOUTHERN SCOTLAND
(see pp80–93)

Borders

Dumfries & Galloway

The Cairngorms (see pp140–41) *cover an area prized for its beauty and diversity of wildlife, though there are also many historical relics to be found, such as this early 18th-century arch at Carrbridge.*

Royal Deeside (see pp144–5) *in the Grampians has been associated with British royalty since Queen Victoria bought Balmoral Castle in 1852.*

Edinburgh (see pp52–79) *is the capital of Scotland. Between its medieval castle and Holyrood Palace stretches the Royal Mile – a concentration of historic sights, ranging from the old Scottish Parliament buildings to the house of John Knox. By contrast, Georgian terraces predominate in the New Town.*

The Burrell Collection (see pp104–5), *on the southern outskirts of Glasgow, is a museum of some of the city's greatest art treasures. It is housed in a spacious, glass building opened in 1983.*

| 0 kilometres | 50 |
| 0 miles | 50 |

EDINBURGH

T HE HISTORIC STATUS *of Edinburgh, the capital of Scotland, is beyond question, with ancient buildings scattered across the city, and the seat of Scotland's new parliament lying close to the royal residence of Holyrood Palace. The astonishing range of historical and artistic attractions draws visitors from all over the world.*

Castle Rock in Edinburgh has been occupied since around 1,000 BC in the Bronze Age, which is no surprise given its strategic views over the Firth of Forth. The Castle itself houses the city's oldest building, St Margaret's Chapel, dating from the 11th century. A few years later, Margaret's son, King David I, founded Holyrood Abbey a mile to the east. The town that grew along the route between these buildings, known as the "Royal Mile", became a popular residence of kings, although not until the reign of James IV (1488–1513) did Edinburgh gain the status of Scotland's capital. James built Holyrood Palace as a royal residence in 1498 and made the city an administrative centre.

Overcrowding made the Old Town a dirty and difficult place to live, and threw rich and poor together. The construction of a Georgian New Town to the north in the late 1700s gave the wealthy an escape route, but even today Edinburgh has a reputation for social extremes. It has major law courts, is second only to London as a financial centre in the British Isles and houses the new Scottish parliament. Bankers and lawyers form the city's establishment, and the most ambitious architectural developments of recent years have been for financial sector companies. Yet outlying housing estates, built in the years following World War II, still have echoes of the Old Town poverty.

Edinburgh is best known today for being a major tourist centre. There are wonderful museums and galleries to visit, and the city enjoys a widely renowned nightlife. At the height of the International Festival, in August, it is estimated that the population actually doubles from 400,000 to 800,000.

A juggler performing at the annual arts extravaganza, the Edinburgh Festival

◁ **The Grassmarket area of the city, dominated by the imposing edifice of Edinburgh Castle**

Exploring Edinburgh

THE CENTRE OF EDINBURGH is divided neatly in half by Princes Street, the principal shopping area. To the south lies the Old Town, site of the ancient city, which grew along the route of the Royal Mile, from the Castle Rock in the west to Holyrood Palace in the east. At the end of the 18th century, building for the New Town started to the north of Princes Street. The area is still viewed today as a world-class example of Georgian urban architecture, with its elegant façades and broad streets. Princes Street itself has lots to offer, including art galleries, the towering Scott Monument and the landmark Balmoral Hotel clock tower, as well as the city's main train station, Waverley.

North Bridge, opened in 1772 – the main route connecting the Old and New Towns

Edinburgh Castle's Royal Scots soldiers

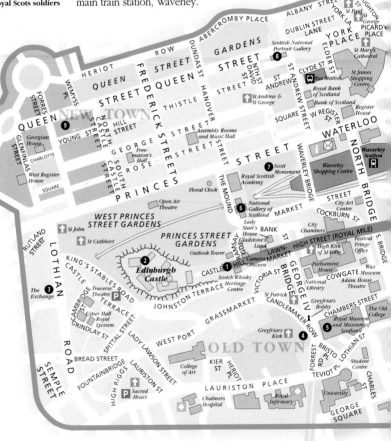

GETTING AROUND

Central Edinburgh is compact, so walking is an excellent way to explore the centre. Other options include a comprehensive bus service and a multitude of black taxis. Avoid exploring the centre by car, because the streets tend to be congested with traffic, and parking may be difficult. Car use has been actively discouraged by the local authority in recent years. On main routes special lanes are provided for buses, taxis and bicycles, and in the suburbs there is also a good network of bicycle paths.

SIGHTS AT A GLANCE

Historic Areas, Streets and Buildings

Edinburgh Castle pp60–61 ❷
The Exchange ❸
Greyfriars Kirk ❹
Holyrood Palace ⓫
New Scottish Parliament ⓭
New Town pp64–5 ❾
The Royal Mile pp56–9 ❶

Monuments

Scott Monument ❼

Landmarks

Calton Hill ❿
Holyrood Park and
   Arthur's Seat ⓮

Museums, Galleries and Exhibitions

Dynamic Earth ⓬
National Gallery of Scotland ❻
The Royal Museum and
   Museum of Scotland ❺
Scottish National Portrait
   Gallery ❽

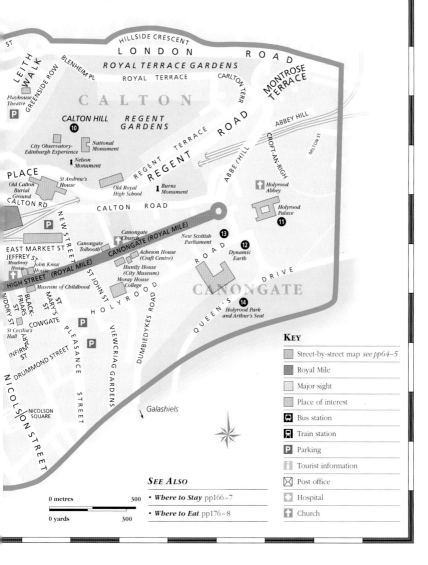

KEY

	Street-by-street map *see pp64–5*
	Royal Mile
	Major sight
	Place of interest
	Bus station
	Train station
P	Parking
	Tourist information
	Post office
	Hospital
	Church

SEE ALSO

- *Where to Stay* pp166–7
- *Where to Eat* pp176–8

0 metres 300
0 yards 300

The Royal Mile ●

Eagle
sign outside
Gladstone's Land

THE ROYAL MILE is a stretch of four ancient streets (from Castlehill to Canongate) which formed the main thoroughfare of medieval Edinburgh, linking the castle to Holyrood Palace. Confined by the city wall, the "Old Town" grew upwards, with some tenements climbing to 20 floors. It is still possible, among the 66 alleys and closes off the main street, to sense Edinburgh's medieval past.

LOCATOR MAP

Gladstone's Land is a preserved 17th-century merchant's house.

The Scotch Whisky Centre introduces visitors to Scotland's national drink.

The Outlook Tower contains an observatory from which to view the city.

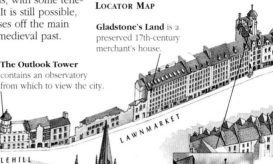

Edinburgh Castle

CASTLEHILL

LAWNMARKET

Lady Stair's House
This 17th-century house is now a museum of the lives and works of writers Burns, Scott and Stevenson.

The Tolbooth Kirk (c.1840) has the city's highest spire.

Outlook Tower
(0131) 226 3709. ☐ daily.
The lower floors of this building date from the early 17th century and were once the home of the Laird of Cockpen. In 1852, Maria Short added the upper floor, the viewing terrace and the Camera Obscura – a large pinhole camera that pictures life in the city centre as it happens. A marvel at the time, it remains one of Edinburgh's most popular attractions.

Gladstone's Land
(NTS) 477B Lawnmarket.
(0131) 226 5856.
☐ Apr–Oct: daily.
This 17th-century merchant's house has been carefully restored. It provides a window on life in a typical Old Town house before over-crowding drove the rich inhabitants north-west to the ever-expanding Georgian New Town. "Lands", as they were then known, were tall,

The bedroom of Gladstone's Land

narrow buildings erected on small plots of land. The six-floor house that is Gladstone's Land was named after Thomas Gledstanes, the merchant who built it in 1617. The house still has the original arcade booths on the street façade as well as a painted ceiling, with fine Scandinavian floral designs.

Although the house is extravagantly furnished, it also contains items, such as wooden overshoes that had to be worn in the dirty streets, which serve as a reminder of the less salubrious features that were part of the old city.

A chest in the beautiful Painted Chamber is said to have been given by a Dutch sea captain to a Scottish merchant who saved him from a shipwreck. A similar house, named Morocco's Land *(see p59)*, can be found further to the east, on Canongate.

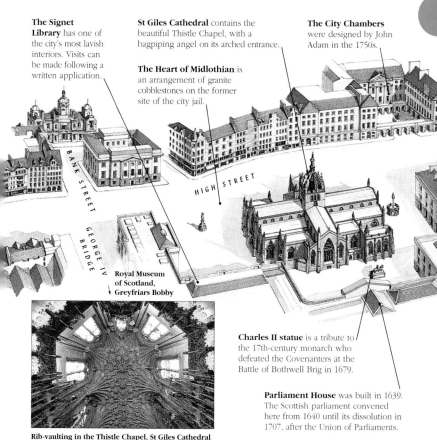

The Signet Library has one of the city's most lavish interiors. Visits can be made following a written application.

St Giles Cathedral contains the beautiful Thistle Chapel, with a bagpiping angel on its arched entrance.

The City Chambers were designed by John Adam in the 1750s.

The Heart of Midlothian is an arrangement of granite cobblestones on the former site of the city jail.

BANK STREET

HIGH STREET

GEORGE IV BRIDGE

Royal Museum of Scotland, Greyfriars Bobby

Charles II statue is a tribute to the 17th-century monarch who defeated the Covenanters at the Battle of Bothwell Brig in 1679.

Parliament House was built in 1639. The Scottish parliament convened here from 1640 until its dissolution in 1707, after the Union of Parliaments.

Rib-vaulting in the Thistle Chapel, St Giles Cathedral

🏛 **Writers' Museum**

Lady Stair's House, Lady Stair's Close. ⓒ *(0131) 529 4901.* ◯ *Mon–Sat.* This fine old town mansion was built in 1622. In the 1720s it was acquired by Elizabeth, Dowager Countess of Stair, and has since been called Lady Stair's House. Its official title reflects its role as a museum of memorabilia from Robert Burns, Sir Walter Scott and Robert Louis Stevenson.

🏛 **Parliament House**

Parliament Sq, High St. ⓒ *(0131) 225 2595.* ◯ *Mon–Fri.* ♿ *limited.* This majestic, Italianate building was constructed in the 1630s for the Scottish Parliament. Parliament House has been home to the Court of Session and the High Court since the Union of Parliaments (*see p45*) in 1707. It is well worth seeing, as much for the spectacle of its many gowned

and wigged advocates as for the beautiful stained-glass window in the Great Hall, commemorating the inauguration of the Court of Session by King James V in 1532.

⛪ **St Giles Cathedral**

Royal Mile. ⓒ *(0131) 225 9442.* ◯ *daily.* 📷 Properly known as the High Kirk (church) of Edinburgh, it is ironic that St Giles is popularly known as a cathedral. Though it was twice the seat of a bishop in the 17th century, it was from here that John Knox directed the Scottish Reformation, with its emphasis on individual worship freed from the authority of bishops. A tablet marks the place

where Jenny Geddes, a local market stallholder, scored a victory for the Covenanters in 1637 by hurling her stool at a preacher who was reading from an English prayer book.

The Gothic exterior of the cathedral is dominated by a 15th-century tower, the only part to escape heavy renovation in the 19th century. Inside, the impressive Thistle Chapel, with its rib-vaulted ceiling and carved heraldic canopies can be seen. The chapel honours the knights, past and present, of the Most Ancient and Most Noble Order of the Thistle. The carved royal pew in the Preston Aisle is used by Queen Elizabeth II when staying in Edinburgh.

Bagpiping angel from the entrance of the cathedral

Exploring Further Down the Royal Mile

THE SECTION of the Royal Mile from High Street to Canongate passes two monuments to the Reformation: John Knox's house and the Tron Kirk. The Canongate was once an independent district, owned by the canons of the Abbey of Holyrood, and sections of its south side have undergone excellent restoration. Beyond Morocco's Land, the road stretches for the final half-mile (800 m) to Holyrood Palace.

LOCATOR MAP

HIGH STREET

SOUTH BRIDGE STREET

The Mercat Cross marks the city centre. It was here that Bonnie Prince Charlie (*see p153*) was proclaimed king in 1745.

The Tron Kirk
was built in 1630 for the Presbyterians who left St Giles Cathedral when it came under the control of the Bishop of Edinburgh.

🕆 John Knox's House

45 High St. 📞 *(0131) 556 9579.*
🕙 *Mon–Sat.* ♿ *limited.* 📷
📷 *by appointment.*

As a leader of the Protestant Reformation and minister at St Giles, John Knox (1513–72) was one of the most important figures in 16th-century Scotland. Ordained as a priest in 1536, Knox later became convinced of the need for religious change. He took part in the Protestant occupation of St Andrews Castle in 1547

and served two years as a galley slave in the French navy as punishment. On release, Knox went to London and Geneva to espouse the Protestant cause, returning to Edinburgh in 1559. The townhouse on the Royal Mile that bears his name dates from 1450 and it was here that he spent the last few months of his life. It is one of the few structures from this period that survive today. Displays tell the story of Knox's life in the context of the political and religious upheavals of his time.

🏛 Museum of Childhood

42 High St. 📞 *(0131) 529 4142.*
🕙 *Mon–Sat (Sun during Edinburgh Festival).* ♿ *limited.* www.cec.org.uk

This museum is not merely a toy collection but a magical insight into childhood, with all its joys and trials. Founded in 1955 by a city councillor, Patrick Murray (who claimed

to eat children for breakfast), it was the world's first museum of childhood. The collection includes medicines, school books and old-fashioned toys. With its nickelodeon, antique slot machines and enthusiastic visitors, this has been called the world's noisiest museum.

🏛 Canongate Tolbooth: The People's Story

163 Canongate. 📞 *(0131) 529 4057.*
🕙 *Mon–Sat (Sun during Edinburgh Festival).*

Edinburgh's social history museum is housed in the Canongate Tolbooth, dating

An 1880 automaton of the Man on the Moon, Museum of Childhood

John Knox's House
Dating from 1450, the oldest house in the city was the home of the preacher John Knox during the 1560s. He is said to have died in an upstairs room. It contains relics of his life.

Morocco's Land is a reproduction of a 17th-century tenement house. It takes its name from the statue of a Moor which adorns the entrance.

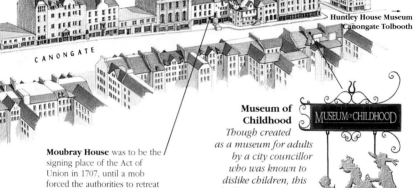

Huntley House Museum
Canongate Tolbooth

CANONGATE

Museum of Childhood
Though created as a museum for adults by a city councillor who was known to dislike children, this lively musem now attracts flocks of young visitors.

MUSEUM OF CHILDHOOD

Moubray House was to be the signing place of the Act of Union in 1707, until a mob forced the authorities to retreat to another venue.

from 1591. With its distinctive clock tower, this was the focal point for life in the Burgh of Canongate. Until the mid-19th century it contained law courts, a jail and the meeting place for the burgh council. It has been a museum since 1954.

Focusing on the lives of ordinary citizens from the late 18th century to the present, it covers subjects such as public health, recreation, trade unions and work. The riots, disease and poverty of the 19th century are also covered, and with subjects as diverse as wartime, football and punk rock, this collection gives a valuable insight into life in Edinburgh.

A prison cell in the Canongate Tolbooth: The People's Story

LIFE BELOW THE OLD TOWN

Until the 18th century most residents of Edinburgh lived along and beneath the Royal Mile and Cowgate. The old abandoned cellars and basements, which lacked any proper water supply, daylight or ventilation, were once centres of domestic life and industry. Under these conditions, cholera, typhus and smallpox were common. Mary King's Close, under the City Chambers, is one of the most famous of these areas – its inhabitants were all killed by the plague around 1645.

You can visit these areas with Robin's Ghost and History Tour – (0131) 661 0125 – or Mercat Walking Tours – (0131) 661 4541 www.mercat-tours.co.uk.

🏛 **Huntly House Museum**
142–146 Canongate. ☎ *(0131) 529 4143.* ◯ *Mon–Sat (Sun during Edinburgh Festival).*
Huntly House was built in the early 16th century and damaged in the English raid on Edinburgh in 1544, although it was later substantially repaired. First used as a family townhouse, it was later divided into apartments but by the 19th

century it was little more than a slum. In 1924 the local authority bought the property and opened the museum in 1932. This local history collection includes exhibits such as Neolithic axe heads, Roman coins, military artifacts and glassware. A section is also dedicated to Field Marshal Earl Haig, Commander-in-Chief of the British Army during World War I.

Edinburgh Castle ❷

Beam support in the Great Hall

Sᴛᴀɴᴅɪɴɢ ᴜᴘᴏɴ the basalt core of an extinct volcano, Edinburgh Castle is an assemblage of buildings dating from the 12th to the 20th century, reflecting its changing role as fortress, royal palace, military garrison and state prison. Though there is evidence of Bronze Age occupation of the site, the original fortress was built by the 6th-century Northumbrian king, Edwin, from whom the city takes its name. The castle was a favourite royal residence until the Union of the Crowns *(see p45)* in 1603, after which the king resided in England. After the Union of Parliaments in 1707, the Scottish regalia were walled up in the Palace for over a hundred years. The Palace is now the zealous possessor of the so-called Stone of Destiny, a relic of ancient Scottish kings which was seized by the English and not returned to Scotland until 1996.

Scottish Crown
Now on display in the palace, the Crown was restyled by James V of Scotland in 1540.

Military Prison

Governor's House
Complete with Flemish-style crow-stepped gables, this building was constructed for the governor in 1742 and now serves as the Officers' Mess for the castle garrison.

 Old Back Parade

Vaults
This French graffiti, dating from 1780, recalls the many prisoners who were held in the vaults during the wars with France in the 18th and 19th centuries.

Mᴏɴs Mᴇɢ

Now kept in the castle vaults, the siege gun (or *bombard*) Mons Meg was made in Belgium in 1449 for the Duke of Burgundy, who gave it to his nephew, James II of Scotland. It was used by James against the Douglas family in their stronghold of Threave Castle *(see p89)* on the Dee in 1455, and later by James IV against Norham Castle in England. After exploding during a salute to the Duke of York in 1682, it was kept in the Tower of London until it was returned to Edinburgh in 1829, at Sir Walter Scott's request.

Sᴛᴀʀ Sɪɢʜᴛs

★ **Great Hall**

★ **Palace**

VISITORS' CHECKLIST

Castle Hill. *(0131) 225 9846.* *Apr–Oct: 9:30am–6pm daily; Nov–Mar: 9:30am–5pm daily (last admission: 45 mins before closing).*
www.historic-scotland.gov.uk

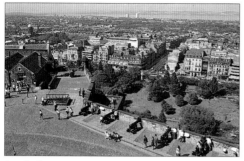

Argyle Battery
This fortified wall commands a spectacular northern view of the city's New Town.

★ Palace
Mary, Queen of Scots, gave birth to James VI in this 15th-century palace, where the Stone of Destiny and Crown Jewels are displayed.

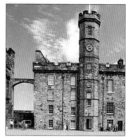

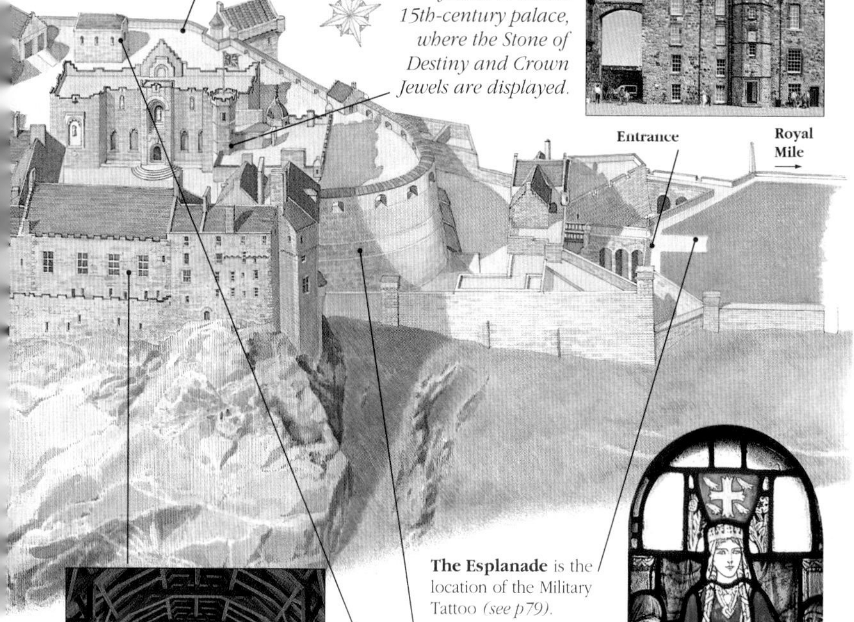

Entrance
Royal Mile

The Esplanade is the location of the Military Tattoo *(see p79)*.

The Half Moon Battery was built in the 1570s as a platform for the artillery defending the eastern wing of the castle.

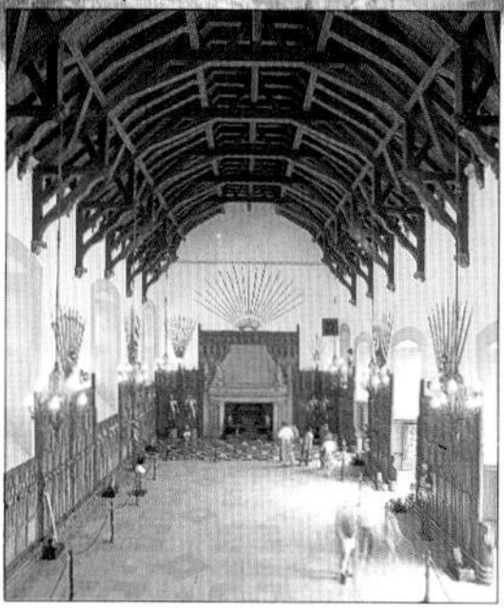

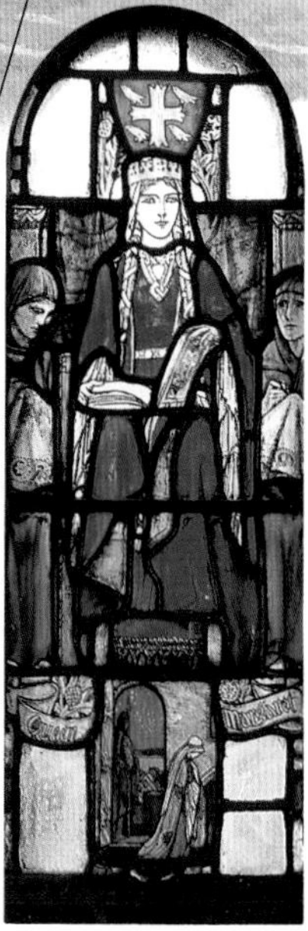

★ Great Hall
With its restored open-timber roof, the hall dates from the 15th century and was the meeting place of the Scottish Parliament until 1639.

St Margaret's Chapel
This stained glass window depicts Malcolm III's saintly queen, to whom the chapel is dedicated. Probably built by her son, David I, in the early 12th century, the chapel is the castle's oldest existing building.

The Standard Life Building, at the heart of the city's financial centre

The Exchange ❸

Lothian Rd, West Approach Rd and Morrison St.

LOCATED WEST of Lothian Road, The Exchange is the most important recent development in central Edinburgh. The once unsightly area was rejuvenated when Festival Square and the Sheraton Grand Hotel were built in 1985. Three years later the local authority published a plan to promote the area as a financial centre. In 1991 investment management firm Baillie Gifford opened Rutland Court on West Approach Road. The ambitious **Edinburgh International Conference Centre**, on Morrison Street, was designed by Terry Farrell and opened in 1995. There has been a fever of construction work ever since. Standard Life opened a new headquarters on Lothian Road in 1997, which has some fine artistic features, and in 1998 Scottish Widows opened a bold new building.

🏢 **Edinburgh International Conference Centre**
📞 (0131) 300 3000. ♿

Greyfriars Kirk ❹

Greyfriars Place. 📞 (0131) 226 5429.
🕐 Easter–Oct: Mon–Sat; Nov–Easter: Thu. ♿ 🚻

GREYFRIARS KIRK occupies a key role in the history of Scotland, as this is where the National Covenant was signed in 1638, marking the Protestant stand against the imposition of an episcopal church by King Charles I. Greyfriars was then a relatively new structure, having been completed in 1620 on the site of a Franciscan friary.

Throughout the 17th century, during years of bloodshed and religious persecution, the kirkyard was used as a mass grave for executed Covenanters. The kirk also served as a prison for Covenanter forces captured after the 1679 Battle of Bothwell Brig. The Martyrs' Monument is a sobering reminder of those times. The original kirk building was severely damaged by fire in 1845 and substantially rebuilt.

But despite this turmoil, Greyfriars is best known for its association with a dog, Bobby, who lived by his master's grave from 1858 to 1872. Bobby's statue stands outside Greyfriars Kirk.

A tribute to Greyfriars Bobby

The Royal Museum and Museum of Scotland ❺

Chambers St. 📞 (0131) 225 7534.
🕐 daily (Sun: pm). 🎫 ♿ 🚻
www.nms.ac.uk

STANDING SIDE BY SIDE on Chambers Street, these two buildings could not be more different from one another. The older of the museums, **The Royal Museum of Scotland**, is a great Victorian palace of self improvement. Designed by Captain Francis Fowke of the Royal Engineers, the building was completed in 1888. Although it started life as an industrial museum, over time its collection was developed to include an eclectic assortment of exhibits, ranging from stuffed animals to ethnographic and technological items. These are all displayed in rooms leading off the large and impressive central hall.

There was, however, no room available to display Scotland's impressive array of antiquities. As a result, they were crammed into inadequate spaces in the National Portrait Gallery in Queen Street, or were hidden away altogether and put into storage.

As far back as the 1950s, recommendations were made that a new facility be built to house the nation's historical treasures. The government did not commit funding to the project until as recently as 1990. Work on a site next door to the Royal Museum of Scotland on Chambers Street started in 1993, and the building took five years to complete. The result was the **Museum of Scotland**, a contemporary flourish of confident design by architects Gordon Benson and Alan Forsyth, which opened to the public in December 1998.

Described as one of the most important buildings erected in Scotland in the second half of the 20th century, the museum tells the story of the country, starting with its geology and natural history. It then moves through to the early peoples of Scotland, the centuries when Scotland was a kingdom in its

The 9th-century Monymusk Reliquary on display at Edinburgh's Museum of Scotland

own right, and then on to later industrial developments. Some stunning items are on show, including St Fillan's Crozier, which was said to have been carried at the head of the Scottish army at Bannockburn in 1314. The Monymusk Reliquary is also on display. Dated to around AD 800, it was a receptacle for the remains of the Christian missionary, St Columba *(see p42)*.

National Gallery of Scotland ❻

The Mound. ☎ *(0131) 556 8921.*
◻ *daily.* ♿ ▣ *by appointment.*

O NE OF SCOTLAND'S finest art galleries, the National Gallery of Scotland is worth visiting for its 15th- to 19th-century British and European paintings alone, though plenty more can be found to delight the enthusiastic art-lover.

Serried ranks of paintings hang on deep red walls behind a profusion of statues and other works of art. Some of the highlights among the Scottish works exhibited are the society portraits by Allan Ramsay and Henry Raeburn, including the latter's *Reverend Robert Walker Skating on Duddingston Loch*, thought to date from the beginning of the 19th century.

Rev Robert Walker Skating on Duddingston Loch

The collection of early German pieces contains Gerard David's almost comic-strip treatment of the *Three Legends of St Nicholas*, from around the beginning of the 16th century. Works by Raphael, Titian and Tintoretto accompany other southern European paintings, including Velazquez's *An Old Woman Cooking Eggs*, from 1620, and there is an entire room devoted to *The Seven Sacraments* by Nicholas Poussin, dating from around 1640. Flemish painters represented include Rembrandt, Van Dyck and Rubens, while among the British offerings are important works by Ramsay, Reynolds and Gainsborough.

Scott Monument ❼

Princes Street Gardens East.
◻ *daily.* ▣

S IR WALTER SCOTT (1771–1832) is one of the most important figures in the history of Scottish literature *(see p86)*. Born in Edinburgh, Scott initially pursued a legal career but he soon turned to writing full time as his ballads and historical novels began to bring him success. His works looked back to a time of adventure, honour and chivalry, and did much to promote this image of Scotland abroad.

In addition to being a celebrated novelist, Sir Walter was also a major public figure – he organized the visit of King George IV to Edinburgh in 1822. After Scott's death in 1832, the Monument was constructed on the south side of Princes Street as a tribute to his life and work. This great Gothic tower was designed by George Meikle Kemp and reaches a height of 61 m (200 ft). It was completed in 1840, and includes a statue of Sir Walter at its base, sculpted by Sir John Steell. Inside the huge structure, which has recently been renovated, are 287 steps up to the top-most platform. The rewards for those keen enough to climb up are excellent views around the city centre and across the Forth to Fife.

The imposing Gothic heights of the Scott Monument on Princes Street

Scottish National Portrait Gallery ❽

1 Queen St. ☎ *(0131) 556 8921.*
◻ *daily.* ♿ ▣ *by appointment.*

A N INFORMATIVE exhibition on the royal house of Stuart is just one of the attractions at the Scottish National Portrait Gallery. The displays detail the history of 12 generations of Stuarts, from the time of Robert the Bruce to Queen Anne. Memorabilia include Mary, Queen of Scots' jewellery and a silver travelling canteen left by Bonnie Prince Charlie *(see p153)* at the Battle of Culloden. The upper gallery has a number of portraits of famous Scots, including a picture of Robert Burns and works by Van Dyck and other artists.

Van Dyck's *Princess Elizabeth and Princess Anne*, **National Portrait Gallery**

Street-by-Street: New Town **9**

THE FIRST PHASE of Edinburgh's "New Town" was built in the 18th century, to relieve the congested and unsanitary conditions of the medieval old town. Charlotte Square at the western end formed the climax of this initial phase, and its new architectural concepts were to influence all subsequent phases. Of these, the most magnificent is the Moray Estate, where a linked series of very large houses forms a crescent, an oval and a twelve-sided circus. The walk shown here explores this area of monumental Georgian town planning.

Albert Monument, Charlotte Square

Moray Place
The crowning glory of the Moray Estate, this circus consists of a series of immense houses and apartments, many still inhabited.

The Water of Leith is a small river running through a delightful gorge below Dean Bridge. There is a riverside walkway to Stockbridge.

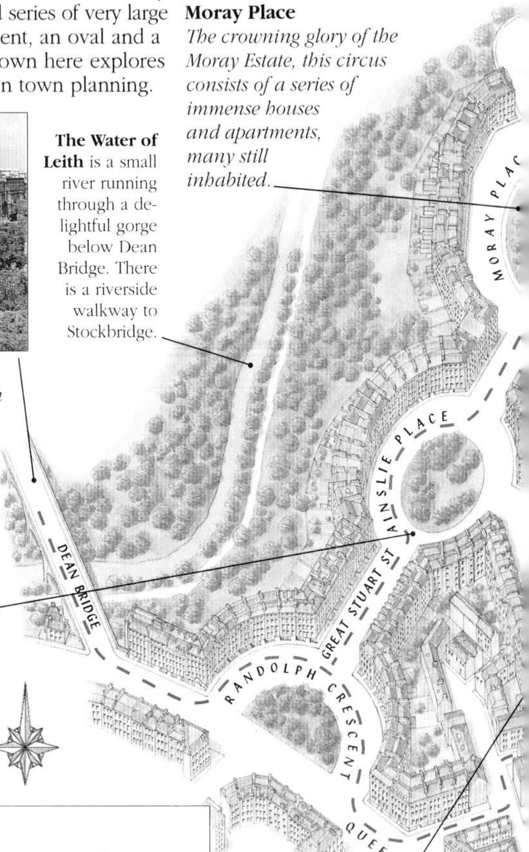

Dean Bridge
This was built in 1829 to the design of Thomas Telford. It gives views down to the Water of Leith and upstream to the weirs and old mill buildings of Dean Village.

Ainslie Place, an oval pattern of town houses, forms the core of the Moray Estate, linking Randolph Crescent and Moray Place.

STAR SIGHTS

★ **Charlotte Square**

★ **The Georgian House**

NEW TOWN ARCHITECTS

The driving force behind the creation of the New Town was George Drummond (1687–1766), the city's Provost, or Mayor. James Craig (1744–95) won the overall design competition in 1766. Robert Adam (1728–92) introduced classical ornamentation to Charlotte Square. Robert Reid (1774–1856) designed Heriot Row and Great King Street, and William Playfair (1790–1857) designed Royal Circus. The monumental development of the Moray Estate was the work of James Gillespie Graham (1776–1855).

Robert Adam

No. 14 was the residence of judge and diarist Lord Cockburn from 1813 to 1843.

| 0 metres | 100 |
| 0 yards | 100 |

KEY

- - - Suggested route

★ The Georgian House
No. 7 is owned by the National Trust for Scotland and is open to the public. It has been repainted in its original colours and furnished with appropriate antiques, and is a testament to the lifestyle of the upper sector of 18th-century Edinburgh society.

LOCATOR MAP
See Edinburgh Map pp54–5

Bute House is the official residence of the Secretary of State for Scotland, the minister of the UK government who represents Scotland.

York Place

★ Charlotte Square
The square was built between 1792 and 1811 to provide a series of lavish town houses for the most successful city merchants. Most of the buildings are now used as offices.

No. 39 Castle Street was the home of the writer Sir Walter Scott (see p86).

Princes Street Gardens
Princes Street was part of the initial building phase of the New Town. The north side is lined with shops; the gardens to the south lie below the castle.

West Register House was originally St George's Church, designed by Robert Adam.

No. 9 was the home of surgeon Joseph Lister (see p23) from 1870 to 1877. He developed methods of preventing infection both during and after surgery.

A view from Edinburgh Castle across the towers and spires of the city to Calton Hill in the distance

Calton Hill ⑩

City centre east, via Waterloo Pl.

CALTON HILL, at the east end of Princes Street, has one of Edinburgh's most memorable and baffling landmarks – a half-finished Parthenon. Conceived as the National Monument to the dead of the Napoleonic Wars, building began in 1822 but funds ran out and it was never finished. Public shame over its condition has given way to affection, as attitudes have softened over the last 170 years or so.

Fortunately, the nearby tower commemorating the British victory at Trafalgar was completed, in 1816. Named the **Nelson Monument**, the

City Observatory, Calton Hill, based on Classical Greek architecture

tower provides a fine vantage point over Edinburgh and the areas surrounding the city.

The Classical theme continues on top of Calton Hill with the old **City Observatory**, designed by William Playfair in 1818 and based on Athens' Temple of the Winds. One of the Observatory's domes has been converted into a theatre showing a slide show called the **Edinburgh Experience**.

Another Classical building, the old **Royal High School**, was created in the 1820s on the Regent Road side of Calton Hill. It was designed by Thomas Hamilton, with the Temple of Theseus at Athens in mind. Often cited as a possible home for a Scottish parliament, the building was the focus for the Vigil for Scottish Democracy, which campaigned from 1992 to 1997 for self government. A discreet cairn marking this effort stands a little way east of the National Monument on Calton Hill. It contains several "gift" stones, including one from Auschwitz in memory of a Scottish missionary who died there.

The final resting place of Thomas Hamilton is the **Old Calton Cemetery**, south of Waterloo Place, which he shares with philosopher David Hume and other celebrated Edinburgh residents.

🏛 **Nelson Monument**
📞 (0131) 556 2716. ⬭ Mon–Sat (Apr–Sep: Mon pm only). 🎟
🏛 **City Observatory**
Calton Hill. 📞 (0131) 556 4365. ⬭ by arrangement only. 🎟
🏛 **Edinburgh Experience**
City Observatory, Calton Hill. 📞 (0131) 337 8530. ⬭ Apr–Oct: 10:30–5:30pm daily (last show 5pm). 🎟 ♿ limited.

The grand façade of Holyrood Palace, renovated in the 17th century following an earlier fire

Holyrood Palace ⑪

East end of the Royal Mile. 📞 (0131) 556 1096. ⬭ daily. ⬤ check for seasonal closures. 🎟 ♿ limited.

KNOWN TODAY AS Queen Elizabeth II's official Scottish residence, Holyrood Palace was built by James IV in the grounds of an abbey in 1498. It was later the home of James V and his wife, Mary of Guise, and was remodelled in the 1670s for Charles II. The Royal Apartments (including the Throne Room and Royal Dining Room) are used for investitures and for banquets whenever the Queen visits the palace. At other times these rooms are open to the public.

A chamber in the so-called James V tower is famously associated with the unhappy reign of Mary, Queen of Scots *(see p44).* It was probably in this room, in 1566, that Mary saw the murder of her trusted Italian secretary, David Rizzio, authorized by her jealous husband, Lord Darnley. She had married Darnley only a year earlier, in Holyrood chapel, and was six months pregnant when she witnessed the murder, during which Rizzio's body was pierced "with fifty-six wounds".

Last of the pretenders to the English throne, Charles Edward Stuart (Bonnie Prince Charlie) held court at Holyrood Palace in 1745. He dazzled

James V's arms, Holyrood Palace

Edinburgh society with his magnificent parties, even while in the early stages of the Jacobite uprising *(see p45).*

Dynamic Earth ⑫

Holyrood Road. (0131) 550 7800.
Apr–Oct: daily; Nov–Mar: Wed–Sun.
www.dynamicearth.co.uk

DYNAMIC EARTH is a permanent exhibition about the planet, which opened in the spring of 1999. Visitors are taken on a journey from the earth's volcanic beginnings to the first appearance of life. Further displays concentrate on the world's climatic zones and dramatic natural phenomena such as tidal waves and earthquakes. State-of-the-art lighting and interactive techniques produce the special effects for 90 minutes of learning and entertainment.

The exhibition building is fronted by a 1,000-seat stone amphitheatre designed by Sir Michael Hopkins, and it incorporates a translucent tented roof. Situated beneath Salisbury Crags, the modern lines of Dynamic Earth contrast sharply with the natural landscape. The project was funded largely by the Millennium Commission, with funds raised by the UK's National Lottery.

New Scottish Parliament ⑬

Holyrood Rd.
www.scottish-devolution.org.uk

FOLLOWING DECADES of Scottish calls for more political self-determination, a referendum in 1997 on the issue of whether or not to have a Scottish parliament, with some powers devolving from the UK parliament in London, resulted in a majority "yes" vote. This site at Holyrood was chosen for the new parliament, and in early 1998 a world-wide competition was held to find a suitable designer for the building. The successful candidate was the innovative Enric Miralles, who gained prominence through his work on buildings at the 1992 Barcelona Olympics. This new parliament is scheduled to open for business in the autumn of 2001.

Holyrood Park and Arthur's Seat ⑭

Main access via Holyrood Park Rd,
Holyrood Rd and Meadowbank Terrace.

HOLYROOD PARK, adjacent to Holyrood Palace, covers over 260 hectares (640 acres) of varying terrain, topped by a rugged 250-m (820-ft) hill. Known as Arthur's Seat, the

hill is actually a volcano that has been extinct for 350 million years. The area has been a royal hunting ground since at least the time of King David I, who died in 1153, and a royal park since the 16th century.

The name Holyrood, which means "holy cross", comes from an episode in the life of David I when, in 1128, he was knocked from his horse by a stag while out hunting. Legend has it that a cross appeared miraculously in his hands to ward off the animal and, in thanksgiving, the king founded the Abbey of the Holy Cross, Holyrood Abbey. The name Arthur's Seat is probably a corruption of Archer's Seat, a more prosaic explanation for the name than any link with the legendary King Arthur.

The park has three small lochs. St Margaret's near the Palace is the most romantic, with its resident swans and position under the ruins of St Anthony's Chapel. Dunsapie Loch is the highest and loneliest, sitting 112 m (367 ft) above sea level under the eastern side of Arthur's Seat. Duddingston Loch, on the south side of the park, is home to a large number of wildfowl.

The **Salisbury Crags** are among the park's most striking features. Their dramatic profile, along with that of Arthur's Seat, can be seen from many kilometres away. The Crags form a parabola of red cliffs that sweep round and up from Holyrood Palace, above a steep supporting hillside. A rough track, called the Radical Road, follows their base.

Arthur's Seat and the Salisbury Crags, looming above the city

Further Afield

A LTHOUGH INEXTRICABLY linked to the rest of Edinburgh, the inhabitants of Leith insist that they do not live in the city itself. More than just a docks area, Leith has plenty of attractions for the visitor. Close by is the magnificent Royal Botanic Garden. Dean Village offers riverside walks, galleries and antique shops. To the west of the city are the historic Hopetoun House and Linlithgow Palace, to the east is Haddington and a dramatic coastline.

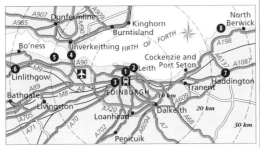

10km = 6miles

KEY

▦	Urban area
✈	Airport
🚉	Train station
—	Intercity train line
▬	Motorway (highway)
▬	Major road
—	Minor road

SIGHTS AT A GLANCE

Dean Village ❸
East Lothian Coast ❽
Forth Bridges ❹
Haddington ❼
Hopetoun House ❺
Leith ❷
Linlithgow Palace ❻
Royal Botanic Garden ❶

A specimen from the Palm House in the city's Royal Botanic Garden

Royal Botanic Garden ❶

Inverleith Row. 🕿 *(0131) 552 7171.*
📷 🔵 *daily.* ♿ 🛒 www.rbge.org.uk

T HIS MAGNIFICENT garden lies a short way to the north of the New Town, across the Water of Leith (a river that runs from the Pentland Hills down through Edinburgh and into the Firth of Forth at Leith).

The garden is a descendant of a Physic Garden near Holyrood House that was created by two doctors in 1670. It was moved to its present location in 1820, and since then has been progressively enlarged and developed. Public access is from the east (well served by buses) and from the west (offering better car parking). The garden benefits from a hill site, giving southerly views across the city.

There is a remarkable rock garden in the southeast corner and an indoor exhibition and interpretation display in the northeast corner. There are also extensive greenhouses in traditional and modern architectural styles, dedicated to different climatic conditions and offering fascinating hideaways on rainy days. Be sure not to miss the alpine display to the northwest of the greenhouses, or the beautiful and fragrant rhododendron walk.

Leith ❷

Northeast of the city centre, linked by Leith Walk.

L EITH IS A HISTORIC port that has traded for centuries with Scandinavia, the Baltic and Holland, and has always been the port for Edinburgh. It was incorporated into the city in 1920, and now forms a northeastern suburb.

The medieval core of narrow streets and quays includes a number of historic warehouses and merchants' houses dating from the 13th and 14th centuries. There was a great expansion of the docks in the 19th century, and many port buildings date from this period.

Shipbuilding and port activities have diminished, but there has been a renaissance in recent years in the form of conversions of warehouse buildings to offices, residences and, most notably, restaurants. The Shore and Dock Place now has Edinburgh's most dense concentration of seafood bistros and varied restaurants *(see pp177–8).*

The tourist attractions have been further boosted by the presence of the former British **Royal Yacht Britannia**, which is on display in Leith's western dock, before moving to a new "Ocean Terminal" in 2000.

⚓ Royal Yacht Britannia
Western Harbour, Leith Docks.
🕿 *(0131) 555 8800.* 🔵 *daily.* 📷 ♿

The British Royal Yacht Britannia, berthed at Leith's western dock

Leger's *The Team at Rest* (1950), Scottish National Gallery of Modern Art

Dean Village ❸

Northwest of the city centre.

THIS INTERESTING area lies in the valley of the Water of Leith, just a few minutes' walk northwest from Charlotte Square *(see map p54)*. A series of water mills along the river have been replaced by attractive buildings of all periods.

Access to Dean Village can be gained by walking down Bell's Brae from Randolph Crescent. A riverside walk threads its way between the historic buildings, crossing the river on a series of footbridges. Upstream from Dean Village the riverside walk leads in a few minutes to a footbridge and a flight of steps giving access to the **Scottish National Gallery of Modern Art**. This gallery offers an excellent collection of modern works of art. The main access for vehicles, as well as less energetic pedestrians, can be found on Belford Road.

Downstream from Dean Village, the riverside walkway passes under the magnificent high level bridge designed by Thomas Telford. It then passes

St Bernard's Well before arriving in the urban village of Stockbridge. Both antiques and curio shops can be found on the south side of the river in St Stephen Street. The riverside walk continues northeast, close to the Royal Botanic Garden. The city centre is a short walk away, via Royal Circus and Howe Street.

17th-century stone houses on the historic Bell's Brae

🏛 **Scottish National Gallery of Modern Art**
Belford Road. 📞 *(0131) 624 6200.*
⭕ *daily.* 📷 *special exhibitions only.* ♿

Forth Bridges ❹

Lothian. 🚊 🚌 *Dalmeny, Inverkeithing.*

THE SMALL TOWN of South Queensferry is dominated by the two great bridges that span 1.5 km (1 mile) across the River Forth to the town of Inverkeithing. The spectacular rail bridge, the first major steel-built bridge in the world, was opened in 1890 and remains one of the greatest engineering achievements of the late Victorian era. Its massive cantilevered sections are held together by more than eight million rivets, and the painted area adds up to some 55 ha (135 acres). The saying "it's like painting the Forth Bridge" has become a byword for non-stop, repetitive endeavour. It was the rail bridge that inspired the book *The Bridge* (1986) by popular Scottish writer Iain Banks *(see p25).*

The neighbouring road bridge was the largest suspension bridge outside the US when it was opened in 1964, a distinction now held by the Humber Bridge in England.

The two bridges make an impressive contrast, best seen from the promenade at South Queensferry. The town received its name from Queen Margaret *(see p61)*, who reigned with her husband, King Malcolm III, in the 11th century. She used the ferry here on her frequent journeys between Edinburgh and her home, the royal palace at Dunfermline in Fife *(see p124).*

The huge, cantilevered Forth Rail Bridge, seen from South Queensferry

Hopetoun House ❺

The Lothians. 🎫 *(0131) 331 2451.*
🚆 *Dalmeny then taxi.* ⭘ *mid-Apr–Sep: daily.* 🏷️ ♿ *limited.* 🚻

AN EXTENSIVE PARKLAND by the Firth of Forth, designed in the style of Versailles, is the setting for one of Scotland's finest stately homes. The original house, of which only the central block remains, was completed in 1707 and later absorbed into William Adam's grand extension. The dignified, horseshoe-shaped plan and lavish interior represent Neo-Classical 18th-century architecture at its best. The red and yellow state drawing rooms, with their Rococo plasterwork and ornate mantelpieces, are particularly impressive. The present Marquess of Linlithgow is a descendant of the first Earl of Hopetoun, for whom the house was originally built.

A wooden panel above the main stairs depicting Hopetoun House

Linlithgow Palace ❻

Kirk Gate, Linlithgow, Lothian.
🎫 *(01506) 842896.* 🚆 🏠 ⭘ *daily.* 🏷️ ♿ *limited.*

STANDING ON THE edge of Linlithgow Loch, the former royal palace of Linlithgow is now one of the country's most visited ruins. It dates back largely to the building commissioned by James V in 1425, following a fire the previous

Ornate fountain in the ruins of Linlithgow Palace

year, though some sections date from the 14th century. The vast scale of the building is demonstrated by the 28-m (94-ft) long Great Hall, with its huge fireplace and windows. The restored fountain in the courtyard was a wedding present in 1538 from James V to his wife, Mary of Guise. His daughter, Mary, Queen of Scots *(see p44)*, was born at Linlithgow in 1542.

The adjacent Church of St Michael is Scotland's largest pre-Reformation church and a fine example of the Scottish Decorated style. Consecrated in the 13th century, the church was damaged by the fire of 1424. The building as it is today was completed in the 16th century.

Haddington ❼

East Lothian. 🚆 *frequent services from Edinburgh and North Berwick.*

THIS ATTRACTIVE county town is situated about 24 km (15 miles) east of Edinburgh. It was destroyed on various occasions during the Wars of Independence in the 13th–14th

centuries, and again in the 16th century. The agricultural revolution brought great prosperity, giving Haddington many historic houses, churches, and other public buildings. A programme of restoration has helped the town to retain its character. The River Tyne encloses the town, and there are attractive riverside walks and parkland. ("A walk around Haddington" guide is available from newsagents.) The parish church of St Mary's, southeast of the centre, dates from 1462 and is one of the largest in the area. Parts of the church have been rebuilt in recent years, having been destroyed in the siege of 1548. A short way south of the town lies **Lennoxlove House**, with its ancient tower house.

🏠 Lennoxlove House
🎫 *(01620) 823720.* ⭘ *Easter–Oct: pm only Wed–Thu & Sat–Sun.* 🏷️

East Lothian Coast ❽

ℹ️ *North Berwick (01620) 892197.*

STRETCHING EAST from Mussel-burgh for some 65 km (40 miles), the coast of East Lothian offers many opportunities for beach activities, windsurfing, golf, viewing seabirds and coastal walks. The coastline is a pleasant mixture of beaches, low cliffs, woodland, golf

The historic and tranquil town of Haddington on the River Tyne

courses and some farmland. Although the A198 and A1 are adjacent to the coast for only short distances, they give easy access to a series of public car parks (a small charge is made in summer), from where it is a short walk to the shore. Among these visitor points are Longniddry Bents, a small west-facing bay favoured by windsurfers, and Gullane, perhaps the best beach for

Tantallon Castle, looking out to the North Sea

seaside activities. Yellowcraig, near Dirleton, is another lovely bay, lying about 400 m (440 yds) from the car park. Lime-tree Walk, near Tyninghame, has the long, east-facing beach of Ravensheugh Sands (a ten-minute walk along a woodland track). Belhaven Bay, just west of Dunbar, is a large beach providing walks along the estuary of the River Tyne. Barns Ness, east of Dunbar, offers a geological nature trail and an impressive lighthouse. Skateraw Harbour is an attractive small bay, despite the presence of Torness nuclear power station to the east. Finally, there is another delightful beach to be found at Seacliff, reached by a private toll road that leaves the A198 about 3 km (2 miles) east of North Berwick. This sheltered bay has spectacular views of the glistening white of the Bass Rock, home to one of the largest gannet (a type of marine bird) colonies in Britain.

The rock itself can be seen at close quarters by taking the boat trip from North Berwick harbour (summer only). Other features of interest along this coastline include **Dirleton Castle** and **Tantallon Castle**, perched on a cliff top near Seacliff beach. There is a small industrial museum at Prestonpans and bird watching in Aberlady Bay. North Berwick and Dunbar are towns worthy of a visit, and **Torness Power Station** has a visitors' centre.

Dirleton Castle
(01620) 850330. ☐ daily.

Tantallon Castle
(01620) 892727. ☐ Apr–Sep: daily; Oct–Mar: Sat–Thu am.

Torness Power Station
(01368) 873000. ☐ mid-Jan–mid-Dec: daily.

EAST LOTHIAN COASTAL WALK

For a very attractive longer coast walk, there is easy public access along the footpath from Gullane Bay to North Berwick. The path follows the coastline, crossing grassy heathland between the alternating sandy bays and low rocky headlands, with views of the coast of Fife to the north. There are small islands along the way. The last part of the walk into North Berwick has wonderful views east to the white slopes of the Bass Rock.

TIPS FOR WALKERS

Starting point: Gullane Bay.
Finishing point: North Berwick.
Length: 10 km (6 miles); 3 hours.
Getting there: by car; a bus service between Edinburgh and North Berwick gives access to both ends.
Level: easy (one steep section).

Gullane Bay

Muirfield

Gullane

Dirleton

North Berwick

KEY

0 kilometres 2
0 miles 1

☐ Urban area
– – Route
▬▬ Major road
═══ Minor road
╫╫╫ Train line
☀ Viewpoint
P Parking

SHOPPING IN EDINBURGH

ESPITE THE GROWTH of new out-of-town malls, Princes Street remains one of the top 12 retail centres in the British Isles. With the ancient Castle rising above the gardens along the street's south side, it is a unique and picturesque place to shop. Although many familiar chain stores can be found here, the capital also boasts its very own

Colourful Wemyssware china

department store, Jenners, a marvellous institution that has been in business for over 150 years. But there are shopping attractions away from Princes Street, too, including Scotland's best delicatessen (Valvona & Crolla), several excellent wine merchants, a selection of Highland clothing outfitters and an appealing collection of specialist stores.

DEPARTMENT STORES

PRINCES STREET has several good department stores, with **House of Fraser** at the west end being one of the best. **Jenners**, located opposite the Scott Monument, is unique to the capital. Founded on a different site in the late 1830s, Jenners established itself at its current premises in 1895. It has gained a reputation as Edinburgh's top store, and during the Christmas season is famed for its central atrium housing a Christmas tree. **John Lewis**, belonging to a nationwide chain of stores, is in a contemporary building of architectural interest on Leith Street.

CLOTHING

DESIGNER LABELS FOR men and women can be found in both Jenners and House of Fraser *(see Department Stores)*. **Corniche** on Jeffrey Street offers more interesting and

Traditional Highland dress and accessories, for sale on the Royal Mile

exciting women's fashion by designers such as Moschino and Mugler, while **Jane Davidson** is home to a more traditional, chic look. George Street contains a number of women's stores, including **Phase Eight**, **Escada** and **Cruise**. Cruise also has a shop catering for men, who can also go to **Smiths** and **Austin Reed** for smart suits. The **Schuh** chain has fashionable footwear for men and women. Several shops on the Royal Mile, including **Judith Glue**, sell interesting knitwear. The Royal Mile also boasts Highland outfitters offering made-to-measure kilts; **Hector Russell** is one of the best. **Kinloch Anderson** in Leith is also a leading example, and the shop has a small display on the history of tartan. **Graham Tiso** is the leading supplier of outdoor gear, with boots, rucksacks and waterproof clothing available at its flagship store in Leith.

FOOD AND DRINK

EDINBURGH HAS A reputation as Scotland's top city for eating out, and it matches this status on the shopping front with some very good food stores. **Valvona & Crolla**, a family-run delicatessen trading since the 1930s, is acknowledged as one of the best of its kind in the UK, let alone Scotland, and stocks good breads and an award-winning Italian wine selection. The **Peckham's** chain is present here, while **Glass & Thompson** is a good deli serving the New Town. Celebrated cheesemonger **Iain Mellis** started his business in Edinburgh, **MacSweens** are master haggis makers, and **Real Foods** is one of Scotland's longest-established wholefood stores.

Specialist wine merchants include **Peter Green** and **Cockburns of Leith**, as well as chains such as **Oddbins**, while **Cadenheads** supplies rare whiskies. **Justerini & Brooks** is the most distinguished wine and spirit

Princes Street from the top of Calton Hill

merchant in the city centre and **Oasts & Toasts** has an extensive range of beers from small independent breweries.

BOOKS AND NEWSPAPERS

THE CITY'S BEST family-run bookshop is **James Thin**. This chain's main branch is at South Bridge near Edinburgh University. The **Waterstone's** chain has virtually taken over the books trade in Princes Street with two branches (the west end branch has a fine coffee shop), while a third Waterstone's is found on George Street nearby. **The International Newsagents** on the High Street has a good selection of foreign newspapers and magazines.

ART, DESIGN AND ANTIQUES

ORIGINAL ART WORKS are on sale at a variety of galleries in the city. **The Scottish Gallery** in the New Town has everything from jewellery for under £100, to pieces by well-known Scottish artists sold at £10,000 or more. The prices at the **Printmakers Workshop** are more affordable, with an innovative range of limited-edition prints for sale, and the **Collective Gallery** offers experimental works. **Inhouse** has some remarkable designer furniture. Browsers looking for antiques should try Victoria Street, St Stephen's Street, the Grassmarket and Causeway-side. For large-scale fixtures

and fittings, the **Edinburgh Architectural Salvage Yard** sells everything from Victorian baths to staircases and doors.

Intricately patterned Edinburgh Crystal, a popular souvenir

DIRECTORY

DEPARTMENT STORES

House of Fraser
145 Princes St, EH2 4YZ.
((0131) 225 2472.

Jenners
48 Princes St, EH2 2YJ.
((0131) 225 2442.

John Lewis
69 St James Centre,
EH1 3SP.
((0131) 556 9121.

CLOTHING

Austin Reed
41 George St, EH2 2HN.
((0131) 225 6703.

Corniche
2 Jeffrey St, EH1 1DT.
((0131) 556 3707.

Cruise (men)
14 St Mary's St, EH1 1SU.
((0131) 556 2532.

Cruise (women)
94 George St, EH2 3DF.
((0131) 226 3524.

Escada
35a George St, EH2 2HN.
((0131) 225 9885.

Graham Tiso
41 Commercial St, EH6 6JD.
((0131) 554 9101.

Hector Russell
137–141 High St,
EH1 1SE.
((0131) 558 1254.

Jane Davidson
52 Thistle St, EH2 1EN.
((0131) 225 3280.

Judith Glue
64 High St, EH1 1TH.
((0131) 556 5443.

Kinloch Anderson
Commercial St, EH6 6EY.
((0131) 555 1390.

Phase Eight
47b George St,
EH2 2HT.
((0131) 226 4009.

Schuh
6 Frederick St, EH2 2HB.
((0131) 220 0290.

Smiths
124 High St, EH1 1QS.
((0131) 225 5927.

FOOD AND DRINK

Cadenheads
172 Canongate,
EH8 8DF.
((0131) 556 5864.

Cockburns of Leith
7 Devon Place, EH12 5HJ.
((0131) 337 6005.

Glass & Thompson
2 Dundas St, EH3 6HZ.
((0131) 557 0909.

Iain Mellis
30a Victoria St, EH1 2JW.
((0131) 226 6215.

Justerini & Brooks
45 George St, EH2 2HT.
((0131) 226 4202.

MacSweens
Dryden Rd, Bilston Glen,
Loanhead, EH20 9LZ.
((0131) 440 2555.

Oasts & Toasts
107 Morrison St,
EH3 8BX.
((0131) 228 8088.

Oddbins
37b George St, EH2 2HN.
((0131) 220 3488.

Peckham's
155 Bruntsfield Place,
EH10 3DG.
((0131) 229 7054.

Peter Green
37a Warrander Park Rd,
EH9 1HJ.
((0131) 229 5925.

Real Foods
37 Broughton St, EH1 3JU.
((0131) 557 1911.

Valvona & Crolla
19 Elm Row, EH7 4AA.
((0131) 556 6066.

BOOKS AND NEWSPAPERS

The International Newsagents
351 High St, EH1 1PW.
((0131) 225 4827.

James Thin
53–59 South Bridge,
EH1 1YS.
((0131) 556 6743.

Waterstone's
128 Princes St, EH2 4AD.
((0131) 226 2666.

ART, DESIGN AND ANTIQUES

Collective Gallery
28 Cockburn St, EH1 1NY.
((0131) 220 1260.

Edinburgh Architectural Salvage Yard
Unit 6,
Couper St, EH6 6HH.
((0131) 554 7077.

Inhouse
28 Howe St, EH3 6TG.
((0131) 225 2888.

Printmakers Workshop
23 Union St, EH1 3LR.
((0131) 557 2479.

The Scottish Gallery
16 Dundas St, EH3 6HZ.
((0131) 558 1200.

What to Buy

Scottish blend tobacco

SCOTLAND OFFERS A WIDE-RANGE of goods and souvenirs to tempt its visitors. Most food and drink items can be found in Edinburgh's food stores and off-licences (liquor stores that also stock tobacco). A number of specialist shops in the city sell more unusual Scottish crafts and products, from handcrafted jewellery to clothing, such as tartan kilts and Arran jumpers (sweaters). Certain areas of Scotland specialize in particular crafts – Orkney is famed for its jewellery, Caithness and Edinburgh for their beautifully engraved glassware.

Caithness glass paperweight   **Edinburgh glass goblet**

Scottish glass is beautifully decorated. The Caithness glass factories in Oban, Perth and Wick offer tours to show how delicate patterns are engraved.

Amethyst brooch   **Celtic brooch**

Celtic earrings

Scottish jewellery reflects either the area in which it was made, a culture (such as Celtic) or an artistic movement such as Art Nouveau. The unbroken, intricate patterns and knotwork in the jewellery pictured above symbolize the wish for eternal life.

Dagger ("dirk")

Sporran   Belt

Stag horn is carved into all manner of objects, both functional, as with this ashtray, and decorative.

Scottish tartan originally existed in the form of large woollen shawls (or plaids) worn by Highlanders in the 15th and 16th centuries. Today, "tartan" refers to the distinctive patterns woven into woolen cloth. Some of these patterns are based on the designs of centuries past. Tartan is used in the making of kilts and many other items.

Tartan tie and scarf

Classic Scottish kilt

Scottish textiles vary greatly, but the most distinctive include chunky woollens from Arran or Shetland; smart tweeds, such as Harris tweed with its fine-toothed check; softest cashmere, used to make jumpers (sweaters), cardigans and scarves; and fluffy sheepskin rugs.

Arran wool jumper (sweater)

Tweed jacket

PACKAGED FOODS

Food is a popular and accessible form of souvenir or gift to purchase during a visit to Scotland. Teatime is a favourite meal with the Scottish, offering such treats as Dundee cake, butter shortbread, Abernethy biscuits, Scotch pancakes and parlies (ginger cookies). Oatcakes are the traditional accompaniment to cheese in Scotland, although they also complement pâté and sweet toppings such as jam or honey. They are also delicious toasted and served with plenty of butter.

Vegetarian haggis   **Original haggis**

Haggis, the most famous of Scottish foods (see p32), traditionally consists of sheep's offal and oatmeal. It is now also available in vegetarian, venison and whisky-laced varieties.

Traditional pure butter shortbread   **Oatcakes**

Scotch Abernethy biscuits

Fudge is an extremely sweet confectionary made almost entirely of sugar and condensed milk. There are many different flavours, from vanilla to rum and raisin, walnut, chocolate and whisky.

Dairy vanilla fudge   **LochRanza whisky fudge**

BOTTLED DRINKS

Home to a large number of distilleries and breweries, Scotland is perhaps associated most with its alcoholic beverages. There is certainly a good range on sale, including locally brewed beers and ales, many varieties of Scotch whisky *(see pp30–31)* and an assortment of spirits and liqueurs, such as Drambuie and Glayva. But Scotland is also famed for its mountain spring water, which is sold still, fizzy (carbonated) or flavoured with fruits such as peach or melon.

Historic Scottish ales

Caledonian spring water

Beers and ales figure prominently in the drink produced in Scotland. Traditionally served by the pint in pubs, they can also be purchased in bottles. Alternative choices include fruit ales and heather ales, brewed using ancient Highland recipes.

Whisky is undoubtedly the most famous of all Scottish spirits. There are a huge number of whiskies from which to choose, each with a unique taste (see pp30–31). Drambuie is a variation on a theme, being a whisky-based, herb flavoured liqueur.

Drambuie   **Glenfiddich**   **LochRanza**   **Glen Ord**   **Bell's**

ENTERTAINMENT IN EDINBURGH

A postcard advertising the
Edinburgh Festival

ALTHOUGH MOST people associate entertainment in Edinburgh with the festivals that take place in August, the city also benefits from its status as the Scottish capital by acting as a centre for drama, dance and music. The Filmhouse is an important venue on the arthouse cinema circuit and some argue that Edinburgh's nightclubs are as good as those in Glasgow these days. Many bars offer an excellent range of Scotch whiskies and cask ales, while the expansion of the café-bar scene in the last few years means it is now possible to find a decent cup of coffee later on in the evening. Edinburgh is home to Scotland's national rugby union stadium, Murrayfield, host to international matches.

ENTERTAINMENT GUIDES

THE TWICE MONTHLY arts and entertainments magazine, *The List*, covers all events in both Edinburgh and Glasgow.

THEATRE AND DANCE

EDINBURGH'S POPULIST **The King's Theatre** hosts pantomimes and performances by touring companies. It is run by the same organization that manages Edinburgh Festival Theatre *(see Classical Music and Opera)*, which dominates in ballet and contemporary dance, although there are children's shows and music hall-style performances there too. **Edinburgh Playhouse** often has runs of internationally successful musicals, such as "Les Miserables", while **The Traverse** is home to more experimental work and has helped launch the careers of young Scottish playwrights. **The Royal Lyceum** tends to

Edinburgh Festival Theatre, venue
for dance, classical music and opera

opt for a more classical repertory with well-known plays and adaptations, but sometimes showcases new work too. Edinburgh University's theatre company stages shows at **Bedlam**, while both **Theatre Workshop** and **St Bride's** present innovative productions.

CLASSICAL MUSIC AND OPERA

VISITS FROM the Glasgow-based Scottish Opera and the Royal Scottish National Orchestra are hosted at the impressive, glass-fronted **Edinburgh Festival Theatre** which opened in 1994. Edinburgh is the home of the internationally acclaimed Scottish Chamber Orchestra, which stages performances at **The Queen's Hall**. Smaller venues throughout the city also host recitals, including Edinburgh University's **Reid Concert Hall** and **St Cecilia's Hall**. **St Giles Cathedral** hosts classical concerts by small groups, such as string quartets.

ROCK, JAZZ AND WORLD MUSIC

FOR MAJOR ROCK concerts by bands such as REM or U2, Murrayfield Stadium *(see Sports)* is called into use from time to time. Edinburgh Playhouse *(see Theatre and Dance)* has also played host to major pop stars. Edinburgh has an eclectic nightclub scene, and intimate sessions – including jazz and world music – often take place at clubs *(see Café-bars, Bars and Clubs)*. The Queen's Hall *(see Classical Music and Opera)* also hosts smaller shows. Folk and jazz musicians appear at the **Tron Ceilidh House** and **Jazz Joint**, respectively.

Some Edinburgh pubs have resident folk musicians and jazz bands – check *The List* magazine for details. **The Assembly Rooms** hosts regular *ceilidhs* (traditional Highland dance evenings).

CINEMA

EDINBURGH, LIKE every other major city, has seen a move to multiplex cinemas lately, although the largest, the **UCI** and the **ABC Multiplex**, are quite far from the centre. More convenient are **The Odeon** and the **ABC Film Centre**, while **The Dominion** is an old-fashioned, family-run affair, less brash than the others. **The Cameo** offers late-night shows and offbeat modern classics. **The Filmhouse** is the arthouse movie theatre for the city, and centre for the International Film Festival.

The ornate, colourful interior of
The King's Theatre, opened in 1906

Logo for the annual
Film Festival

Opening ceremony of a Five Nations rugby union match at Murrayfield

SPORTS

THE IMPRESSIVE **Murrayfield Stadium** is the national centre for Scottish rugby; internationals are played from late January to March. The **Scottish Claymores**, part of the NFL European league, play American football from April to June. There are two association football (soccer) sides, **Heart of Midlothian** in the west and **Hibernian** in Leith. **Meadowbank Stadium and Sports Centre** hosts league basketball.

CAFÉ-BARS, BARS AND CLUBS

CAFÉ-BARS have become a common sight in Edinburgh, and Broughton Street is an obvious centre. Some are associated more with nightlife, including **The Iguana**, **Indigo Yard**, **Po-Na-Na** and **The City Café**. Good examples of more traditional Edinburgh bars are **The Café Royal**, **Bennet's**, **The Cumberland** or **The Bow Bar**. All serve good cask ales, many brewed in Scotland, and an extensive selection of single malt Scotch whiskies. Some of the city's acclaimed club venues, which also host live bands from time to time, are **The Bongo Club**, **The Liquid Room** and **The Venue**.

DIRECTORY

THEATRE AND DANCE

Bedlam
11b Bristow Place, EH1 1E2.
(0131) 225 9893.

Edinburgh Playhouse
18–22 Greenside Place,
EH1 3AA.
(0131) 557 2590.

The King's Theatre
2 Leven St, EH3 9QI.
(0131) 529 6000.

The Royal Lyceum
30b Grindlay St, EH3 9AX.
(0131) 248 4848.

St Bride's
10 Orwell Terrace,
EH11 2DZ.
(0131) 346 1405.

Theatre Workshop
34 Hamilton Place,
EH3 5AX.
(0131) 226 5425.

The Traverse
10 Cambridge St, EH1 2ED.
(0131) 228 1404.

CLASSICAL MUSIC AND OPERA

Edinburgh Festival Theatre
13-29 Nicolson St, EH8 9FT.
(0131) 529 6000.

The Queen's Hall
Clerk St, EH8 9JG.
(0131) 668 2019.

Reid Concert Hall
Bristo Sq, EH19 1HD.
(0131) 650 4367.

St Cecilia's Hall
Cowgate, EH1 1LJ.
(0131) 650 2423.

St Giles Cathedral
Royal Mile, EH1 1RE.
(0131) 225 9442.

ROCK, JAZZ AND WORLD MUSIC

Assembly Rooms
George St, EH2 2LR.
(0131) 220 4349.

Jazz Joint
8–16a Morrison St,
EH3 8JB.
(0131) 221 1288.

Tron Ceilidh House
9 Hunter Sq, EH1 1RR.
(0131) 226 0931.

CINEMA

ABC Film Centre
120 Lothian Rd, EH3 8BG.
(0131) 228 1638.

ABC Multiplex
120 Wester Hailes Rd,
EH14 1SW.
(0131) 453 1569.

The Cameo
38 Home St, EH39LZ.
(0131) 228 4141.

The Dominion
18 Newbattle Terrace,
EH10 4RT.
(0131) 447 4771.

The Filmhouse
88 Lothian Rd, EH3 9BZ.
(0131) 228 2688.

The Odeon
7 Clerk St, EH8 9JH.
(0131) 667 0971.

UCI
Kinnaird Park,
Newcraighall, EH15 3RD.
(0131) 669 0777.

SPORTS

Heart of Midlothian
Tynecastle Stadium,
Gorgie Rd, EH11 2NL.
(0131) 200 7200.

Hibernian
Easter Road Stadium,
12 Albion Place, EH7 5QG.
(0131) 661 2159.

Meadowbank Stadium and Sports Centre
139 London Rd, EH7 6AE.
(0131) 661 5351.

Murrayfield Stadium
Murrayfield, EH12 5PJ.
(0131) 346 5000.

Scottish Claymores
137 George St, EH2 0BR.
(0131) 478 7200.

CAFÉ-BARS, BARS AND CLUBS

Bennet's
8 Leven St, EH3 9LG.
(0131) 229 5143.

The Bongo Club
14 New St, EH8 8DW.
(0131) 558 7604.

The Bow Bar
80 West Bow, EH1 2HH.
(0131) 226 7667.

The Café Royal
19 W Register St, EH2 2AA.
(0131) 556 1884.

The City Café
19 Blair St, EH1 1QR.
(0131) 220 0127.

The Cumberland
1–3 Cumberland St,
EH3 6RT.
(0131) 558 3134.

The Iguana
41 Lothian St, EH1 1HB.
(0131) 220 4288.

Indigo Yard
7 Charlotte Lane, EH2 4QZ.
(0131) 220 5603.

The Liquid Room
9c Victoria St, EH1 2HE.
(0131) 225 2564.

Po-Na-Na
43b Frederick St, EH2 1EP.
(0131) 226 2224.

The Venue
15–21 Calton Rd, EH8 8DL.
(0131) 557 3073.

The Edinburgh Festival

A masked Fringe street performer

AUGUST IN EDINBURGH means "the Festival". The Edinburgh International Festival is one of the world's premier arts jamborees, covering drama, dance, opera, music and ballet. The more eclectic "Fringe" developed in parallel with the official event, but has now exceeded it in terms of size. Both have been going strong for over 50 years, as has the Edinburgh International Film Festival. The British Army contributes with the Military Tattoo and, more recently, the Edinburgh Book Festival and Jazz & Blues Festival have also been staged in August. A total of half a million people visit these events.

Entrance to the Fringe information office, located on the Royal Mile

EDINBURGH INTERNATIONAL FESTIVAL

AS A CULTURAL antidote to the austerity of post-war Europe, where many cities were devastated and food rationing was common even in the victorious countries, Edinburgh held its first arts festival in 1947. Over the years it grew in scope and prestige, and it is now one of the top events in the world calendar of performing arts. It boasts a strong programme of classical music, traditional ballet, contemporary dance, opera and drama, and is held in major venues across the city *(see Directory p77)*.

The grand finale of the International Festival is a breathtaking spectacle, with some 250,000 crowding into the city centre to see a magnificent fireworks display based at the Castle. The lucky few with tickets for the Ross Bandstand in Princes Street Gardens also experience the fireworks concert by the Scottish Chamber Orchestra.

THE FRINGE

THE FRINGE started with a few performances providing an alternative to the official events of the International Festival, in the first year it was staged. A decade later, coming to Edinburgh to appear "on the Fringe" was an established pastime for amateurs, student drama companies or anyone else. All that was needed was a space to perform in the city in August. This haphazard approach has long since given way to a more formal one, with an administrative body running the Fringe and, in recent years, a core of professionally-run venues attracting the bulk of the Fringe audiences. The Assembly Rooms in George Street *(see Directory p77)* and the Pleasance Theatre in The Pleasance host shows by television celebrities whose stand-up comedy or cabaret fails to fit the International Festival format.

The original vibrancy of the Fringe still exists, and in church halls and other odd venues across Edinburgh, including the city's streets, Fringe-goers can find everything from musicals performed by school children to experimental adaptations of Kafka's works.

Enjoying the August sun and street entertainment on the Royal Mile

EDINBURGH INTERNATIONAL FILM FESTIVAL

LIKE THE OTHER long established festivals that take place in Edinburgh, the International Film Festival dates from 1947. Although it started with a focus on documentary cinema, it soon began to widen and encompass both arthouse and popular movies.

The Festival invented "the retrospective" as a means of studying a film-maker's work. It has seen premieres by such noted directors as Woody Allen and Steven Spielberg. Since its 1995 relaunch, the

Crowds throng around the colourful Fringe street performers

The Military Tattoo at Edinburgh Castle, with an audience of thousands

Festival has been broken down into four main sections. There is a showcase for young British talent, a world premieres section, a film study category, and a major retrospective.

Although the showings are screened primarily at The Filmhouse on Lothian Road, every city centre cinema now takes part in the festival to some extent *(see Directory p77 for details of all the cinemas).*

EDINBURGH MILITARY TATTOO

THE ENDURING popularity of the Military Tattoo never fails to surprise some people, or to charm others. It has been running since 1950, when the British Army decided to contribute to Edinburgh's August events with displays of martial prowess and music on the picturesque Castle Esplanade.

Temporary stands are built on the Esplanade each summer in preparation for the 200,000 visitors who watch the Tattoo over its three-week run. This enormous spectacle heralds the approach of the other, assorted August arts festivals. Marching bands and musicians from the

A painted street performer showing his skill at staying as still as a statue

armed forces of other countries are invited every year to enhance the show. For many, the highlight of the Tattoo is a solo piper playing a haunting pibroch lament *(see p28)* from the Castle battlements.

A temporary marquee selling books at the Edinburgh Book Festival

EDINBURGH BOOK FESTIVAL

EVERY AUGUST, a mini-village of marquees is erected in the beautiful Georgian surroundings of Charlotte Square Gardens in the city centre. This temporary village plays host to two weeks of book-related events and talks by a variety of writers, from novelists and poets to those who specialize in cook books or children's fiction. Scottish authors are always well represented.

Originally held every other year, the Book Festival became so popular that since 1998 it has been an annual event coinciding with the other festivals.

EDINBURGH JAZZ & BLUES FESTIVAL

FOR AROUND NINE days in early August a selection of international jazz performers comes to Edinburgh to give concerts, accompanied by Scotland's principal jazz musicians.

The Queen's Hall on Clerk Street *(see p76)* is the main centre, although other venues in the city are used. There is also a free, open-air Mardi Gras day in the Grassmarket, in the Old Town, on the opening Saturday. The Blues element of the Festival is held in its own separate venue and is also very successful, attracting many UK and American performers.

DIRECTORY

Edinburgh International Festival
21 Market St, EH1 1BW.
(0131) 473 2001.
www.go-edinburgh.co.uk

The Fringe
The Fringe Office,
180 High St, EH1 1QS.
(0131) 226 5257.
www.edfringe.com

Edinburgh International Film Festival
88 Lothian Rd, EH3 9BZ.
(0131) 228 4051.
www.edfilmfest.org.uk

Edinburgh Book Festival
Scottish Book Centre,
137 Dundee St, EH11 1BG.
(0131) 228 5444.
www.edinburghfestivals.co.uk

Edinburgh Jazz & Blues Festival
Assembly Direct,
89 Giles St, EH6 6BZ.
(0131) 553 4000.
Box office: (0131) 667 7776.
www.jazzmusic.co.uk

Military Tattoo
Edinburgh Tattoo,
32 Market St, EH1 1QB.
(0131) 225 1188.
www.edintattoo.co.uk

SOUTHERN SCOTLAND

*S*OUTHERN SCOTLAND *is a blend of attractive landscapes and historic houses, castles and abbeys. Sadly, many of these ancient buildings exist only in fortified or ruined form due to the frontier wars that dated from the late 13th century. The rounded hills of the Borders region and the more rugged peaks of Dumfries & Galloway bore the brunt of this fierce conflict between Scotland and England.*

In 1296 Scotland committed itself to the Wars of Independence against the English, and it was Southern Scotland that suffered the most. The strife caused by the many battles lasted for three centuries, as first Scottish self-determination, and then alliances with France, led to strained relations between Scotland and its southern neighbour, England. Dryburgh, one of the area's magnificent 12th-century abbeys, was burned twice, first by the English in 1322 and then again in 1544.

The virtual independence of the Borders district brought further conflict. Powerful families had operated under local laws set in place since the mid-12th century, and when Scottish kings were not fighting the English, they led raids into the Border country to try and bring it back under central control.

Over the years, some of the great dramas of Scottish history have been played out in the South. Robert the Bruce's guerrilla army defeated an English force at Glen Trool in 1307, but Flodden, near Coldstream, was the scene of the country's worst military reverse in 1513, when King James IV of Scotland and thousands of his men fell in battle. Today, the quiet countryside around the Borders market towns, and the beautiful mountain scenery in Dumfries & Galloway, seem to belie such violent history. The area is now known for its manufacturing of textiles and for promoting its literary associations, as Sir Walter Scott lived at Abbotsford, near St Boswells. But it is the ruins of the great Border abbeys, castles and battlegrounds that serve as a reminder of Southern Scotland's turbulent past.

Fishing in the tranquil waters of the River Tweed, which weaves its way through the Border country

◁ **The majestic ruins and colourful gardens of Melrose Abbey, one of the four great Border abbeys**

Exploring Southern Scotland

Southern scotland has a variety of landscapes and small towns of great character, but the region is often over-looked by visitors keen to reach Edin-burgh, Glasgow or the Highlands. The hills around Glen Trool in Dumfries & Galloway are beautiful and dramatic while, further east, the Border hills are less rugged but offer some classic pan-oramas such as Scott's View, near Mel-rose. The Ayrshire coast has a string of holiday resorts; the Solway Firth coast is fine touring country, quiet and pic-turesque; and St Abb's Head in the east is one of Scotland's most impor-tant wildlife reserves.

The Gothic abbey church at Melrose, once one of the richest abbeys in Scotland

GLASGOW

M8

A70

HAMILTON

PENTLAND HILLS

M74

NEW LANARK **11**

10

A77

A78

BIGGAR

ARDROSSAN

KILMARNOCK

A70

PRESTWICK

A70

AYR

SANQUHAR **12**

MOFFAT

CULZEAN CASTLE **21**

DRUMLANRIG CASTLE **13**

BURNS HERITAGE TRAIL **15**

GALLOWAY FOREST PARK **19**

16

CAERLAVEROCK CASTLE

STRANRAER

THREAVE CASTLE **14**

THE RHINNS OF GALLOWAY **20**

17 KIRKCUDBRIGHT

Solway Firth

WHITHORN **18**

| 0 kilometres | 20 |
| 0 miles | 20 |

Getting Around

Travelling east to west and vice versa can be problematic as all the main routes run north/south from Edinburgh and Glasgow to England. There are rural bus services but these tend to be infrequent and slow. Rail links down the east coast from Edinburgh, and from Glasgow to Ayrshire, are good, and there is also a train service from Glasgow to Stranraer, the ferry port for Northern Ireland. Exploring scenic areas away from the coasts is best done by car.

Key

- Motorway (highway)
- Major road
- Scenic route
- Scenic path
- River
- Viewpoint

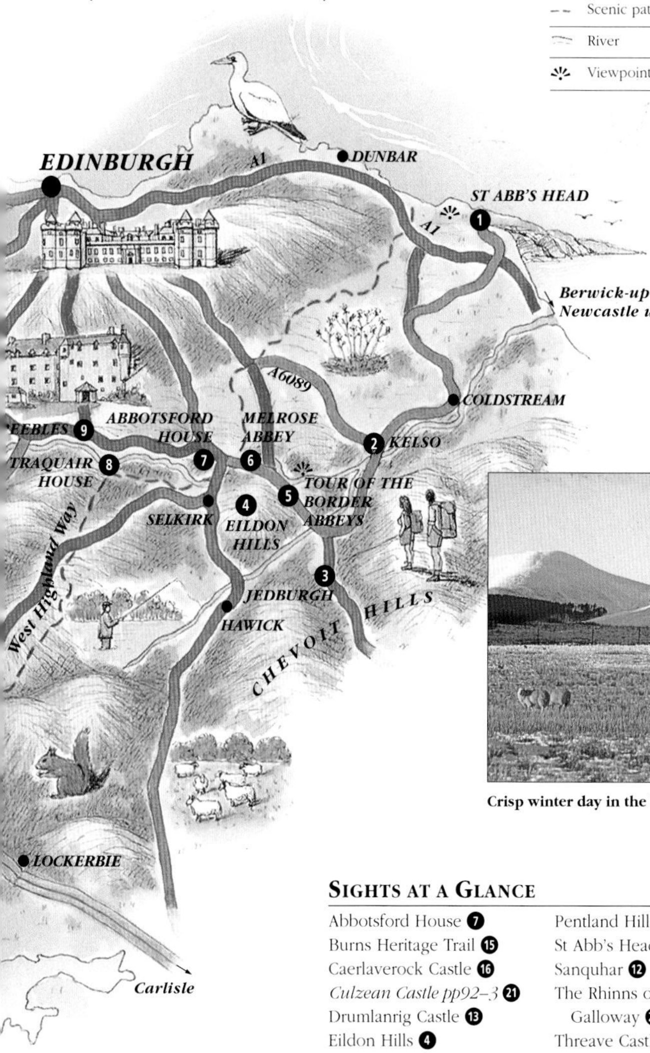

EDINBURGH
A1
DUNBAR
ST ABB'S HEAD
1
A1
Berwick-upon-Tweed,
Newcastle upon Tyne
A6089
COLDSTREAM
PEEBLES 9
ABBOTSFORD HOUSE 7
MELROSE ABBEY 6
2 KELSO
TRAQUAIR HOUSE 8
TOUR OF THE BORDER ABBEYS 5
SELKIRK
4 EILDON HILLS
3
JEDBURGH
HAWICK
CHEVIOT HILLS
West Highland Way
LOCKERBIE
Carlisle

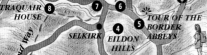

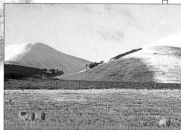

Crisp winter day in the Pentland Hills

Sights at a Glance

Abbotsford House 7
Burns Heritage Trail 15
Caerlaverock Castle 16
Culzean Castle pp92–3 21
Drumlanrig Castle 13
Eildon Hills 4
Galloway Forest Park 19
Jedburgh 3
Kelso 2
Kirkcudbright 17
Melrose Abbey 6
New Lanark 11
Peebles 9
Pentland Hills 10
St Abb's Head 1
Sanquhar 12
The Rhinns of Galloway 20
Threave Castle 14
Traquair House 8
Whithorn 18

Tour
Tour of the Border Abbeys 5

See Also

- ***Where to Stay*** pp167-8
- ***Where to Eat*** p178

The shattered crags and cliffs of St Abb's Head

St Abb's Head ❶

The Borders. 🚊 Berwick-upon-Tweed. 🚌 from Edinburgh. 🚆 (01890) 771443. ⭘ Easter–Oct: daily.

THE JAGGED CLIFFS of St Abb's Head, rising 91 m (300 ft) from the North Sea, offer a spectacular view of thousands of seabirds wheeling and diving below. This nature reserve is an important site for cliff-nesting sea birds and, during the May to June breeding season, it becomes the home of more than 50,000 birds, including fulmars, guillemots, kittiwakes and puffins.

St Abb's village has one of the few unspoiled working harbours on Scotland's east coast. A clifftop trail begins at the visitors' centre, where displays include identification boards and a touch table where young visitors can get to grips with wings and feathers.

Kelso ❷

The Borders. 🚶 6,035. 🚆 🚹 The Square (01573) 223464, Easter–Oct.

KELSO HAS a charming centre, with a cobbled square surrounded by Georgian and Victorian buildings. Nearby **Kelso Race Course** holds regular horse races and is a popular attraction. The focus of the town, however, is the ruin of the 12th-century **abbey**. This was the oldest and wealthiest of the four Border Abbeys founded by David I, but it suffered from wars with England and was severely damaged in

1545. **Floors Castle** on the northern edge of Kelso is more complete. Designed by William Adam in the 1720s, it was then substantially reworked by William Playfair after 1837.

🚹 **Kelso Race Course**
🚆 (01573) 224767. 🖼 ♿
♣ **Floors Castle**
🚆 (01573) 223333. ⭘May–Oct: daily. 🖼 ♿ 📷

Jedburgh ❸

The Borders. 🚶 4,250. 🚆
🚹 Murray's Green (01835) 863435.

THE TOWN IS home to the mock-medieval **Jedburgh Castle**. Built in 1820, the castle was once the local jail but now serves as a museum with some good displays on the area's history, and an exhibition on life in a 19th-century prison.

Built around 1500, **Mary, Queen of Scots' House** is so-called due to a visit by the queen in 1566. The house was converted into a general museum in the 1930s, and in 1987

Jedburgh's medieval Abbey church at the centre of the attractive town

(on the 400th anniversary of Mary's execution) it became a centre dedicated to telling her life story. Exhibits include a copy of her death mask.

Jedburgh Abbey is one of the great quartet of 12th-century Border Abbeys, along with Dryburgh, Kelso and Melrose. The Abbey church has some interesting features including a rose window, and there is an excellent visitors' centre.

♣ **Jedburgh Castle**
🚆 (01835) 863254. ⭘ Easter–Oct: daily (Sun: pm). 🖼
🚩 **Mary, Queen of Scots' House**
🚆 (01835) 863331. ⭘ Mar–Nov: daily. 🖼
🚩 **Jedburgh Abbey**
🚆 (01835) 863925. ⭘ daily. 🖼

A picturesque view of the Eildon Hills in late summer sunshine

Eildon Hills ❹

The Borders. 🚆 🚹 Melrose (01896) 822555, Easter–Oct.

THE THREE PEAKS of the Eildon Hills dominate the central Borders landscape. Mid Hill is the tallest at 422 m (1,385 ft), while North Hill once had a Bronze Age hill fort dating from before 500 BC, and later a Roman fort. In this part of the country the most celebrated name is Sir Walter Scott *(see p86)*, who had a particular affection for these hills. A panorama of the Eildons called **Scott's View** lies just east of Melrose, near Dryburgh Abbey, and this is the best location to see the hills' position as they rise above the Tweed Valley.

Tour of the Border Abbeys ⑤

T HE SCOTTISH BORDERS are scattered with the ruins of ancient buildings destroyed in conflicts between England and Scotland. Most poignant of all are the Border Abbeys, whose magnificent architecture bears witness to their former spiritual and political power. Founded during the 12th-century reign of David I, the abbeys were destroyed by Henry VIII in 1545. This tour takes in the abbeys and some other sights.

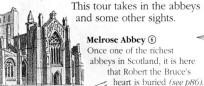

Melrose Abbey ⑥
Once one of the richest abbeys in Scotland, it is here that Robert the Bruce's heart is buried *(see p86)*.

Kelso Abbey ②
The largest of the four Border Abbeys, Kelso was founded in 1128 and took 84 years to complete.

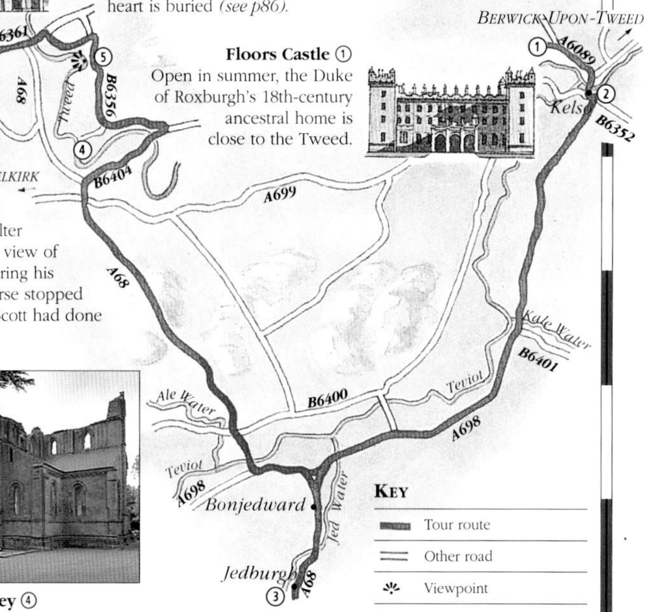

Floors Castle ①
Open in summer, the Duke of Roxburgh's 18th-century ancestral home is close to the Tweed.

Scott's View ⑤
This was Sir Walter Scott's favourite view of the Borders. During his funeral, the hearse stopped here briefly as Scott had done so often in life.

Dryburgh Abbey ④
Also set on the bank of the Tweed, Dryburgh is considered the most evocative monastic ruin in Scotland. Sir Walter Scott is buried here.

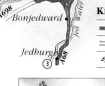

KEY

▬▬	Tour route
══	Other road
☀	Viewpoint

TIPS FOR DRIVERS

Length: 50 km (32 miles).
Stopping-off points: Leave the car at Dryburgh Abbey and take a walk northwards to the footbridge over the River Tweed.

0 kilometres   5

0 miles   3

Jedburgh Abbey ③
The abbey was established in 1138, though fragments of 9th-century Celtic stonework survive from an earlier structure. The visitors' centre illustrates the lives of Augustinian monks.

The ruins of Melrose Abbey, viewed from the southwest

Melrose Abbey ❻

Abbey St, Melrose, The Borders.
C (01896) 822562. **O** daily. 🖾
& limited.

T HE ROSE-PINK RUINS of this,
one of the most beautiful
of the Border Abbeys, bear
testimony to the devastation
of successive English invasions.
Built by David I in 1136 for
Cistercian monks from Yorkshire, and also to replace a
7th-century monastery, Melrose
was repeatedly ransacked by
English armies, most notably
in 1322 and 1385. The final
blow, from which none of
the abbeys recovered, came
in 1545 when Henry VIII of
England implemented his
destructive Scottish policy

known as the "Rough Wooing".
This resulted from the failure
of the Scots to ratify a marriage
treaty between Henry VIII's
son and the infant Mary,
Queen of Scots. What remains
of the abbey are the outlines
of cloisters, the kitchen, monastic buildings and the shell
of the abbey church with its
soaring east window and
profusion of medieval carvings. The rich decorations of
the south exterior wall include
a gargoyle shaped like a pig
playing the bagpipes and several animated figures, including a cook with his ladle.
An embalmed heart, found
here in 1920, is probably that
of Robert the Bruce, the
abbey's chief benefactor, who
had decreed that his heart be

taken on a crusade to the
Holy Land. It was returned
to Melrose Abbey after its
bearer, Sir James Douglas,
was killed in Spain.

Abbotsford House ❼

Galashiels, The Borders. **C** (01896)
752043. 🚌 from Galashiels. **O**
mid-Mar–May & Oct: daily (Sun: pm);
Jun–Sep: daily. 🖾 🗹 **&** limited.

F EW HOUSES BEAR the stamp
of their creator so intimately
as Abbotsford House, the
home of Sir Walter Scott for
the final 20 years of his life.
He bought a farm here in 1811,
known as Clarteyhole ("dirty
hole" in Borders Scots), though
he soon renamed it Abbotsford, in memory of the monks
of Melrose Abbey who used
to cross the River Tweed nearby. He later demolished the
house to make way for the
turreted building we see today,
its construction funded by the
sales of his popular novels.
Scott's library contains more
than 9,000 rare books and his
collections of historic relics
reflect his passion for the heroic past. The walls bristle with
an extensive collection of arms
and armour, including Rob
Roy's broadsword (see p117).
Stuart mementoes include one
of many crucifixes belonging
to Mary, Queen of Scots and a
lock of Bonnie Prince Charlie's
hair. The surprisingly small
study, in which Scott wrote
his Waverley novels, is open
to the public, as is the room
overlooking the river, in
which he died in 1832.

SIR WALTER SCOTT

Sir Walter Scott (1771–1832)
was born in Edinburgh and
trained as a lawyer. He is
best remembered as a major
literary figure and champion
of Scotland, whose poems
and novels (most famously
his Waverley series) created
enduring images of a heroic
wilderness filled with the
romance of the clans. His
orchestration, in 1822, of the
state visit of George IV to
Edinburgh was an extrava-
ganza of Highland culture that helped establish tartan as the
national dress of Scotland. He served as Clerk of the Court
in Edinburgh's Parliament House and for 30 years was Sheriff
of Selkirk. He loved Central and Southern Scotland, putting
the Trossachs (see pp116–17) firmly on the map with the
publication of the Lady of the Lake (1810). His final years
were spent writing to pay off a £114,000 debt following the
failure of his publisher in 1827. He died with his debts
paid, and was buried at Dryburgh Abbey in 1832.

The Great Hall at Abbotsford, adorned with arms and armour

Traquair House ⑧

Peebles, The Borders. ☎ *(01896) 830323.* 🚌 *from Peebles.* ◯ *Apr–Sep: daily; Oct: Fri–Sun.* 🏷 🚹 *limited.*

A S SCOTLAND'S OLDEST contin- uously inhabited house, Traquair has deep roots in Scottish religious and political history stretching back over 900 years. Evolving from a fortified tower to a stout-walled 17th-century mansion *(see p19)*, the house was a Catholic Stuart strong-hold for 500 years. Mary, Queen of Scots was among the many monarchs to have stayed here. Her crucifix is kept in the house and her bed is covered by a counter-pane that she made. Family letters and a collection of engraved Jacobite drinking glasses are among the relics recalling the period of the Highland rebellions.

Following a vow made by the fifth Earl, Traquair's Bear Gates (the "Steekit Yetts"), which closed after Bonnie Prince Charlie's visit in 1745, will not reopen until a Stuart reascends the throne. A secret stairway leads to the Priest's Room, which, with its clerical vestments that

Mary's crucifix, Traquair House

could be disguised as bed-spreads, attests to the prob-lems faced by Catholic families until Catholicism was legalized in 1829. Traquair House Ale is still produced in the adjacent 18th-century brewhouse.

Peebles ⑨

The Borders. 🏠 *8,000.* 🚍 *from Gala-shiels.* 🚹 *23 High St (01721) 720138.*

A CHARMING BORDERS town, Peebles has some fascin-ating sights, including the **Tweeddale Museum** which houses full-scale plaster casts of part of the Parthenon Frieze, and casts of an 1812 frieze depicting the entry of Alexander the Great into Babylon. Nearby, the **Scottish Museum of Ornamental Plasterwork** is housed in a quaint work-shop full of ceiling deco-rations and cornices. The walled **Kailzie Gardens**, near Peebles, attract day-trippers from Edinburgh.

🏛 **Tweeddale Museum** ☎ *(01721) 724820.* ◯ *Easter–Oct: Mon–Sat; Nov–Mar: Mon–Fri.* 🖼
🏛 **Scottish Museum of Ornamental Plasterwork** ☎ *(01721) 720212.* ◯ *Mon–Fri.* ● *First 2 weeks in Aug.* 🖼 🚹
🌼 **Kailzie Gardens** ☎ *(01721) 720007.* ◯ *daily.* 🖼 🖼

Pentland Hills ⑩

The Lothians. 🚆 *Edinburgh, then bus.* 🚹 *Regional Park Headquarters, Edinburgh (0131) 445 3383.*

T HE WILDS OF the Pentland Hills stretch for 26 km (16 miles) southwest of Edin-burgh, and offer some of the best hill-walking country in Southern Scotland. Walkers can saunter along the many sign-posted footpaths, while the more adventurous can take the chairlift at the Hillend dry ski slope to reach the higher ground leading to the 493 m (1,617 ft) hill of Allermuir. Even more ambitious is the classic scenic route along the ridge from Caerketton to West Kip.

To the east of the A703, in the lee of the Pentlands, stands the exquisite and ornate 15th-century **Rosslyn Chapel**. It was originally intended as a church, but after the death of its founder, William Sinclair, it was used as a burial ground for his descendants. The delicately wreathed Apprentice Pillar recalls the legend of the apprentice carver who was killed by the master stone-mason in a fit of jealousy at his pupil's superior skill.

🚹 **Rosslyn Chapel** ☎ *(0131) 440 2159.* ◯ *daily.* 🖼 🚹 *www.rosslynchapel.org.uk*

Details of the highly ornate, decorative carved-stone vaulting in Rosslyn Chapel

The Classical 18th-century tenements of New Lanark on the banks of the Clyde

New Lanark ⓫

Clyde Valley. 👥 *150.* ⬆ 🏠 *Lanark.*
ℹ️ *Horsemarket, Ladyacre Rd, Lanark
(01555) 661661.* 🅿️ *Mon.*

SITUATED BY THE beautiful
falls of the River Clyde,
with three separate waterfalls,
the village of New Lanark was
founded in 1785 by the industrial entrepreneur David Dale.

DAVID LIVINGSTONE

Scotland's great missionary
doctor and explorer was
born in Blantyre where he
began working life as a
mill boy at the age of ten.
Livingstone (1813–73)
made three epic journeys
across Africa, from 1840,
promoting "commerce and
Christianity". He became
the first European to see
Victoria Falls, and died in
1873 while searching for
the source of the Nile. His
body is buried in West-
minster Abbey in London.

Ideally located alongside the
river for the working of its
water-driven mills, the village
had become the largest producer of cotton in Britain by
1800. Dale and his successor,
and son-in-law, Robert Owen,
were philanthropists whose
reforms demonstrated that
commercial success need not
undermine the wellbeing of
the workforce. The manu-
facturing of cotton continued
here until the late 1960s.

Preserved as a museum,
New Lanark is a window on to
working life in the early 19th
century. The **Annie McLeod
Experience** provides a
special-effects ride into the
past, illustrating the life of a
10-year-old mill girl in 1820.

ENVIRONS: 24 km (15 miles)
north, the town of Blantyre
has a memorial to the Clyde
Valley's most famous son, the
explorer David Livingstone.

🏛 **Annie McLeod Experience**
New Lanark Visitor Centre.
📞 *(01555) 661345.* ⭕ *daily.*
🈺 ♿ 🎫 *by appointment.*

Sanquhar ⓬

Dumfries & Galloway. 👥 *2,500.*
⬆ 🏠 ℹ️ *The Post Office, High St
(01659) 50185.*

NOW OF CHIEFLY historic
interest, the town of
Sanquhar was famous in the
history of the Covenanters.

In the 1680s, two declarations
opposing the rule of bishops
were pinned to the Mercat
Cross, the site of which is
now marked by a granite
obelisk. The first protest was
led by a local teacher, Richard
Cameron, whose followers
became the Cameronian regiment. The Georgian **Tolbooth**
was designed by architect
William Adam in 1735 and
houses a local interest museum
and tourist centre. The Post
Office, opened in 1763, is the
oldest in Britain, predating
the mail coach service.

Drumlanrig Castle ⓭

Thornhill, Dumfries & Galloway.
ℹ️ *(01848) 330248.* ⬆ 🏠 *Dumfries,
then bus.* ⭕ *May–Aug: Mon–Sun pm.*
🈺 ♿

RISING SQUARELY from a grassy
platform, the massive
fortress-palace of **Drumlanrig
Castle** was built from pink
sandstone between 1679 and
1691 on the site of a 15th-
century Douglas stronghold.
The castle's multi-turreted,

**The Baroque front steps and
doorway of Drumlanrig Castle**

formidable exterior conceals a priceless collection of art treasures as well as such Jacobite relics as Bonnie Prince Charlie's camp kettle, sash and money box. Hanging within oak-panelled rooms are paintings by Leonardo da Vinci, Holbein and Rembrandt. The emblem of a crowned and winged heart recalls Sir James, the "Black Douglas", who lived here. He bore Robert the Bruce's heart while on crusade to fulfil a vow made by the former king. After being mortally wounded he threw the heart at his enemies with the words "forward brave heart!"

The exterior of Burns Cottage, birthplace of Robert Burns

The sturdy island fortress of Threave Castle on the Dee

Threave Castle ⑭

(NTS) Castle Douglas, Dumfries & Galloway. 【 (01556) 502611.
🚆 Dumfries. ◯ Apr–Sep: daily. ▨

A MENACING GIANT of a tower, this 14th-century Black Douglas stronghold on an island in the Dee (accessed by rowing boat) commands the most complete medieval riverside harbour in Scotland. Douglas's struggles against the early Stewart kings culminated in his surrender here after a two-month siege in 1455 – but only after James II had brought the cannon Mons Meg to batter the castle. Threave was finally dismantled after an army of Protestant Covenanters defeated its Catholic defenders in 1640. Only the shell of the kitchen, great hall and domestic levels remains.

Burns Heritage Trail ⑮

South Ayrshire, Dumfries & Galloway.
🛈 Dumfries (01387) 253862, Ayr (01292) 288688.

R OBERT BURNS (1759–91) left behind a remarkable body of work ranging from satirical poetry to tender love songs. His status as national bard is unchallenged and an official Burns Heritage Trail leads visitors around sights in southwest Scotland where he lived.

In Dumfries, the **Robert Burns Centre** focuses on his years in the town, while **Burns House**, where he lived from 1793 to 1796, contains memorabilia. His Greek-style mausoleum can be found in St Michael's Churchyard.

At **Ellisland Farm** on the River Nith there are further displays, with some of Burns' family possessions, along with the opportunity for riverside walks. Mauchline, some 18 km (11 miles) east of Ayr, has the **Burns House and Museum** in another former residence.

Alloway, just south of Ayr, is the real centre of the Burns

Trail. The **Tam O'Shanter Experience** is a contemporary film and video centre based on his poem about witches. **Burns Cottage**, the poet's birthplace, houses memorabilia and a collection of manuscripts. The ruins of Alloway Kirk, where Burns' father is buried, and the 13th-century Brig o' Doon have the best period atmosphere.

🏛 **Robert Burns Centre**
Mill Rd, Dumfries. 【 (01387) 264808.
◯ Apr–Sep: daily; Oct–Mar: Tue–Sat.
🏛 **Burns House**
Burns St, Dumfries. 【 (01387) 255297. ◯ Apr–Sep: daily; Oct–Mar: Tue–Sat.
🏛 **Ellisland Farm**
Holywood Rd, Auldgirth. 【 (01387) 740426. ◯ Apr–Sep: daily; Oct–Mar: Tue–Sat. ▨ ♿ ▨
🏛 **Burns House and Museum**
Castle St, Mauchline. 【 (01290) 550045. ◯ May–Oct: Tue–Sun. ▨ ♿ limited.
🏛 **Tam O'Shanter Experience**
Murdoch's Lane, Alloway. 【 (01292) 443700. ◯ daily. ▨ ♿ ▨ by appointment.
🏛 **Burns Cottage**
Alloway. 【 (01292) 443700. ◯ daily. ▨ ♿

SCOTTISH TEXTILES

Weaving in the Scottish Borders goes back to the Middle Ages, when monks from Flanders established a thriving woollen trade with the Continent. Cotton became an important source of wealth in the Clyde Valley during the 19th century, when handloom weaving was overtaken by power-driven mills. The popular Paisley patterns were based on original Indian designs.

A colourful pattern from Paisley

The moated fairy-tale Caerlaverock Castle with red stone walls

Caerlaverock Castle ⑯

Near Dumfries, Dumfries & Galloway.
ℹ️ *Historic Scotland, Edinburgh
(0131) 668 8800.* ⭕ *daily.* 🎒 ♿

THIS IMPRESSIVE, three-sided, red stone structure, with its distinctive moat, is the finest example of a medieval castle in southwest Scotland. It stands 14 km (9 miles) south of Dumfries, and was built in around 1270 using masonry from an older castle situated close by.

Caerlaverock came to prominence in 1300, during the Wars of Independence, when it was besieged by Edward I, king of England, setting a precedent for more than three centuries of

strife. Surviving chronicles of Edward's adventures describe the castle in much the same form as it stands today, despite being partially demolished and rebuilt on many occasions, due to the clashes between the English and Scottish forces during the 14th and 16th centuries. Throughout these troubled times, Caerlaverock Castle remained the stronghold of the Maxwell family, and the Maxwell crest and motto remain over the door. It was the struggle between Robert Maxwell, who was the first Earl of Nithsdale and a supporter of Charles I, and a Covenanter army that caused the castle's ruin in 1640.

Kirkcudbright ⑰

Dumfries & Galloway. 🚶 *3,600.* 🚌
ℹ️ *Harbour Sq (01557) 330494.*
⭕ *Easter–Oct: daily.*

BY THE mouth of the River Dee, at the head of Kirkcudbright Bay, this attractive town has an artistic heritage. The Tolbooth, dating from the late 16th century, is now the **Tolbooth Art Centre**, which houses studios, and exhibits work by Kirkcudbright's 19th-century artists. The most celebrated of these artists was Edward Hornel (1864–1933), a friend of the Glasgow Boys,

who painted striking images of Japanese women. Some of his work is displayed in his former home, Broughton House, on the High Street.

MacLellan's Castle in the town centre was built in 1582 by the then Provost of Kirkcudbright, while outside, the ruins of Dundrennan Abbey date from the 12th century. Mary, Queen of Scots spent her last night there before fleeing to England in May 1568.

🏛 **Tolbooth Art Centre**
High St. ☎️ *(01557) 331556.* ⭕ *May–Aug: daily; Oct–Apr: Mon–Sat.* 🎒 ♿
♠ **MacLellan's Castle**
☎️ *(0131) 668 8800.* ⭕ *Apr–Sep: daily; Oct–Mar: Sat & Sun.* 🎒

Whithorn ⑱

Dumfries & Galloway. 🚶 *1,000.*
🚇 *Stranraer.* 🚌 ℹ️ *Dashwood Sq, Newton Stewart (01671) 402431.*

THE EARLIEST SITE of continuous Christian worship in Scotland, Whithorn (meaning white house) takes its name from the white chapel built by St Ninian in 397. Though nothing remains of the chapel, a guided tour of the archaeological dig reveals evidence of Northumbrian, Viking and Scottish settlements ranging from the 5th to the 19th centuries. **Whithorn: Cradle of Christianity** is a centre that provides audio-visual information on the excavations, and contains a fine collection of carved stones, one of which dates from 450 AD.

🏛 **Whithorn: Cradle of Christianity**
45–47 George St. ☎️ *(01988) 500508.*
⭕ *Apr–Oct: daily.* 🎒 🎫 ♿

Galloway Forest Park ⑲

Dumfries & Galloway. 🚇 *Stranraer.*
ℹ️ *Clatteringshaws Forest Wildlife Centre, New Galloway (01644) 420285.* ⭕ *Easter–Oct: daily.*

THIS IS THE WILDEST stretch of country in Southern Scotland, with points of historical interest as well as great beauty. The park extends to 670 sq km

Traditional stone buildings on the shore at Kirkcudbright

Loch Trool, Galloway Forest Park, site of one of Robert the Bruce's victories

The Rhinns of Galloway ⑳

Dumfries & Galloway. ≷ *Stranraer.*
🚌 *Stranraer, Portpatrick.* ⛴ *Stranraer.* ℹ *28 Harbour St, Stranraer (01776) 702595.*

IN THE EXTREME southwest of Scotland, this peninsula is almost separated from the rest of the country by Loch Ryan and Luce Bay. It has a number of attractions, including the **Logan Botanic Garden**, near Port Logan. Established in 1900, subtropical species in the garden benefit from the area's mild climate.

Stranraer on Loch Ryan is the main centre and ferry port for Northern Ireland. The nearby **Portpatrick** is a prettier town, featuring a ruined church dating from 1629 and the remains of 16th-century Dunskey Castle.

♣ **Logan Botanic Garden**
Near Port Logan, Stranraer. 📞 *(01776) 860231.* ⬜ *Mar–Oct: daily.* 🅿 ♿

(260 sq miles) just north of Newton Stewart. Clatteringshaws Loch, to the northeast, has a visitors' centre, but the principal focal point is Loch Trool. By Caldons Wood, to the west end of the loch, the Martyrs' Monument marks the spot where six Covenanters were killed at prayer in 1685. Bruce's Stone, above the north shore, commemorates an occasion in 1307 when Robert the Bruce routed English forces.

The hills to the north of Loch Trool are a considerable size, and worthy of note. Bennan stands at 562 m (1,844 ft), Benyellary at 719 m (2,359 ft), while Merrick, at 843 m (2,766 ft), is the tallest mountain in Southern Scotland. A round trip from Loch Trool to Merrick's summit and back, via the silver sands of Loch Enoch to the east, is a total of 15 km (9 miles) over rough but very rewarding ground.

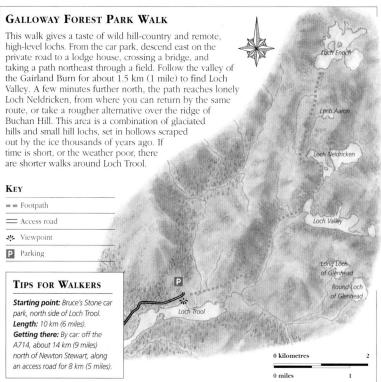

GALLOWAY FOREST PARK WALK

This walk gives a taste of wild hill-country and remote, high-level lochs. From the car park, descend east on the private road to a lodge house, crossing a bridge, and taking a path northeast through a field. Follow the valley of the Gairland Burn for about 1.5 km (1 mile) to find Loch Valley. A few minutes further north, the path reaches lonely Loch Neldricken, from where you can return by the same route, or take a rougher alternative over the ridge of Buchan Hill. This area is a combination of glaciated hills and small hill lochs, set in hollows scraped out by the ice thousands of years ago. If time is short, or the weather poor, there are shorter walks around Loch Trool.

KEY

▪▪ Footpath

— Access road

🔆 Viewpoint

🅿 Parking

TIPS FOR WALKERS

Starting point: *Bruce's Stone car park, north side of Loch Trool.*
Length: *10 km (6 miles).*
Getting there: *By car: off the A714, about 14 km (9 miles) north of Newton Stewart, along an access road for 8 km (5 miles).*

Loch Enoch

Loch Aaron

Loch Neldricken

Loch Valley

Long Loch of Glenhead

Round Loch of Glenhead

Loch Trool

0 kilometres   2

0 miles   1

Culzean Castle ㉑

Robert Adam by George Willison

Sᴛᴀɴᴅɪɴɢ ᴏɴ ᴀ ᴄʟɪꜰꜰ'ꜱ ᴇᴅɢᴇ in an extensive parkland estate, the 16th-century keep of Culzean (pronounced Cullayn), home of the Earls of Cassillis, was remodelled between 1777 and 1792 by the Neo-Classical architect Robert Adam. Restored in the 1970s, it is now a major showcase of Adam's later style of work. The grounds became Scotland's first public country park in 1969 and, with farming flourishing alongside ornamental gardens, they reflect both the leisure and everyday activities of life on a great country estate.

View of Culzean Castle (c.1815), by Nasmyth

Lord Cassillis' Rooms contain typical mid-18th-century furnishings, including a gentleman's wardrobe of the 1740s.

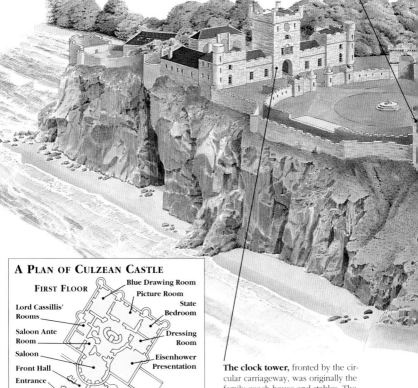

A Pʟᴀɴ ᴏꜰ Cᴜʟᴢᴇᴀɴ Cᴀꜱᴛʟᴇ

Fɪʀꜱᴛ Fʟᴏᴏʀ

- Blue Drawing Room
- Picture Room
- State Bedroom
- Lord Cassillis' Rooms
- Saloon Ante Room
- Saloon
- Front Hall
- Entrance
- Dressing Room
- Eisenhower Presentation

- Shop
- Ship Model Room
- Benefactor's Room
- Old Eating Room
- Dining Room
- Armoury
- Oval Staircase

Gʀᴏᴜɴᴅ Fʟᴏᴏʀ

The clock tower, fronted by the circular carriageway, was originally the family coach house and stables. The clock was added in the 19th century, and today the buildings are used for residential and educational purposes.

Star Sights
★ Saloon
★ Oval Staircase

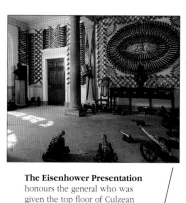

Armoury
On the walls are the bayonet blades and flintlock pistols issued to the West Lowland Fencible Regiment when Napoleon threatened to invade in the early 1800s.

VISITORS' CHECKLIST

(NTS) 6 km (4 miles) west of Maybole, Ayrshire. (01655) 760269. Ayr, then bus. Castle Apr–Oct: daily 10am–5:30pm. Grounds dawn until dusk daily.

The Eisenhower Presentation
honours the general who was given the top floor of Culzean in gratitude for his role in World War II.

Fountain Court
This sunken garden is a good place to begin a tour of the grounds to the east.

Carriageway

★ Saloon
With its restored 18th-century colour scheme and Louis XVI chairs, this elegant saloon perches on the cliff's edge 46 m (150 ft) above the Firth of Clyde. The carpet is a copy of one designed by Adam.

★ Oval Staircase
Illuminated by an overarching skylight, the staircase, with its Ionic and Corinthian pillars, is considered one of Adam's finest design achievements.

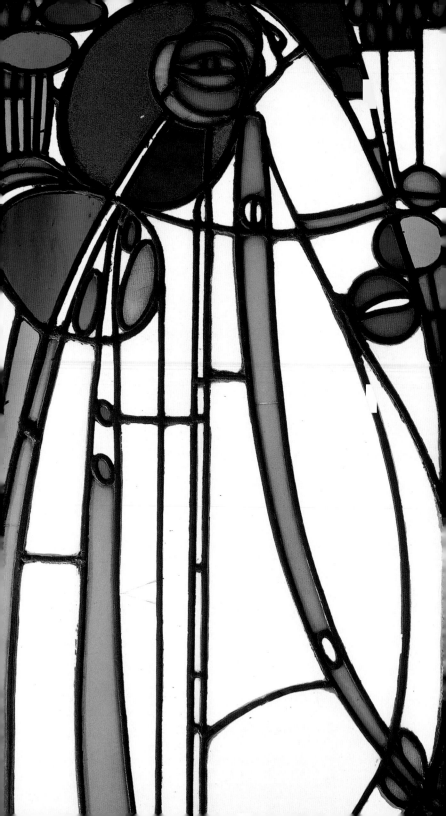

GLASGOW

LASGOW DISPLAYS *audacity in everything, from the profile of its new buildings, such as the Armadillo-like extension to the Scottish Exhibition and Conference Centre, to the presence of designer clothes shops and the wit of its people. As recently as the 1970s, this was a city with a fading industrial history and little sense of direction, but much has changed since then.*

Glasgow's city centre, on the north bank of the River Clyde, has been occupied since ancient times. The Romans already had a presence in the area some 2,000 years ago, and there was a religious community here from the 6th century. Records show Glasgow's growing importance as a merchant town from the 12th century onwards.

Historic buildings such as Provand's Lordship, a 15th-century townhouse, remind visitors of its pre-industrial roots, but modern Glasgow grew from the riches of the British Empire and the Industrial Revolution. In the 18th century the city imported rum, sugar and tobacco from the colonies, while in the 19th century Glasgow reinvented itself as a cotton manufacturing centre. It then became a site for shipbuilding and for heavy engineering, attracting many incomers from poverty-stricken districts in the Scottish Highlands and islands, and in Ireland, in the process. Between the 1780s and the 1880s the population exploded from around 40,000 to over 500,000. The city boundaries expanded, and, despite an economic slump between the two World Wars, Glasgow clung on to its status as an industrial giant until as late as the 1970s, when its traditional skills were no longer needed. This was a bad time, but the city has bounced back with an International Garden Festival in 1988, European City of Culture status in 1990, refurbished buildings and a reputation for excellent nightlife. It finished the millennium as UK City of Architecture, 1999.

Fashionable brasseries in the rejuvenated Merchant City area of Glasgow

◁ Stained glass by architect and designer Charles Rennie Mackintosh, whose work can be seen all over the city

Exploring Glasgow

GLASGOW CITY CENTRE is a neat grid of streets running east to west and north to south on the north bank of the River Clyde. This small area includes the main train stations, the principal shopping facilities and, at George Square, the tourist information office. Outside the centre, Byres Road to the west of Kelvingrove Park is the focus of the district known as "the West End", with its bars and restaurants near the University. Pollok Country Park, in the southwest, is home to the wonderful Burrell Collection.

Detail of St Mungo Museum's deceptively modern façade

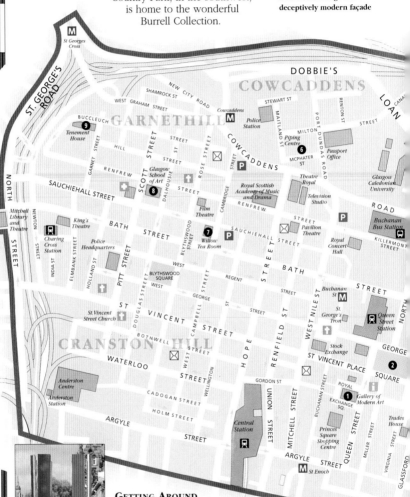

The distinctive "U" sign for the Glasgow Underground

GETTING AROUND

An extensive regional train service links Glasgow with its suburbs. In the city itself there is an underground system that operates daily in a simple loop around the centre, both north and south of the River Clyde (limited hours on Sundays). The M8 motorway (highway) cuts through central Glasgow, linking Inverclyde and the airport in the west with Edinburgh in the east. Buses and black cabs are other options.

SIGHTS AT A GLANCE

Historic Streets and Buildings
George Square **2**
Glasgow Cathedral
  and Necropolis **5**
Pollok House **17**
Willow Tea Room **7**

Museums and Galleries
Burrell Collection pp104–5 **18**
Gallery of Modern Art **1**
Hunterian Art Gallery **13**
Kelvingrove Art Gallery
  and Museum **11**
Museum of Transport **12**

People's Palace **15**
Provand's Lordship **3**
St Mungo Museum of
  Religious Life and Art **4**
Tenement House **9**

Parks and Gardens
Botanic Gardens **14**

Arts Centres
Glasgow School of Art **8**
House for an Art Lover **16**
Piping Centre **6**
Scottish Exhibition Centre **10**

**Sauchiehall Street, the heart of
the city's busy shopping district**

SEE ALSO

• *Where to Stay* pp168–9

• *Where to Eat* pp178–80

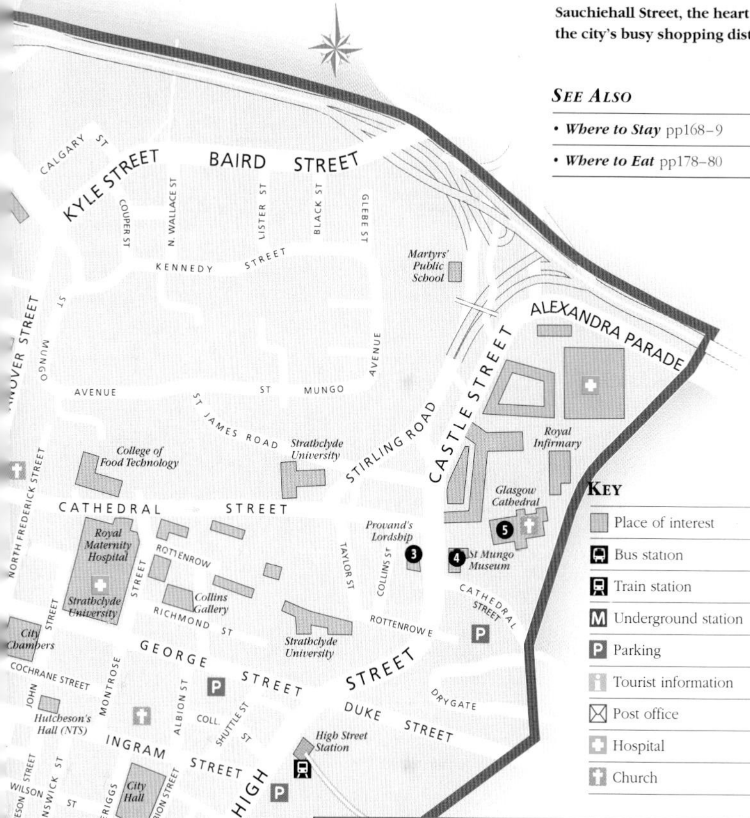

KEY

▢	Place of interest
🚌	Bus station
🚉	Train station
M	Underground station
P	Parking
i	Tourist information
⊠	Post office
✚	Hospital
✝	Church

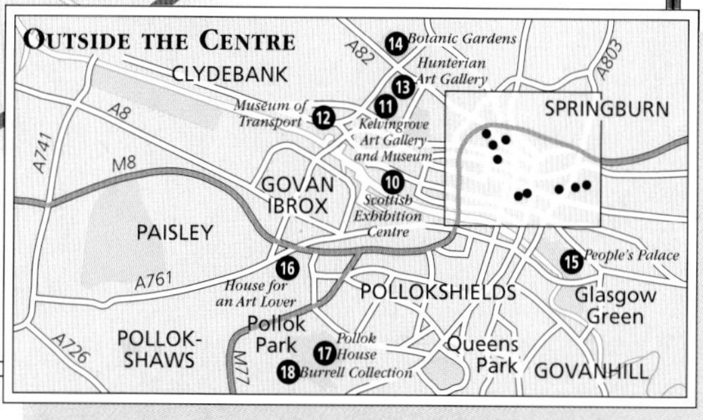

OUTSIDE THE CENTRE

0 metres	300
0 yards	300

The imposing City Chambers in George Square, where a statue of Sir Walter Scott stands atop the central column

Gallery of Modern Art ❶

Queen Street. **(** (0141) 229 1996.
◻ daily. **♿ ✉**
www.goma.glasgow.gov.uk

ONCE THE HOME of Glasgow's Royal Exchange (the city's centre for trade), this building dates from 1829 and also incorporates a late 18th-century mansion that formerly occupied the site. The local authority took over the Exchange just after World War II, and for many years it served as a library. It finally opened its doors as the Gallery of Modern Art in 1996. A controversial acquisitions policy and a somewhat limited budget has led

Ornate tower of the Gallery of Modern Art

the gallery to concentrate on the works of living artists, while a desire to attract a wide audience means the roly-poly figures of Beryl Cook hang alongside the stark photographic images of Jo Spence. Works of art by contemporary Scots, such as John Bellany, Elizabeth Blackadder and the new generation of Glasgow Boys, are displayed on the

four themed floors that represent each of the elements – air, water, earth and fire.

George Square ❷

City centre. **City Chambers (** (0141) 287 2000. **◻** Mon–Wed & Fri, 10:30am and 2:30pm for guided tours. **♿ ✉** **Merchant House (** (0141) 221 8272. **✉** by appointment.

GEORGE SQUARE was laid out in the late 18th century as a residental area, but re-development during Victorian times conferred its enduring status as the city's focal point. The only building not to be affected by the later 19th-century makeover is the Copthorne Hotel (1807) on the north side of the Square.
The 1870s saw a building boom, with the construction of the former Post Office (1876) at the southeast corner, and the **Merchant House** (1877) to the west side. The latter is home to Glasgow's Chamber of Commerce. Founded in 1781, it is the oldest organization of its kind in the UK. The most dominant structure in George Square, however, is the **City Chambers** on the east side. Designed by William Young, in an Italian Renaissance

style, the imposing building was opened in 1888 by Queen Victoria. With the elegant proportions of the interior decorated with marble and mosaic, the opulence of this building makes it the most impressive of its kind in Scotland.

Provand's Lordship ❸

3 Castle St. **(** (0141) 287 2699.
● for renovation until the year 2000.

PROVAND'S LORDSHIP was originally built as a canon's house in 1471, and is now Glasgow's oldest surviving house, as well as a museum. Its low ceilings and austere wooden furnishings create a vivid impression of life in a wealthy 15th-century household. Mary, Queen of Scots (see p44) may have stayed here when she visited Glasgow in 1566 to see her cousin, and husband, Lord Darnley.

Provand's Lordship, Glasgow's only medieval house

St Mungo Museum of Religious Life and Art ❹

2 Castle St. 📞 (0141) 553 2557.
⬤ daily. ♿ 🎫 by appointment.

GLASGOW HAS strong religious roots, and the settlement that grew to become today's city started with a monastery founded in the 6th century AD by a priest called Mungo. He died in the early years of the 7th century, and his body lies buried underneath Glasgow Cathedral. The building itself dates from the 12th century, and stands on ground blessed by St Ninian as long ago as 397 AD.

In recent years, the ever-growing numbers of visitors to the cathedral prompted plans for an interpretive centre. Despite the efforts of the Society of Friends of Glasgow Cathedral, however, sufficient funds could not be raised. The local authority decided to step in with money, and with the idea for a more extensive project – a museum of religious life and

Detail from the St Mungo Museum

art. The site chosen was adjacent to the cathedral, where the 13th-century Castle of the Bishops of Glasgow once stood. The museum has the appearance of a centuries-old fortified house, despite the fact that it was completed as recently as 1993.

The top floor tells the story of the country's religion from a nondenominational perspective. Both Protestant and Catholic versions of Christianity are represented, as well as the other faiths of modern Scotland. The many, varied displays touch on the lives of communities as extensive as Glasgow's Muslims, who have had their own Mosque in the city since 1984, as well as local converts to the Baha'i faith.

The other floors are given over to works of art. The star of the show is Salvador Dali's *Christ of St John of the Cross* (1951), which was brought to Glasgow in 1952 despite controversy over its subject matter. The painting was vandalized in 1961 but was subsequently restored. It now sits alongside religious artifacts and artworks, such as burial discs from Neolithic China (2000 BC), contemporary paintings by Aboriginal Australians, and some excellent Scottish stained glass from the early part of the 20th century.

Further displays in the museum examine issues of fundamental concern to people of all religions – war, persecution, death and the afterlife – and from cultures as far afield as West Africa and Mexico. In the grounds surrounding the building, there is a permanent Zen Garden, created by Yasutaro Tanaka. Such gardens have been a traditional aid to contemplation in Japanese Buddhist temples since the beginning of the 16th century.

Dali's *Christ of St John of the Cross* at the St Mungo Museum of Religious Life and Art

Glasgow's medieval cathedral viewed from the southwest

Glasgow Cathedral and Necropolis ❺

Cathedral Square. **Cathedral**
📞 (0141) 552 6891. ⬤ daily. ♿
Necropolis ⬤ daily.

AS ONE OF THE FEW cathedrals to escape destruction during the Scottish Reformation (*see p44*) by adapting itself to Protestant worship, Glasgow Cathedral is a rare example of an almost complete original 13th-century church.

It was built on the site of a chapel founded by the city's patron saint, St Mungo, a 6th-century bishop of Strathclyde. According to legend, Mungo placed the body of a holy man, named Fergus, on a cart yoked to two wild bulls, telling them to take it to the place ordained by God. In the "dear green place" at which the bulls stopped, he built his church.

Because of its sloping site, the cathedral is built on two levels. The crypt contains the tomb of St Mungo, surrounded by an intricate forest of columns springing up to end in delicately carved rib-vaulting. The Blacader Aisle, which is reputed to have been built over a cemetery blessed by St Ninian, has a ceiling thick with decorative bosses.

Behind the cathedral, a likeness of Protestant reformer John Knox (*see p44*) surveys the city from his Doric pillar, overlooking a Victorian cemetery. The necropolis is filled with crumbling monuments to the dead of Glasgow's wealthy merchant families.

Piping Centre ❻

30–34 McPhater St. ▐ *(0141) 353 0220.* ⬜ *daily.* 🖼 ♿

THE PIPING CENTRE, which opened its doors in a refurbished church in 1996, aims to promote the study and history of piping in Scotland. It offers tuition at all levels, and houses the **National Museum of Piping**, which traces the development of the instrument. Displays show that bagpipes were first introduced to Scotland as early as the 14th century, although the golden age of piping in the Highlands and islands was the 17th and 18th centuries. This was the era of the MacCrimmons of Skye (hereditary pipers to the chiefs of Clan MacLeod), when complex, extended tunes (*ceol mor*, or "the big music") were written for clan gatherings, battles and in the form of laments.

The exterior of the Glasgow School of Art, Mackintosh's masterpiece

Traditional bagpipes with brass drones

Willow Tea Room ❼

217 Sauchiehall St. ▐ *(0141) 332 0521.* ⬜ *Mon–Sat, Sun (pm).*

THIS IS THE SOLE survivor of a series of delightfully frivolous tea rooms created by the designer Charles Rennie Mackintosh (*see opposite page*) at the turn of the century for

the celebrated restaurateur Miss Kate Cranston. Everything in the tearoom, from the high-backed chairs to the tables and cutlery, was of Mackintosh's own design. In particular, the 1904 **Room de Luxe** sparkles with eccentricity: striking mauve and silver furniture, coloured glass and a flamboyant leaded door create a remarkable venue in which to enjoy an afternoon tea of cakes and muffins.

The Mackintosh-designed interior of the Willow Tea Room

Glasgow School of Art ❽

167 Renfrew St. ▐ *(0141) 353 4526.* ⬜ *Mon–Sat (by appointment).* ⬛ *26 Jun–2 Jul, 20 Dec–4 Jan.* 🖼 🚫 ♿ *limited.* www.gsa.ac.uk

WIDELY CONSIDERED to be the greatest architectural work in the illustrious career of Charles Rennie Mackintosh, the Glasgow School of Art was built between 1897 and 1909 to a design he submitted in a competition. Due to financial constraints, it was built in two stages. The earlier eastern half displays a severity of style, likened by a contemporary critic to a prison. The later western half is characterized by a softer architectural style.

An art student will guide you through the building to the Furniture Gallery, Board Room and the Library, the latter being a masterpiece of spatial composition. Each room is an exercise in contrasts between

height, light and shade, with innovative details echoing the architectural themes of the structure. How much of the school can be viewed depends on curricular requirements at the time of visiting, as it still functions as an active and highly successful art college.

Tenement House ❾

(NTS) 145 Buccleuch St. ▐ *(0141) 333 0183.* ⬜ *Mar–Oct: daily (pm).* 🖼 🚫 *by appointment.*

MORE A TIME CAPSULE than a museum, the Tenement House is an almost undisturbed record of life as it was in a modest Glasgow flat on a tenement estate in the early 20th century. Glasgow owed much of its vitality and neighbourliness to tenement life, though in later years many of these Victorian and Edwardian apartments were to earn a bad name for poverty and overcrowding, and many of them have been pulled down.

The Tenement House was first owned by Miss Agnes Toward, who lived here from 1911 until 1965. It remained largely unaltered during that time and, since Agnes threw very little away, the house has become a treasure-trove of social history. In the parlour, which would have been used only on formal occasions, afternoon tea is laid out on a white lace cloth. The kitchen, with its coal-fired range and box bed, is filled with the tools of a vanished era, such as a goffering-iron for crisping waffles, a washboard and a stone hot-water bottle.

Agnes's lavender water and medicines are still arranged in the bathroom, and it feels almost as though she stepped out of the house 70 years ago and simply forgot to return.

The preserved Edwardian kitchen of the Tenement House

Glasgow Artists

Detail from House for an Art Lover

THE LATE 19TH CENTURY was a time of great artistic activity in Glasgow, with influential painters such as Sir James Guthrie, Robert McGregor and others rising to prominence. But due to snobbery on the part of the Edinburgh-based arts establishment, these men often had to seek recognition outside Scotland. Only after a London exhibition in 1890 was the term "Glasgow School" coined, although the artists generally called themselves the "Glasgow Boys". Art Nouveau designer Charles Rennie Mackintosh was a contemporary, contributing his genius to the creative life of the city as well as to a new Glasgow School of Art, completed in two stages – 1899 and 1909. More recently, the term Glasgow Boys has been used to describe the generation of artists who attended the School of Art in the 1970s and '80s.

Stirling Station, by William Kennedy (1859–1918), depicts the crowded platform with people waiting for a train. The rich colours, and steam from the trains, contribute to the atmosphere of this bustling station.

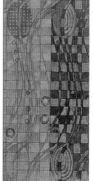

A Star (1891) by Sir John Lavery is indicative of the artist's dashing, fluid, style as a portraitist. Born in Belfast, Lavery studied at Glasgow and was part of the Whistler- and Impressionist-influenced Glasgow School.

Mackintosh's stylized tulips on a checkered background provide a striking example of Art Nouveau decoration, juxtaposing the organic with the geometric.

In The Wayfarer, by Edward Arthur Walton (1860–1922), the winding path leads the viewer into the distance, in the direction of the wayfarer's gaze.

Designed by Mackintosh in 1901, the House for an Art Lover (see p103) was finally built in 1996. The design of the building and all of the furniture remains true to the original plans.

Mackintosh's unique fluidity of form is seen in this detail from a stained glass door in the House for an Art Lover.

CHARLES RENNIE MACKINTOSH

Glasgow's most celebrated designer (1868–1928) entered Glasgow School of Art at the age of 16. After his success with the Willow Tea Room, he became a leading figure in the Art Nouveau movement. His characteristic straight lines and flowing detail are the hallmark of early 20th-century style.

Scottish Exhibition Centre ⑩

Finnieston. **(** (0141) 248 3000. **Ġ**
☑ by appointment. www.secc.co.uk

W HEN THE SECC opened in 1985, it gave Glasgow a world-class facility for conferences, exhibitions and entertainment. The main auditorium holds up to 9,000 people and regularly hosts major rock concerts. The centre revitalized a derelict stretch of the Clyde, and, for the Glasgow Garden Festival in 1988 on the opposite bank, Bell's Bridge was built as a pedestrian link.

The exterior of the SECC has always left much to be desired, and has been described as an "ignominious shed", but an extension, completed in 1997, reclaimed a lot of design kudos. Named the Armadillo, the extension is a breathtaking building, reminiscent of a symmetrical, metallic Sydney Opera House, and contains a 3,000-seat auditorium. The nearby Clyde Navigation Trustees Crane No. 7 is a reminder of Glasgow's industrial past.

Kelvingrove Art Gallery and Museum ⑪

Argyle St, Kelvingrove. **(** (0141) 287 2699. ☐ daily. **Ġ** **☑**

A N IMPOSING red sandstone building, Kelvingrove is Scotland's most popular gallery, housing a magnificent art collection. Best known for its

George Henry's *Japanese Lady with a Fan* **(1894), at Kelvingrove**

17th-century Dutch and 19th-century French paintings, the collection began as the gift of a Glasgow coachbuilder who died in 1854, leaving works by Botticelli, Giorgione and Rembrandt. Prominent among Continental artists are Degas, Millet and Monet, while in the Scottish Gallery, the famous work *Massacre of Glencoe* by James Hamilton (1853–94) is on display *(see p134)*, alongside works by the Glasgow Boys *(see p101)*. Other exhibitions in the museum cover an extraordinary number of subjects, including ceramics, silver, European arms and armour, and the geology of Scotland. The archaeological display includes a reconstruction of the Antonine Wall, which was built by the Romans to mark the boundary of their occupied area of Scotland.

Museum of Transport ⑫

1 Bunhouse Rd. **(** (0141) 287 2000.
☐ daily. **Ġ** **☑**

H OUSED IN Kelvin Hall, this imaginative museum conveys much of the optimism and vigour of the city's industrial heyday. Model ships and ranks of gleaming Scottish-built steam engines, cars and motorcycles recall the 19th and early 20th centuries, when Glasgow's supremacy in shipbuilding, trade and manufacturing made her the "second city" of the British Empire. Old Glasgow can be seen through fascinating footage of the town in the cinema and through a reconstruction of a 1938 street, with Art Deco shop fronts, cinema and Underground station.

The Museum of Transport's 1938 street, with a reconstructed Underground station

Hunterian Art Gallery ⑬

82 Hillhead St. **(** (0141) 330 5431.
☐ Mon–Sat. ● 24 Dec–5 Jan.

B UILT TO HOUSE a number of paintings bequeathed to Glasgow University by an ex-student and physician, Dr William Hunter (1718–83), the Hunterian Art Gallery contains Scotland's largest print collection. There are also works by many major European artists, dating from the 16th century. A collection of work by the designer Charles Rennie Mackintosh *(see p101)* is supplemented by a complete reconstruction of No. 6 Florentine Terrace, where he lived from 1906 to 1914. A major collection of 19th- and

Kelvingrove Art Gallery and the Glasgow University buildings, seen from the south

20th-century Scottish art includes work by William McTaggart (1835–1910), but by far the most famous collection is of work by the Paris-trained American painter, James McNeill Whistler (1834–1903), who influenced so many of the Glasgow School painters.

Whistler's *Sketch for Annabel Lee* (c.1869), Hunterian Art Gallery

Botanic Gardens ⑭

Great Western Rd. 🔳 (0141) 334 2422. ⭕ daily. ♿ 🔲 by appointment.

THESE GARDENS form a peaceful space in the heart of the city's West End, by the River Kelvin. Originally founded at another site in 1817, they were moved to the current location in 1839 and opened to the public three years later. Aside from the main range of greenhouses, with assorted displays including palm trees and an area given over to tropical crops,

one of the most interesting features is the **Kibble Palace**. Built at Loch Long in the Highlands by John Kibble, a Victorian engineer, the glass palace was moved to its present site in the early 1870s but its splendour is now much reduced.

People's Palace ⑮

Glasgow Green. 🔳 (0141) 554 0223. ⭕ daily. ♿

THIS VICTORIAN, sandstone structure was purpose-built in 1898 as a cultural museum for the people of Glasgow's East End. It houses everything from temperance tracts to trade-union banners, suffragette posters to the comedian Billy Connolly's banana-shaped boots, and thus provides a social history of the city from the 12th to the 20th century. A superb conservatory at the back of the building contains an exotic winter garden, with tropical plants and birds.

House for an Art Lover ⑯

Bellahouston Park, Dumbreck Rd. 🔳 (0141) 353 4791. ⭕ daily. ⬤ during functions (telephone for details). 🔲 ♿

PLANS FOR THE House for an Art Lover were submitted by Charles Rennie Mackintosh and his partner Margaret Macdonald in response to a competition in a German magazine in the summer of 1900.

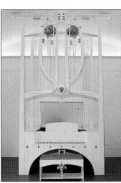

Distinctive Mackintosh piano in the Music Room, House for an Art Lover

The competition brief was to create a country retreat for someone of elegance and taste who loved the arts. As it was a theoretical exercise, the couple were unrestrained by logistics or budget and won a special prize for their efforts.

The plans lay unused for over 80 years until consulting engineer Graham Roxburgh, who had worked on the refurbishment of other Mackintosh interiors in Glasgow (including Craigie Hall), decided to try to build the House for an Art Lover. Work began in 1989 and was successfully completed in 1996. The House is host to a digital design studio and postgraduate study centre for students at the Glasgow School of Art, as well as a café.

It is the rooms on the main floor, however, that give a real insight into the vision of Mackintosh and the artistic talent of Macdonald. The Oval Room is a beautifully proportioned space in a single light colour, meant as a tranquil retreat for ladies, while the Music Room and its centrepiece piano that is played to add to the atmosphere is also bright and inspiring.

The Main Hall is darker than the other rooms and it leads into the Dining Room, with its long table, sideboard and relief stone fireplace. The great attention to detail shown throughout the House, in the panelling, light fixtures and other elements, is enormously impressive. The exterior of the building is no exception, as that too is an extraordinary achievement in art and design.

One of the greenhouses in Glasgow's peaceful Botanic Gardens

The Georgian Pollok House, viewed from the south

Pollok House ⑰

(NTS) 2060 Pollokshaws Rd. ▐ (0141) 616 6410. ○ Apr–Oct: 10am–5pm daily, Nov–Mar: 11am–4pm daily.

POLLOK HOUSE is Glasgow's finest 18th-century domestic building and contains one of Britain's best collections of Spanish paintings. The Neo-Classical central block was finished in 1750, the sobriety of its exterior contrasting with the exuberant plasterwork within. The Maxwells have lived at Pollok since the mid-13th century, but the male line ended with Sir John Maxwell, who added the grand entrance hall in the 1890s. A keen plant collector, he also designed most of the terraced gardens and parkland beyond.

Hanging above the family silver, porcelain, hand-painted Chinese wallpaper and Jacobean glass, the Stirling Pollok paintings are strong on British and Dutch schools, including William Blake's *Sir Geoffrey Chaucer and the Nine and Twenty Pilgrims* (1745) as well as William Hogarth's portrait of James Thomson, who wrote the words to *Rule Britannia*.

Spanish 16th- to 19th-century art predominates: El Greco's *Lady in a Fur Wrap* (1541) hangs in the library, while the drawing room contains works by Francisco de Goya and Esteban Murillo. In 1966 Anne Maxwell Macdonald gave the house and 146 ha (361 acres) of parkland to the City of Glasgow. The park provides the site for the city's fascinating Burrell Collection.

Burrell Collection ⑱

GIVEN TO THE CITY in 1944 by Sir William Burrell (1861–1958), a wealthy shipping owner, this internationally acclaimed collection is the star of Glasgow's renaissance, with objects of major importance in numerous fields of interest. The building housing these pieces was purpose-built in 1983. When the sun shines in, the stained glass blazes with colour, while the shaded tapestries seem a part of the surrounding woodland.

Bull's Head
Dating from the 7th century BC, this bronze head from Turkey was once part of a cauldron handle.

Hutton Castle Dining Room
This is a reconstruction of the Dining Room at Burrell's own home – the 16th-century Hutton Castle, near Berwick-upon-Tweed. The Hall and Drawing Rooms can also be seen nearby.

Hornby Portal
This 14th-century arch, with its heraldic display, comes from Hornby Castle in Yorkshire.

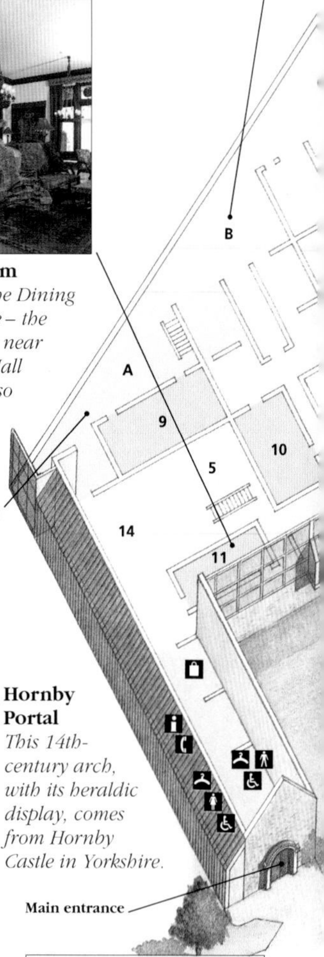

Main entrance

STAR EXHIBITS

★ **Stained Glass**

★ **Tapestries**

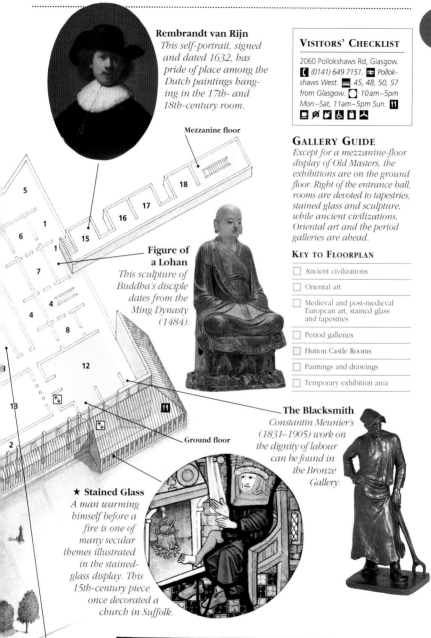

Rembrandt van Rijn
This self-portrait, signed and dated 1632, has pride of place among the Dutch paintings hanging in the 17th- and 18th-century room.

Mezzanine floor

GALLERY GUIDE
Except for a mezzanine-floor display of Old Masters, the exhibitions are on the ground floor. Right of the entrance hall, rooms are devoted to tapestries, stained glass and sculpture, while ancient civilizations, Oriental art and the period galleries are ahead.

KEY TO FLOORPLAN

☐ Ancient civilizations

☐ Oriental art

☐ Medieval and post-medieval European art, stained glass and tapestries

☐ Period galleries

☐ Hutton Castle Rooms

☐ Paintings and drawings

☐ Temporary exhibition area

Figure of a Lohan
This sculpture of Buddha's disciple dates from the Ming Dynasty (1484).

Ground floor

The Blacksmith
Constantin Meunier's (1831–1905) work on the dignity of labour can be found in the Bronze Gallery.

★ Stained Glass
A man warming himself before a fire is one of many secular themes illustrated in the stained-glass display. This 15th-century piece once decorated a church in Suffolk.

★ Tapestries
A detail from the Swiss work in wool, Scenes from the Life of Christ and of the Virgin (c.1450), is one of many tapestries on show.

Shopping in Glasgow

WHILE GLASGOW itself is home to some 625,000 people, as the focal point of a great conurbation in west central Scotland it provides the main shopping centre for almost half of the country's population. The large number of potential customers is allied to Glasgow's reputation as Scotland's most

Ortak brooch

fashion-conscious city. This, plus the revival of the city's fortunes throughout the 1990s, has seen the arrival of some very smart stores and malls. In contrast, a trip to the colourful Barras street market, which is held every weekend, offers a more traditional, if somewhat anarchic, Glaswegian shopping experience.

St Enoch Centre, one of the city's malls

DEPARTMENT STORES AND MALLS

IN 1988, GLASGOW saw the opening of **Princes Square**, which has earned itself the title of Scotland's smartest shopping mall. The **Italian Centre**, in the Merchant City area, houses designer boutiques. Leading department stores are **House of Fraser** and **John Lewis**, which opened in Spring 1999.

MARKETS

NO VISIT TO GLASGOW is complete without a trip to **The Barras**, a weekend market in the east end of the city centre. The name is a dialect version of "The Barrows", and dates from a time when goods were sold from barrows.

The current site, between the Gallowgate and London Road, has been an official market since the 1920s. Every Saturday and Sunday, thousands of bargain hunters

descend on stalls that sell virtually everything from old junk to cheap clothes and CDs.

FASHION

MANY OF Glasgow's designer fashion stores are housed in the malls in the city centre. Outside the malls, **Cruise** sells all the well-known designer names for men and women while **Diesel**, one of the more streetwise fashion labels, has an outlet on Buchanan Street. Further along Buchanan Street, **Karen Millen** is the store for the chic professional woman, with **Smiths** on Renfield Street offering the same style for men. **Schuh** is a chain of stores selling a wide range of fashionable footwear for both men and women; **Pied à Terre** sells smart shoes for women. **Pandora's Hats** is the best place to buy accessories. For a luxurious range of underwear, try **Pampas Lingerie**.

Second-hand clothes stores are common throughout the city. **Flip** offers items with 1950s American chic, whereas the clothing on sale at **Starry Starry Night** is more classic and traditional in its style.

Graham Tiso is the city's best outdoors shop, selling everything from boots and jackets to rock-climbing equipment. Serious tartan souvenir-hunters should seek out **Hector Russell**, a Highland outfitter that produces made-to-measure kilts.

FOOD AND DRINK

GLASGOW's finest independent delicatessen is **Fratelli Sarti**, a traditional Italian food store also offering a good selection of wines. **Peckham's**, a chain of delis, has an excellent branch at Central Station, and its scope goes far beyond Italy. A man once described as the UK's top cheesemonger, **Iain Mellis**

Glenlivet whisky

Traditional, "barrow-style" fruit stall in Glasgow's Barras Market

opened an outlet in Glasgow in 1995. It is the best place in the entire west of Scotland for artisan cheeses made from unpasteurized milk. **Roots and Fruits** is Glasgow's leading fruit and vegetable store, and **Le Petit Sablis** does superb breads. Aside from national chains selling beer, wine and spirits, such as **Oddbins**, there is **The Whisky Shop** in the Princes Square mall, and the **Ubiquitous Chip Wine Shop**.

Shopping on Argyle Street, with its profusion of high-street stores

BOOK STORES

GLASGOW's long-established bookshop, **John Smith & Son**, dates from 1751 and its main branch is in St Vincent Street. The well-known chain **Waterstone's** has a huge store with five floors on Sauchiehall Street, including an Internet café and a coffee shop.

ART AND DESIGN

THERE ARE A NUMBER of small galleries where art on display can be purchased. Many are concentrated in the streets behind the Tron Theatre, such as the **Glasgow Print Studio** and **Art Exposure**. The **Glasgow Art Fair**, held annually in mid-April in galleries across the city, also provides an opportunity to buy contemporary art. Fans of antiques should try the extensive **Heritage House** at Yorkhill Quay or **Lansdowne Antiques** on Park Road. For furniture and interior design ideas, visit **Designworks** or **Inhouse**.

DIRECTORY

DEPARTMENT STORES AND MALLS

House of Fraser
21–45 Buchanan St,
G1 3HR.
(0141) 221 3880.

Italian Centre
7 John St, G1 1HP.
(0141) 552 6368.

John Lewis
Buchanan Galleries,
G1 2GF.
(0141) 353 6677.

Princes Square
48 Buchanan St, G1 3JX.
(0141) 221 0324.

FASHION

Cruise
180 Ingram St, G1 1DN.
(0141) 552 9989.

Diesel
116–121 Buchanan St,
G1 2JW.
(0141) 221 5255.

Flip
70–72 Queen St, G1 3EN.
(0141) 221 2041.

Graham Tiso
129 Buchanan St, G1 2JA.
(0141) 248 4877.

Hector Russell
110 Buchanan St, G1 2JN.
(0141) 221 0217.

Karen Millen
36 Buchanan St, G1 3JX.
(0141) 243 2136.

Pampas Lingerie
78 Hyndland Rd, G12 9UT.
(0141) 357 2383.

Pandora's Hats
5 Sinclair Drive, G42 9PR.
(0141) 649 7714.

Pied à Terre
Unit 20 Princes Square,
Buchanan St, G1 3JD.
(0141) 221 0463.

Schuh
118–120 Argyle St,
G2 8BH.
(0141) 248 7331.

Smiths
14–16 Renfield St, G2 5AL.
(0141) 221 0603.

Starry Starry Night
19–21 Dowanside Lane,
G12 9BZ.
(0141) 337 1837.

FOOD AND DRINK

Fratelli Sarti
133 Wellington St, G2 2XD.
(0141) 248 2228.

Iain Mellis
492 Great Western Rd,
G12 8EW.
(0141) 339 8998.

Le Petit Sablis
493 Great Western Rd,
G12 8HL.
(0141) 576 0220.

Oddbins
26 Hope St, G2 6AA.
(0141) 248 3082.

Peckham's
Caledonian Centre,
Central Station, G1 3SH.
(0141) 248 4012.

Roots & Fruits
351 Byres Rd, G12 8AU.
(0141) 339 5164.

Ubiquitous Chip Wine Shop
12 Ashton Lane, G12 8SJ.
(0141) 334 5007.

The Whisky Shop
Unit 12 Princes Square,
48 Buchanan St, G1 3JX.
(0141) 226 8446.

BOOK STORES

John Smith & Son
57 St Vincent St, G2 5TB.
(0141) 221 7472.

Waterstone's
153–157 Sauchiehall St,
G2 3EW.
(0141) 332 9105.

ART AND DESIGN

Art Exposure
19 Parnie St, G1 5RJ.
(0141) 552 7779.

Designworks
38 Gibson St, G12 8NX.
(0141) 339 9520.

Glasgow Art Fair
(0141) 552 6027.

Glasgow Print Studio
22 King St, G1 5QP.
(0141) 552 0704.

Heritage House
3b Yorkhill Quay Estate,
G3 8QE.
(0141) 334 4924.

Inhouse
24–26 Wilson St, G1 1SS.
(0141) 552 3322.

Lansdowne Antiques
10 Park Rd, G4 9JG.
(0141) 339 7211.

ENTERTAINMENT IN GLASGOW

T HE DANCE MUSIC that has emerged during the 1990s has found a natural home in Glasgow, which has possibly the most exuberant nightlife in Scotland. With the Scottish Exhibition and Conference Centre housing two major rock venues, and Barrowlands still a fixture on the concert circuit, popular music is very prominent. There are a number of mainstream cinemas in the city,

A flag celebrating Glasgow as "the friendly city"

as well as the Glasgow Film Theatre, a centre for arthouse releases. The annual Celtic Connections Festival in January is an international folk music event and there is plenty of culture in the city as a whole. Some major orchestras, the Scottish Ballet and Scottish Opera are based here. The Citizens' is a highly-acclaimed theatre and the Tramway and the Arches both stage large, innovative productions.

Scottish Opera performing *Eugene Onegin* on stage at the Theatre Royal

SOURCES OF INFORMATION

T HE TWICE MONTHLY arts and entertainment magazine *The List* covers all events in Glasgow and Edinburgh.

CLASSICAL MUSIC AND OPERA

S COTLAND'S NATIONAL opera company, Scottish Opera, is based at the **Theatre Royal** and stages some eight productions each season.

Glasgow Royal Concert Hall, with a capacity of 2,400, hosts visits from major international orchestras and is also home to the Royal Scottish National Orchestra. When the Royal Concert Hall opened in 1990, it replaced **City Hall** as the main classical venue, but the Scottish Chamber Orchestra still performs at the latter.

For more intimate shows, the **Royal Scottish Academy of Music and Drama** has two smaller halls, while various venues across the city host occasional recitals and concerts.

ROCK, JAZZ AND WORLD MUSIC

R OCK BANDS HAVE a choice of venues. There is the main auditorium at the **Scottish Exhibition and Conference Centre**, and the **Armadillo** in the same centre. It is **Barrowlands**, however, that remains the city's principal rock venue. Jazz sessions take place at City Hall and at **Cottier's Theatre**.

Musicians outside City Chambers during a Festival of Jazz

The Royal Concert Hall holds a Celtic Connections Festival. It also hosts international music, as does the **Old Fruitmarket**.

CINEMA

T HERE IS NO SHORTAGE of cinema screens in the city. The **ABC Film Centre** boasts six, as does **Odeon City Centre**, and the **Odeon at the Quay** has 12 screens. The **Glasgow Film Theatre**, known by its initials GFT, shows arthouse and foreign-language movies. The **Grosvenor** shows both commercial and arthouse films.

The stylish café-bar at the Tron Theatre in the city centre

THEATRE AND DANCE

T HE SCOTTISH BALLET stages its Glasgow performances at the Theatre Royal *(see Classical Music and Opera)*. Visiting dance companies, from classical to contemporary, also perform here and it is a noted stop on the touring circuit for major theatre companies from the rest of the UK and overseas.

The **Citizens' Theatre** is the main venue for serious drama, from Greek tragedies to modern pieces, and it rightly claims to be Scotland's best.

Both the **Tramway** and the **Arches** have staged extraordinary avant-garde shows, and are acclaimed for their experimental works. Smaller-scale productions can be seen at the **Tron** and Cottier's Theatre *(see Rock, Jazz and World Music)*. Commercial productions, such as musicals and pantomimes, are a staple at the popular **King's**.

Original road sign for the West End

BARS AND CLUBS

VISITORS CAN CHOOSE from traditional pubs, which give a flavour of the old city, or fashionable bars with a contemporary atmosphere. Old-fashioned pubs have long been popular in Glasgow. These include the **Horseshoe**, in the city centre, the **Griffin** on Bath Street and the **Halt** on Woodlands Road. Modern venues are harder to find, but two bars that are thriving are **Bargo**, in Merchant City, and the first floor bar at the **Cul de Sac** in the West End. The city's club culture is one of the best in the UK. Each venue has different styles of music on different nights, including house, hip-hop, techno or drum-and-bass. The Arches *(see Theatre and Dance)*, **The Sub Club**, **The Tunnel** and **Archaos** are among the best.

SPORTS

GLASGOW IS HOME to the country's most successful football (soccer) clubs, **Celtic** and **Glasgow Rangers**, and each has a large, impressive stadium. The football season runs from August to May, and there is usually a game at least once a week during that time. Scotland's refurbished **Hampden National Stadium** hosts the finals of domestic cup competitions in November and May each year, and major international games.

Celtic fans cheering on their football (soccer) team from the stands

---

DIRECTORY

CLASSICAL MUSIC AND OPERA

City Hall
Candleriggs, G1 1NQ.
(0141) 287 5511.

Glasgow Royal Concert Hall
2 Sauchiehall St,
G2 3NY.
(0141) 287 5511.

Royal Scottish Academy of Music and Drama
100 Renfrew St, G2 3DB.
(0141) 332 5057.

Theatre Royal
282 Hope St, G2 3QA.
(0141) 332 9000.

ROCK, JAZZ AND WORLD MUSIC

Barrowlands
244 Gallowgate, G4 0TS.
(0141) 552 4601.

Cottier's Theatre
93 Hyndland St, G11 5PX.
(0141) 357 3868.

Old Fruitmarket
Albion St, G1 1NQ.
(0141) 287 5511.

Scottish Exhibition and Conference Centre/Armadillo
Finnieston,
G3 8YW.
(0141) 248 3000.

CINEMA

ABC Film Centre
326 Sauchiehall St,
G2 3JB.
(0141) 332 9513.

Glasgow Film Theatre
12 Rose St, G3 6RB.
(0141) 332 8128.

Grosvenor
Ashton Lane,
G12 8SJ.
(0141) 339 4298.

Odeon at the Quay
Paisley Road West, G5 8NP.
(0141) 418 0111.

Odeon City Centre
56 Renfield St, G2 1NF.
(0141) 332 3413.

THEATRE AND DANCE

Arches
30 Midland St, G1 4PR.
(0141) 221 4001.

Citizens' Theatre
119 Gorbals St, G5 9DS.
(0141) 429 0022.

King's
294 Bath St, G2 4JN.
(0141) 287 5511.

Tramway
25 Albert Drive, G41 2PE.
(0141) 422 2023.

Tron
63 Trongate, G1 5HB.
(0141) 552 4267.

BARS AND CLUBS

Archaos
25–27 Queen St, G1 3EF.
(0141) 204 3189.

Bargo
80 Albion St, G1 1NY.
(0141) 553 4771.

Cul de Sac
44–46 Ashton Lane,
G12 8SJ.
(0141) 334 8899.

Griffin
226 Bath St, G2.
(0141) 331 5171.

Halt
160 Woodlands Rd,
G3 6LF.
(0141) 564 1527.

Horseshoe
17 Drury St, G2 5AE.
(0141) 229 5711.

The Sub Club
22 Jamaica St, G1 4QD.
(0141) 248 4600.

The Tunnel
84 Mitchell St, G1 3NA.
(0141) 204 1000.

SPORTS

Celtic
Celtic Park,
95 Kerrydale St, G40 3RE.
(0141) 551 8653.

Glasgow Rangers
Ibrox Stadium,
G51 2YX.
(0141) 427 8800.

Hampden National Stadium
Hampden Park,
Letherby Drive, G42 9BA.
(0141) 632 1275.

CENTRAL SCOTLAND

C ENTRAL SCOTLAND *is a contrast of picturesque countryside and major urban centres, where a modern industrialized country meets an older and wilder landscape. Historically, it was here that the English-speaking Lowlands bordered the Gaelic Highlands, and there is still a strong sense of transition for anyone travelling north.*

The Highland Boundary Fault is a geological feature running through Central Scotland from Arran in the southwest to Stonehaven on the northeast coast. The Fault divides the Highlands from the Lowlands, making Central Scotland an area of contrasts, with both mountainous areas and green farmland. For hundreds of years, this line was also a meeting place, or border, between two very different cultures. To the north and west was a Gaelic-speaking people, who felt loyalty to their local clan chiefs. This way of life began to be marginalized in the late 18th century, as the more Anglicized Lowlands established their dominance.

In the Lowlands, Scotland's industry developed, drawing on coal reserves in districts such as Lanarkshire and the Lothians, while the Highlands were depopulated and eventually set aside for sporting estates and sheep farming.

Because Central Scotland is so compact, the opposing characteristics of Highland and Lowland, industrial and pre-industrial, exist side by side. Stirling Castle, parts of which date from the 16th century, is sited close to the petro-chemical plants and power plants on the upper reaches of the Forth. The tranquillity of the Trossachs and the hills of Arran are easily accessible from Glasgow, Scotland's largest, and largely industrial, city. The country's first coal-run ironworks was built at Carron in 1759, very close to Falkirk where Bonnie Prince Charlie had enjoyed one of his last military successes as claimant to the British throne 13 years earlier. Perth and Dundee are important centres of commerce positioned a short distance from the relative wildness of the Southern Highlands. There is no other area of Scotland that displays so many profound contrasts.

The view from Goat Fell Ridge, near Brodick, across to the spectacular mountains of Arran

◁ A golfer in the grounds of a stately home, one of a number in Central Scotland providing golfing facilities

Exploring Central Scotland

CENTRAL SCOTLAND presents some
remarkable contrasts. The Goat
Fell ridge on the Isle of Arran, off the
west coast, has one of the most inspiring island hill walks in the entire
country while, just to the north, the
Isle of Bute is a more placid tourist
destination. On the mainland, the
Trossachs, near Callander, is an area
of outstanding mountain beauty, very
different from the lowlands of the Forth
Valley further east. Stirling Castle
stands at the head of the Forth under
the shadow of the Ochil Hills, while
Perth occupies a similar position on
the Tay. The Firth of Tay, with its
open views, is home to Dundee,
Scotland's fourth city.

Loch Katrine seen from the Trossachs

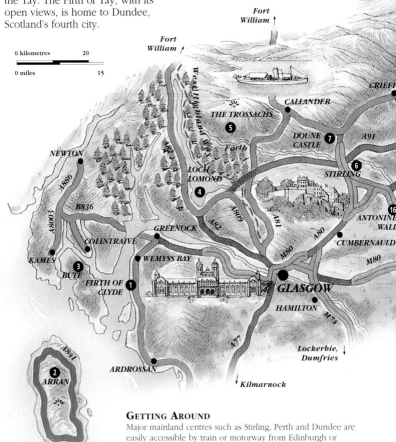

0 kilometres 20

0 miles 15

GETTING AROUND

Major mainland centres such as Stirling, Perth and Dundee are
easily accessible by train or motorway from Edinburgh or
Glasgow but, for the mountain areas in Central Scotland (the
Trossachs or minor ranges), a car is recommended. Reaching
Arran or Bute is best done by car or train from Glasgow, then car
ferry from ports on the Ayrshire coast (Ardrossan, Wemyss Bay).
The islands are small enough to make bicycle touring possible.

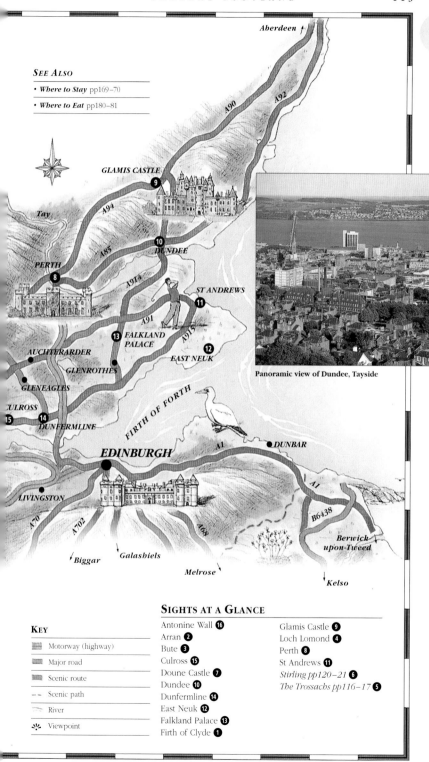

SEE ALSO

- *Where to Stay* pp169–70
- *Where to Eat* pp180–81

GLAMIS CASTLE ❾

DUNDEE ❿

PERTH ❽

ST ANDREWS ⓫

FALKLAND PALACE ⓭

EAST NEUK ⓬

Tay

AUCHTERARDER

GLENROTHES

GLENEAGLES

CULROSS ⓯

DUNFERMLINE ⓮

FIRTH OF FORTH

EDINBURGH

LIVINGSTON

DUNBAR

Biggar   Galashiels   Melrose

Berwick-upon-Tweed

Kelso

Aberdeen

Panoramic view of Dundee, Tayside

SIGHTS AT A GLANCE

Antonine Wall ⓰
Arran ❷
Bute ❸
Culross ⓯
Doune Castle ❼
Dundee ❿
Dunfermline ⓮
East Neuk ⓬
Falkland Palace ⓭
Firth of Clyde ❶

Glamis Castle ❾
Loch Lomond ❹
Perth ❽
St Andrews ⓫
Stirling pp120–21 ❻
The Trossachs pp116–17 ❺

KEY

▬▬ Motorway (highway)

▬▬ Major road

▬▬ Scenic route

-- Scenic path

〰 River

☼ Viewpoint

Firth of Clyde ❶

Numerous counties west of Glasgow. *Helensburgh and Dumbarton in the north; Troon and Ayr in the south.* *from Largs to Great Cumbrae; from Gourock to Dunoon.* *Largs (01475) 673765; Dumbarton (01389) 742306.*

As might be expected of a waterway that leads from Glasgow, a former economic powerhouse of the British Empire *(see p46)*, to the Irish Sea and the Atlantic, the Firth of Clyde has many reminders of its industrial past. **Greenock**, some 40 km (25 miles) west of Glasgow, was once a shipbuilding centre. Few go there for the town's beauty, but the **McLean Museum and Art Gallery**, with its exhibits and information on the engineer James Watt *(see p22)*, a native of Greenock, is worth a visit. Princes Pier is a departure point for cruises along the Clyde. **Dumbarton**, 24 km (15 miles) from Glasgow on the northern bank, dates from the 5th century AD. Its ancient castle perches on a rock overlooking the rest of the town.

The Firth itself is L-shaped, heading northwest as it opens up beyond the Erskine Bridge. On reaching Gourock, just west of Greenock, the Firth branches south to more open water. Kip Marina at nearby **Inverkip** is a major yachting centre, while many towns on the Ayrshire coast have served as holiday resorts for Glasgow since Victorian times. **Largs**, site of the clash between Scots and Vikings in 1263, has a multimedia centre about the Vikings in Scotland, as well as a modern monument to the 1263 battle. A ferry service is offered to **Great Cumbrae Island**, which lies just off the coast. The main town on the island is Millport, which is built around a picturesque bay. The western side of the Firth of Clyde is much less developed, bordered by the Cowal Peninsula with its hills and lochs. The only town of note in this wild country is **Dunoon**. Again once a Victorian holiday resort, it still relies on tourism for its income. For many years there was a strong American influence in Dunoon due to the US nuclear submarine base at Holy Loch that is now closed.

The old harbour at Brodick, with Goat Fell Ridge in the distance

McLean Museum and Art Gallery

Union St, Greenock. *(01475) 723741.* *Mon–Sat.*

Largs seafront, the departure point for ferries to Great Cumbrae Island

Arran ❷

North Ayrshire. *4,500.* *from Ardrossan to Brodick; from Claonaig (Isle of Mull) to Lochranza (Apr–Oct only).* *Brodick (01770) 302140.*

Arran is thought to have been populated as long ago as the end of the last Ice Age. The island's neolithic chambered burial tombs, such as the one at **Torrylinn** near Lagg in the south, indicate this. Bronze Age stone circles can also be seen around **Machrie** on the west coast. Vikings arrived from about AD 800 and exerted an influence for more than four centuries. After the Battle of Largs in 1263, when Alexander III defeated the Norsemen, Scotland bought Arran from the Vikings in 1266.

Today, visitors tend to come to Arran for outdoor pursuits. Golf is especially popular, with 18-hole courses at Brodick, Whiting Bay and Lamlash *(see p189)*. Fishing is also popular.

Golfer on the island of Arran

Brodick is the island's only real town. The more mountainous parts offer some of the most spectacular hillwalking in Central Scotland. **The Goat Fell Ridge** to the east of Glen Rosa and **Beinn Tarsuinn** to the west have a particular rugged beauty.

Robert the Bruce stayed on Arran on his return to Scotland in 1307. His followers had already been harrassing the garrison at **Brodick Castle**, then occupied by supporters of the King of England. Legend states that it was from Arran that Bruce saw a signal fire on the Ayrshire coast that told him it was safe to return to the mainland and launch the campaign against the English *(see p43)*. Parts of the Castle still date from the 13th century, though it has had many later additions.

Brodick Castle

(NTS) Brodick. *(01770) 302202.*
Castle *Apr–Oct: daily.*
Gardens *daily.*

The snowy peak of Ben Lomond rising majestically over Loch Lomond, part of the West Highland Way

Bute ❸

Argyll & Bute. 7,000. from Wemyss Bay to Rothesay; from Colintraive to Rhubodach. from Dunoon. Rothesay (01700) 502151.

BUTE IS ALMOST an extension of the Cowal Peninsula, and the small ferry from Colintraive takes only five minutes to cross the Kyles of Bute to Rhubodach on the island. This route is a long drive from Glasgow, however, and most people choose to travel via Wemyss Bay on the Firth of Clyde across to the island's main town, Rothesay.

Just 25 km (16 miles) long by 8 km (5 miles) at its widest point, Bute has been occupied since at least the Bronze Age. The remains of the chapel at St Ninian's Point on the west coast date from around the 6th century, while **Rothesay Castle**, now ruined, is mostly

a 12th-century structure and was the site of struggles between islanders and Vikings in the 13th century. Over the last 120 years or so, Bute has played a more placid role as a popular holiday resort.

One of Bute's main attractions is **Mount Stuart House**, 5 km (3 miles) south of Rothesay. This great aristocratic house, built in 1877 by the third Marquess of Bute, is set in 18th-century gardens. The features of this wonderful Gothic edifice reflect the Marquess's interests in mythology, religion and astronomy.

♦ Rothesay Castle

Castle Hill St, Rothesay. (01700) 502691. Apr–Sep: daily; Oct–Mar: Sat–Thu am (Sun: pm only).

♦ Mount Stuart House

Mount St. (01700) 503877. May–mid-Oct: Wed, Fri–Mon; mid-Oct–Apr: Mon–Fri by appointment.

View of Bute with the 14th-century Kames Castle, at the head of Kames Bay

Loch Lomond ❹

West Dunbartonshire, Argyll & Bute, Trossachs. Balloch, Tarbet. Balloch, Balmaha. Dumbarton (01389) 742306.

OF SCOTLAND'S many lochs, Lomond is perhaps the most popular and best loved. Lying just 30 km (19 miles) northwest of Glasgow, its accessibility has helped its rise to prominence. The loch is the largest body of fresh water in the British Isles, 35 km (22 miles) long and 8 km (5 miles) at its widest point in the south, where there are a scattering of over 30 islands, some with ancient ruins. The northern end is narrower and deeper.

Duncryne, a small hill some 5 km (3 miles) northeast of **Balloch** on the southern shore, gives an excellent view of the Loch. In general, the western shore is the more developed, with villages such as **Luss** and **Tarbet** attracting large numbers of visitors.

The contrast between the Loch and the surrounding mountains adds to the spectacle. **Ben Ime** in the Arrochar Alps, to the northwest of Lomond, stands at 1,011 m (3,317 ft) while **Ben Lomond** on the east side is 974 m (3,196 ft). Many walkers pass this way since Scotland's most popular long-distance footpath, the West Highland Way (see p191) from Glasgow to Fort William, skirts the eastern shore. Boat trips around the loch operate regularly from Balloch Pier. The area is also good for water sports enthusiasts – speed boats, kayaks and jet skis can all be rented.

The Trossachs ❺

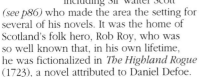

COMBINING THE RUGGEDNESS of the Grampians with the pastoral tranquillity of the Borders, this beautiful region of craggy hills and sparkling lochs is the colourful meeting place of the Lowlands and Highlands. Home to a wide variety of wildlife, including the golden eagle, peregrine falcon, red deer and the wildcat, the Trossachs have inspired numerous writers, including Sir Walter Scott

Golden eagle

(see p86) who made the area the setting for several of his novels. It was the home of Scotland's folk hero, Rob Roy, who was so well known that, in his own lifetime, he was fictionalized in *The Highland Rogue* (1723), a novel attributed to Daniel Defoe.

Loch Katrine
The setting of Sir Walter Scott's Lady of the Lake *(1810), this freshwater loch can be explored on the Victorian steamer* Sir Walter Scott, *which cruises from the Trossachs Pier.*

Loch Lomond
Britain's largest freshwater lake was immortalized in a ballad composed by a local Jacobite soldier, dying far from home. He laments that though he will return home before his companions who travel on "the high road", he will be doing so on "the low road" (of death).

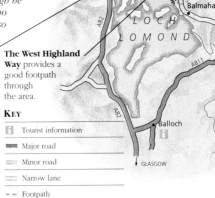

FORT WILLIAM

Inveruglas

LOCH ARKLET

LOCH

Tarbet

BEN LOMOND
974 m
(3,195 ft)

Kinlochard

BEN UIRD
596 m
(1,955 ft)

Luss

Balmaha

L O C H
L O M O N D

The West Highland Way provides a good footpath through the area.

Balloch

GLASGOW

KEY

ℹ	Tourist information
▬▬	Major road
▭▭	Minor road
═══	Narrow lane
‑ ‑	Footpath
⚶	Viewpoint

0 kilometres   5

0 miles   5

Luss
With its exceptionally picturesque cottages, Luss is one of the prettiest villages in Central Scotland. Surrounded by grassy hills, it occupies one of the most scenic parts of Loch Lomond's western shore.

Inchmahome Priory

Mary, Queen of Scots was hidden in this island priory to escape the armies of King Henry VIII, before fleeing for France.

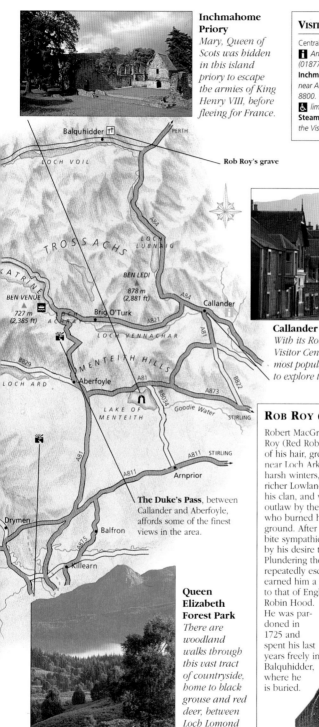

Balquhidder

LOCH VOIL

PERTH

Rob Roy's grave

TROSSACHS

LOCH LUBNAIG

A84

BEN LEDI
878 m
(2,881 ft)

KATRINE

BEN VENUE
727 m
(2,385 ft)

Brig O'Turk

A821

Callander

A84

LOCH ACHRAY

LOCH VENNACHAR

A81

MENTEITH HILLS

B829

LOCH ARD

Aberfoyle

A81

A873

B8034

Goodie Water

STIRLING

LAKE OF MENTEITH

A811 STIRLING

A811

Arnprior

Drymen

A81

Balfron

The Duke's Pass, between
Callander and Aberfoyle,
affords some of the finest
views in the area.

Killearn

Callander

*With its Rob Roy and Trossachs
Visitor Centre, Callander is the
most popular town from which
to explore the Trossachs.*

ROB ROY (1671–1734)

Robert MacGregor, known as Rob
Roy (Red Robert) from the colour
of his hair, grew up as a herdsman
near Loch Arklet. After a series of
harsh winters, he took to raiding
richer Lowland properties to feed
his clan, and was declared an
outlaw by the Duke of Montrose
who burned his house to the
ground. After this, Rob Roy's Jacobite sympathies became inflamed
by his desire to avenge the crime.
Plundering the duke's lands and
repeatedly escaping from prison
earned him a reputation similar
to that of England's
Robin Hood.
He was par-
doned in
1725 and
spent his last
years freely in
Balquhidder,
where he
is buried.

Queen Elizabeth Forest Park

*There are
woodland
walks through
this vast tract
of countryside,
home to black
grouse and red
deer, between
Loch Lomond
and Aberfoyle.*

The 17th-century town house of the Dukes of Argyll

Stirling ❻

Central. 🏛 28,000. 🚊 🚌
ℹ 41 Dunbarton Rd (01786) 475019.

SITUATED BETWEEN the Ochil Hills and the Campsie Fells, the town of Stirling grew up around its castle, historically one of Scotland's most important fortresses. Below the castle the Old Town is still protected by the original walls, built in the 16th century to keep Mary, Queen of Scots safe from Henry VIII. The medieval **Church of the Holy Rude**, on Castle Wynd, where the infant James VI was crowned in 1567, has one of Scotland's few surviving hammerbeam oak roofs. In front of the church, the ornate façade of **Mar's Wark** is all that remains of a grand palace which, though never completed, was commissioned in 1570 by the first Earl of Mar. It was destroyed by the Jacobites in 1746. Opposite stands the beautiful 17th-century town house of the Dukes of Argyll.

ENVIRONS: Three kilometres (2 miles) south of Stirling, the **Bannockburn Heritage Centre** stands by the field where Robert the Bruce defeated the English in 1314 *(see p43)*. After the battle, he dismantled the castle so it would not fall back into English hands. A bronze equestrian statue commemorates the man who became an icon of Scottish independence.

ℹ **Bannockburn Heritage Centre**
(NTS) Glasgow Rd. 📞 *(01786) 812664.* ☐ *Mar–23 Dec: daily.* ⬤ *24 Dec–Feb.* 📷 ♿

Stirling Castle

R ISING HIGH on a rocky crag, this magnificent castle, which dominated Scottish history for centuries, now remains one of the finest examples of Renaissance architecture in Scotland. Legend says that King Arthur wrested the original castle from the Saxons, but there is no evidence of a castle before 1124. The present building dates from the 15th and 16th centuries and was last defended, against the Jacobites, in 1746. From 1881 to 1964 the castle was used as a depot for recruits into the Argyll and Sutherland Highlanders, though it now serves no military function.

Gargoyle on castle wall

Robert the Bruce
In the esplanade, this modern statue shows Robert the Bruce sheathing his sword after the Battle of Bannockburn in 1314.

Prince's Tower

Forework

Entrance

***Stirling Castle in the Time of the Stuarts**, painted by Johannes Vorsterman (1643–99)*

◁ **Loch Ard, near Stirling, in the Trossachs**

★ **Palace**
The otherwise sparse interiors of the royal apartments contain the Stirling Heads. These Renaissance roundels depict 38 figures, thought to be members of the royal court at that time.

VISITORS' CHECKLIST

Castle Wynd, Stirling. ☎ (01786) 450000. ☐ Apr–Sep: 9:30am–6pm daily; Oct–Mar: 9:30am–5pm daily (last admission: 45 mins before closing). 🅿 🅿 museum. 🅰 limited. ✉ 🍴 ☐ ☐

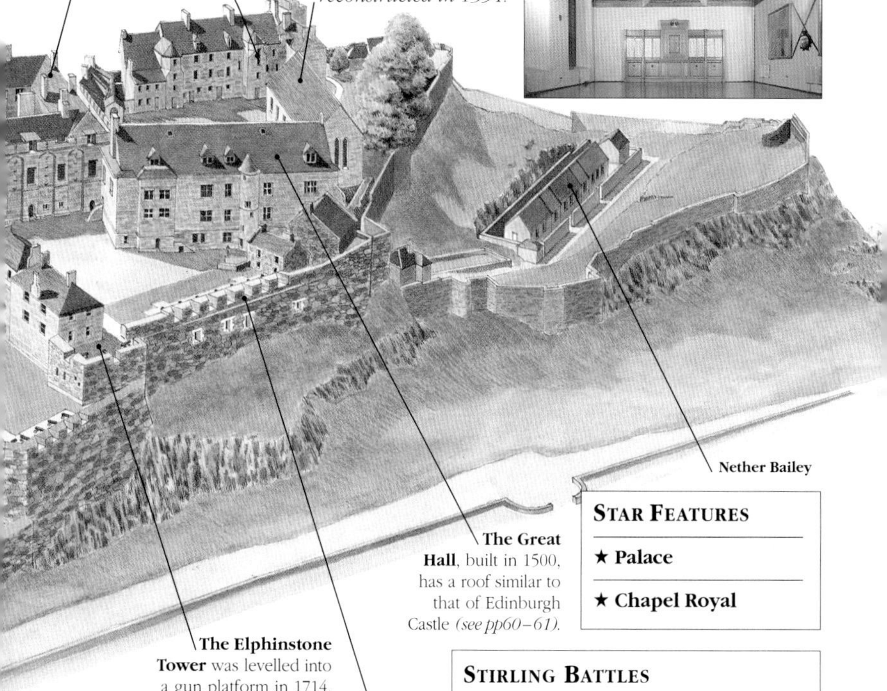

The King's Old Building houses the Regimental Museum of the Argyll and Sutherland Highlanders.

★ **Chapel Royal**
Seventeenth-century frescoes by Valentine Jenkins adorn the chapel, reconstructed in 1594.

Nether Bailey

The Great Hall, built in 1500, has a roof similar to that of Edinburgh Castle *(see pp60–61).*

STAR FEATURES

★ **Palace**

★ **Chapel Royal**

The Elphinstone Tower was levelled into a gun platform in 1714.

STIRLING BATTLES

At the highest navigable point of the Forth and holding the pass to the Highlands, Stirling occupied a key position in Scotland's struggles for independence. Seven battlefields can be seen from the castle; the 67-m (220-ft) Wallace Monument at Abbey Craig recalls William Wallace's defeat of the English at Stirling Bridge in 1297, foreshadowing Bruce's victory in 1314.

The Victorian Wallace Monument

Grand Battery
Following the unrest after the deposition of the Stuarts (see p45), this parapet was built in 1708, to strengthen the castle's defences.

Perth seen from the east across the Tay

Doune Castle ❼

Doune, Central. ☎ *(01786) 841742.*
🚆 🚌 *Stirling then bus.* ⏰ *Apr–Oct:
daily; Nov–Mar: Sat–Thu.*
⏺ *21 Dec–8 Jan.* 🎟 ♿ *limited.*

BUILT AS THE residence of
Robert, Duke of Albany,
in the late 14th century,
Doune Castle was a Stuart
stronghold until it fell into ruin
in the 18th century. Now fully
restored, it is one of the most
beautifully complete castles
of its time and offers a unique
view into the life of the medieval royal household.
　The Gatehouse, once a self-
sufficient residence, leads
through to the central courtyard from which the Great
Hall can be entered. Complete
with its reconstructed open-
timber roof, minstrels' gallery
and central fireplace, the
Hall adjoins the Lord's Hall
and Private Room with its
original privy and well-hatch.
A number of private stairs and

narrow passages illustrate the
ingenious means by which the
royal family tried to protect
itself during times of danger.

Perth ❽

Perthshire. 🏘 *45,000.* 🚆 🚌
ℹ *45 High St (01738) 638353.*

ONCE THE CAPITAL of medi-
eval Scotland, Perth's rich
heritage is reflected in many
of its buildings. It was in the
Church of St John, founded
in 1126, that the preacher
John Knox delivered the fiery
sermons which led to the destruction of many local mon-
asteries. The Victorianized
Fair Maid's House (c.1600),
on North Port, is one of the
oldest houses in town and
was the fictional home of the
heroine of Sir Walter Scott's
The Fair Maid of Perth (1828).
　In **Balhousie Castle**, the
Museum of the Black Watch
commemorates the first ever

Highland regiment, while the
Art Gallery and Museum has
displays on local industry and
exhibitions of Scottish painting.

ENVIRONS: Three km (2 miles)
north of Perth, the Gothic
Scone Palace stands on the
site of an abbey destroyed by
John Knox's followers in 1559.
Between the 9th and 13th
centuries, Scone guarded the
sacred Stone of Destiny, now
housed in Edinburgh Castle
(see pp60–61), on which the
Scottish kings were crowned.
The embroideries of Mary,
Queen of Scots are among the
many priceless artifacts on
display within the palace.

♠ **Balhousie Castle**
RHQ Black Watch, Hay St.
☎ *(0131) 310 8530.* ⏰ *Apr–Sep:
Mon–Sat; Oct–Apr: Mon–Fri.*
⏺ *23 Dec–6 Jan, last Sat in Jun.*
🏛 **Art Gallery and Museum**
78 George St. ☎ *(01738) 632488.*
⏰ *Mon–Sat.* ⏺ *24 Dec–4 Jan.* ♿
♠ **Scone Palace**
A93 to Braemar. ☎ *(01738) 552300.*
⏰ *Good Fri–mid-Oct: daily.* 🎟 ♿

Glamis Castle ❾

Glamis, outside Forfar, Tayside.
☎ *(01307) 840242.* 🚆 🚌 *Dundee
then bus.* ⏰ *Apr–Oct: daily.* 🎟 🎟
♿ *grounds.*

WITH THE pinnacled out-
line of a Loire chateau,
the imposing medieval tower-
house of **Glamis Castle**

Glamis Castle with statues of James VI (left) and Charles I (right)

began as a royal hunting lodge in the 11th century but underwent reconstruction in the 17th century. It was the childhood home of Queen Elizabeth the Queen Mother, and her former bedroom can be seen with a youthful portrait by Henri de Laszlo (1878–1956).

Behind the castle's grey-pink walls, many rooms are open to the public, including Duncan's Hall, the oldest in the castle and Shakespeare's setting for the king's murder in *Macbeth*. Together, the rooms present an array of china, paintings, tapestries and furniture spanning 500 years. In the grounds stand a pair of wrought-iron gates made for the Queen Mother on her 80th birthday in 1980.

View of St Andrews over the ruins of the cathedral

Dundee ❿

Tayside. 🏛 150,000. ✈ ➹ 🚉
🛈 7–21 Castle St (01382) 527527.
🗓 Tue, Fri–Sun.

Famous for its cake and marmalade, **Dundee** was also a major ship-building centre in the 18th and 19th centuries, a period which is recreated at the Victoria Docks.

HMS Unicorn, built in 1824, is the oldest British-built warship still afloat and is fitted as it was on its last voyage. Berthed at Craig Pier is the royal research ship **Discovery**. Built here in 1901 for the first of Captain Scott's voyages to the Antarctic, the *Discovery* was one of the last sailing ships to be made in Britain. Housed in a Victorian Gothic building, the **McManus Galleries** provide a

glimpse of Dundee's industrial heritage, with exhibitions of archaeology and Victorian art.

ENVIRONS: Along the coast, the pretty town of **Arbroath** is famed for its red stonework, ancient Abbey and "Arbroath Smokies" (smoked haddock). St Vigean's Museum displays a copy of *The Declaration of Arbroath*, attesting Scotland's independence.

🏛 **HMS Unicorn**
Victoria Docks.
🛈 (01382) 200900.
🕐 10am–5pm daily.
🔴 late Dec–early Jan.
♿ limited.
www.frigateunicorn.org
🏛 **Discovery**
Discovery Point.
🛈 (01382) 201245.
🕐 daily. ♿ ♿
📷 by appointment.
🏛 **McManus Galleries**
Albert Institute, Albert Square.
🛈 (01382) 432020. 🕐 Mon–Sun.

Insignia of St Mary's College, St Andrews University

St Andrews ⓫

Fife. 🏛 14,000. ➹ Leuchars. 🚉
🛈 70 Market St (01334) 472021.

Scotland's oldest university town and one-time ecclesiastical capital, **St Andrews** is now a shrine to golfers from all over the world. Its main streets and cobbled alleys, full of crooked housefronts, dignified university buildings and medieval churches, converge on the venerable ruins of the 12th-century **cathedral**. Once the largest cathedral in Scotland, it was later pillaged for its stones, which were used to build the town. **St Andrew's Castle** was built for the town's bishops in the year 1200. The dungeon, in which many religious Reformers were held prisoner, can still be seen. St Andrews' golf courses occupy the land to the west of the city, and each is open for a modest fee. The **British Golf Museum**, which tells how the city's Royal and Ancient Golf Club became the ruling arbiter of the game, will delight golf enthusiasts.

♣ **St Andrew's Castle**
The Scores. 🛈 (01334) 477196.
🕐 daily. ♿ ♿ ♿
🏛 **British Golf Museum**
Bruce Embankment. 🛈 (01334)
478880. 🕐 Easter–mid-Oct: daily;
mid-Oct–Easter: Thu–Mon. ♿ ♿

THE BIRTHPLACE OF GOLF

Scotland's national game *(see pp188–9)* was pioneered on the sandy links around St Andrews. The earliest record of the game being played dates from 1457, when golf was banned by James II because it was interfering with his subjects' archery practice. Mary, Queen of Scots was berated in 1568 for playing immediately after her husband, Darnley, had been murdered.

Mary, Queen of Scots at St Andrews in 1563

The central courtyard of Falkland Palace, bordered by rose bushes

East Neuk ⑫

Fife. 🚆 Leuchars. 🚌 Glenrothes & Leuchars. 🛈 St Andrews (01334) 472021.

A STRING of pretty fishing villages peppers the shoreline of the **East Neuk** (the eastern "corner") of Fife, stretching from Earlsferry to Fife Ness. Much of Scotland's medieval trade with Europe passed through these ports, a connection reflected in the Flemish-inspired crow-stepped gables of many of the cottages. Although the herring industry has declined and the area is now a peaceful holiday centre, the sea still dominates village life. The harbour is the heart of St Monans, a charming town of narrow twisting streets, while Pittenweem is the base for the East Neuk fishing fleet.

The town is also known for **St Fillan's Cave**, the retreat of a 9th-century hermit whose relic was used to bless the army of Robert the Bruce before the Battle of Bannockburn. A church stands among

the cobbled lanes and colourful cottages of Crail; legend goes that the stone by the church gate was hurled across to the mainland from the Isle of May by the Devil.

A number of 16th- to 19th-century buildings in the village of Anstruther contain the **Scottish Fisheries Museum**, which tells the area's history with the aid of cottage interiors, boats and displays on whaling. From the village you can also embark for the nature reserve on the **Isle of May**, which teems with seabirds and a colony of grey seals. The statue of Alexander Selkirk in Lower Largo recalls the local boy whose seafaring adventures inspired Daniel Defoe's novel *Robinson Crusoe* (1719). After disagreeing with his captain, he was put ashore on an uninhabited island where he survived for four years.

⋔ Scottish Fisheries Museum
Harbour Head, St Ayles, Anstruther. ☏ (01333) 310628. ☐ daily. 🌐 📷 🛥

THE PALACE KEEPER

Due to the size of the royal household and the necessity for the king to be itinerant, the office of Keeper was created by the medieval kings who required custodians to maintain and replenish the resources of their many palaces while they were away. Now redundant, it was a hereditary title and gave the custodian permanent and often luxurious lodgings.

James VI's bed in the Keeper's Bedroom at Falkland Palace

Falkland Palace ⑬

(NTS) Falkland, Fife. 🅿 (01337) 857397. 🚆 🚌 Ladybank, Kirkcaldy, then bus. ☐ Apr–Oct: daily (Sun: pm). 🌐

T HIS STUNNING Renaissance palace was designed as a hunting lodge for the Stuart kings. Although its construction was begun by James IV in 1500, most of the work was carried out by his son, James V, in the 1530s. Under the influence of his two French wives, he employed French workmen to redecorate the façade of the East Range with dormers, buttresses and medallions, and to build the beautifully proportioned South Range. The palace fell into ruin during the years of the Commonwealth and was occupied briefly by Rob Roy (*see p117*) in 1715.

After buying the estates in 1887, the third Marquess of Bute became the Palace Keeper and subsequently restored the building. The richly panelled interiors are filled with superb furniture and contemporary portraits of the Stuart monarchs. The royal tennis court, built in 1539 for King James V, is the oldest in Britain.

Dunfermline ⑭

Fife. 🚶 45,000. 🚆 🅿 🛈 13–15 Maygate (01383) 720999. ☐ Apr–Oct.

S COTLAND'S CAPITAL until 1603, Dunfermline is dominated by the ruins of the 12th-century abbey and palace, which recall its royal past. The town first came to prominence in the 11th century as the seat of King Malcolm III, who founded a priory on the present site of the **Abbey Church**. With its Norman nave and 19th-century choir, the abbey church contains the tombs of 22 Scottish kings and queens, including that of the renowned Robert the Bruce.

The ruins of the **palace**, where Malcolm married his queen, Margaret, soar over the beautiful gardens of Pittencrieff Park. Dunfermline's most famous son, the philanthropist Andrew Carnegie (1835–1919),

The 12th-century Norman nave of Dunfermline Abbey Church

had been forbidden entrance to the park as a boy. After making his fortune, however, he bought the entire Pittencrieff estate and gave it to the people of Dunfermline. He was born in the town, but moved with his family to Pennsylvania in his teens. There, he made a vast fortune in the iron and steel industry, becoming one of the wealthiest men in the world, and donating some $350 million for the benefit of mankind. The **Carnegie Birthplace Museum** is still furnished as it was when he lived there, and tells the story of his meteoric career and many charitable donations.

🏛 Carnegie Birthplace Museum
Moodie St. **🚗** (01383) 724302.
🕐 daily. **🅿 ♿**

Culross ⑮

Fife. **🚶** 450. **🚆** Dunfermline. **🚌** Dunfermline. **ℹ** National Trust, The Palace (01383) 880359. **🕐** Apr–Sep: daily. **🅿 ♿** limited.

A**N IMPORTANT** religious centre in the 6th century, the town of Culross is reputed to have been the birthplace of St Mungo in 514. Now a beautifully preserved 17th- and 18th-century village, Culross prospered in the 16th century due to the growth of its coal and salt industries, most notably under the genius of Sir George Bruce. Descended from the family of Robert the Bruce, Sir George took charge of the Culross colliery in 1575 and created a drainage system called the "Egyptian Wheel" which cleared a mine 1.5 km (1 mile) long, running underneath the River Forth.

Throughout its subsequent decline of more than 150 years, Culross stood unchanged. The National Trust for Scotland began restoring the town in 1932 and now provides a guided tour. This starts at the **Visitors' Centre**, housed in the one-time village prison.

Built in 1577, Bruce's **palace** has the crow-stepped gables, decorated windows and red pantiles typical of the period. The interior retains its original early 17th-century painted ceilings, which are among the finest in Scotland. Crossing the square past the **Oldest**

House, dating from 1577, head for the **Town House** to the west. Behind it, a cobbled street known as the Back Causeway (with its raised section for nobility) leads to the turretted **Study**, built in 1610 as a house for the Bishop of Dunblane. The main room is open to visitors and should be seen for its original Norwegian ceiling. Continuing northwards to the ruined abbey, fine church and Abbey House, don't miss the Dutch-gabled **House with the Evil Eyes**.

The 17th-century study, with its decorated ceiling, at Culross

Antonine Wall ⑯

Falkirk. **ℹ** 2–4 Glebe St (01324) 620244. **🚆** Falkirk. **🕐** Mon–Sat.

T**HE ROMANS** were in Scotland from around AD 80; they withdrew south and built Hadrian's Wall between the Solway and the Tyne some 40 years later. They moved north once again around AD 140, in the reign of Emperor Antonius. His governor, Lollius Urbicus, supervised the building of a forward defence that ran from Old Kilpatrick on the Firth of Clyde through Central Scotland to east of Bo'ness on the Forth. The Antonine Wall is an earth rampart measuring 60 km (37 miles) with a ditch and forts at strategic points. There are a number of sites that give a good impression of its original condition, the best being Rough Castle, west of Falkirk, which not only has a very well-preserved section of wall and ditch but was also the location of a major Roman fortification.

The 16th-century palace of industrialist George Bruce, at Culross

The Highlands and Islands

OST OF THE *stock images of Scottishness – clans and tartans, whisky and porridge, bagpipes and heather – originate in the Highlands, and enrich the popular picture of Scotland as a whole. But for many centuries the Gaelic-speaking, cattle-raising Highlanders had little in common with their southern neighbours.*

Clues to the non-Celtic ancestors of the Highlanders lie scattered across the Highlands and islands in the form of stone circles, brochs and cairns spanning over 5,000 years. By the end of the 6th century, the Gaelic-speaking Celts had arrived from Ireland, as had St Columba who introduced Christianity by establishing Scotland's first church on the island of Iona. It was the fusion of Christianity with Viking culture in the 8th and 9th centuries that produced the beautiful St Magnus Cathedral in the Orkney Islands.

For over 1,000 years, Celtic Highland society was founded on a clan system, built on family ties to create loyal groups dependent on a feudal chief. However, the clans were systematically broken up by England after 1746, following the defeat of the Jacobite attempt on the British crown, led by Bonnie Prince Charlie *(see p153)*. A more romantic vision of the Highlands began to emerge in the early 19th century. Its creation was largely due to Sir Walter Scott, whose novels and poetry depicted the majesty and grandeur of a country previously considered merely poverty-stricken and barbaric. Another great popularizer was Queen Victoria, whose passion for Balmoral Castle helped to establish the trend for acquiring Highland sporting estates. But behind the sentimentality lay harsh economic realities that drove generations of Highland farmers to seek a new life overseas.

Today, over half the inhabitants of the Highlands and islands still live in communities of less than 1,000 people. But thriving oil and tourist industries have supplemented fishing and whisky, and population figures are rising.

A group of puffins congregating on the rocks, a common sight on Scottish islands

◁ **The castle of Eilean Donan, Loch Duich in Glen Shiel**

Exploring the Highlands and Islands

To the north and west of Stirling, the historic gateway to the Highlands, lie the magnificent mountains and glens, fretted coastlines and lonely isles that are the epitome of Scottish scenery. Inverness, the Highland capital, makes a good starting point for exploring Loch Ness and the Cairngorms, while Fort William holds the key to Ben Nevis. Inland from Aberdeen lie Royal Deeside and the Spey Valley whisky heartland. The romantic Hebridean Islands are a ferry-ride from Oban, Mallaig or Ullapool.

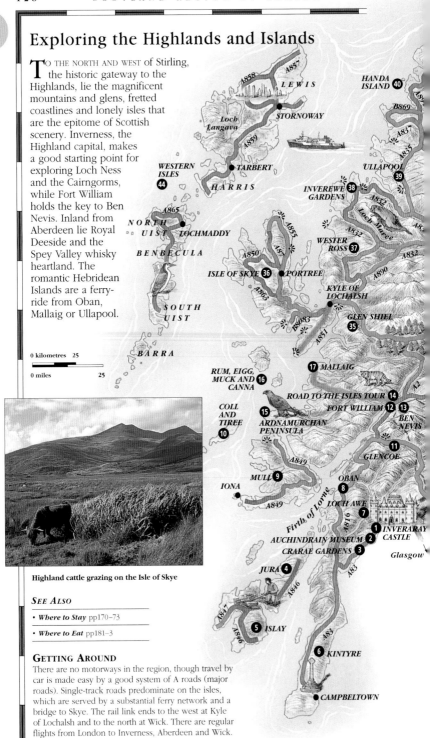

Highland cattle grazing on the Isle of Skye

SEE ALSO

• *Where to Stay* pp170–73

• *Where to Eat* pp181–3

GETTING AROUND

There are no motorways in the region, though travel by car is made easy by a good system of A roads (major roads). Single-track roads predominate on the isles, which are served by a substantial ferry network and a bridge to Skye. The rail link ends to the west at Kyle of Lochalsh and to the north at Wick. There are regular flights from London to Inverness, Aberdeen and Wick.

CAPE WRATH AND THE NORTH COAST ④①

THURSO

JOHN O' GROATS

WICK

DORNOCH ㉞

STRATHPEFFER ㉝

INVERNESS ㉚

BLACK ISLE ㉜

ELGIN ㉖

FORT GEORGE ㉗

CAWDOR CASTLE ㉙

CULLODEN ㉘

THE GREAT GLEN ㉛

SPEYSIDE MALT WHISKY TRAIL ㉕

THE CAIRNGORMS ㉒

BALLATER

ABERDEEN ㉓

ROYAL DEESIDE TOUR ㉔

BLAIR CASTLE ⑲

KILLIECRANKIE WALK ⑱

PITLOCHRY ⑳

DUNKELD ㉑

Dundee

Perth

Stirling

SHETLAND ISLANDS ㊸

LERWICK

ORKNEY ISLANDS ㊷

KIRKWALL

JOHN O'GROATS

0 kilometres 50

0 miles 25

KEY

▦	Major road
▦	Scenic route
– –	Scenic path
▱	River
☀	Viewpoint

Inveraray Castle ❶

Inveraray, Argyll & Bute. *Arrochar, then bus.* *(01499) 302203.* *Apr–Jun, Sep–Oct: Sat–Thu; Jul–Aug: daily.* *limited.*

THIS MULTI-TURRETED mock Gothic palace is the family home of the powerful Clan Campbell, who have been the Dukes of Argyll since 1701. It was built in 1745 by architects Roger Morris and William Adam on the site and ruins of a 15th-century castle. The conical towers were added later, after a fire in 1877.

The magnificent interiors, designed by Robert Mylne in the 1770s, form a backdrop to such treasures as Regency furniture, a huge collection of Oriental and European porcelain and portraits by Ramsay, Gainsborough and Raeburn. One of the most impressive displays is the Armoury Hall; the Campbells collected early weaponry to fight the Jacobite rebels. In the stables, the Combined Operations Museum commemorates the 250,000 allied troops who trained at Inveraray during World War II.

The pinnacled Gothic exterior of Inveraray Castle

Auchindrain Museum ❷

Inveraray, Argyll & Bute. *(01499) 500235.* *Inveraray, then bus.* *Apr–Sep: daily.* *limited.*

THE FIRST OPEN-AIR museum in Scotland, Auchindrain illuminates the working lives of the kind of farming community typical of the Highlands until the late 19th century. Constituting a township of some 20 thatched cottages, the site was communally farmed by its tenants until the last one retired in 1962. Visitors can wander through the houses, most of which combine living space, kitchen and a cattle shed all under one roof. They are furnished with box beds and rush lamps, and edged by herb gardens. These homes of Auchindrain are a truly fascinating memorial to a time before the Highland farmers made the transition from subsistence to commercial farming.

A traditional crofter's plough at the Auchindrain Museum

Crarae Gardens ❸

Crarae, Argyll & Bute. *Easter–Oct: (01546) 886614; Nov–Mar: (01546) 886388.* *Inveraray, then bus.* *daily.* *by appointment.* *limited.* www.crarae-gardens.ork

WIDELY CONSIDERED the most beguiling of the many gardens of the West Highlands, the Crarae Gardens *(see also pp20–21)* were created in the 1920s by Lady Grace Campbell. She was the aunt of explorer Reginald Farrer, whose specimens from Tibet were the beginnings of a collection of exotic plants. The gardens now resemble a Himalayan ravine, nourished by the warmth of the Gulf Stream and the high rainfall of the region. Although many unusual Himalayan rhododendrons flourish here, the gardens are also home to exotic plants from Tasmania, New Zealand and the United States. Great plant collectors still contribute to the gardens, which are at their best in late spring.

Jura ❹

Argyll & Bute. *250.* *from Kennacraig to Islay, Islay to Jura.* *Bowmore (01496) 810254.*

BARREN, MOUNTAINOUS and overrun by red deer, the Isle of Jura has only one road, which connects the single village of Craighouse to the Islay ferry. Though walking is restricted from August to October during the stalking (deer-hunting) season, Jura offers superb hill-walking, especially on the slopes of the three main peaks known as the Paps of Jura. The tallest of these is Beinn An Oir at 784 m (2,572 ft). Beyond the northern tip of the isle are the notorious whirlpools of Corryvreckan, virtually impossible to see. The author George Orwell, who came to the island to write his final novel, *1984*, nearly lost his life here in 1946 when he fell into the water. A legend tells of Prince

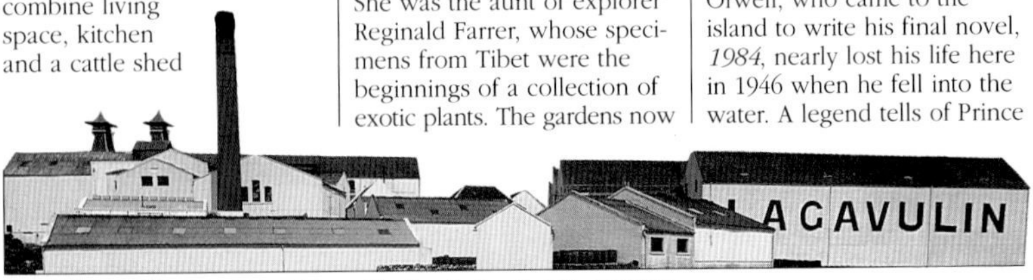

Lagavulin distillery, producer of one of Scotland's finest malts, on Islay

Mist crowning the Paps of Jura, seen at sunset across the Sound of Islay

Breackan who was drowned in his attempt to win the hand of a princess. He tried to keep his boat anchored in the whirlpool for three days, held by ropes made of hemp, wool and maidens' hair, until one rope, containing the hair of an unfaithful girl, finally broke.

Islay ❺

Argyll & Bute. 🚶 *3,500.* 🚢 *from Kennacraig.* 🛈 *Bowmore (01496) 810254.*

THE MOST SOUTHERLY of the Western Isles, Islay (pronounced 'Eyeluh') is the home of such respected Highland single malt whiskies *(see p30)* as Lagavulin and Laphroaig. Most of the island's distilleries produce heavily-peated malts with a distinctive tang of the sea. The Georgian village of Bowmore has the island's oldest distillery and a circular church designed to minimize the Devil's possible lurking-places. The **Museum of Islay Life** in Port Charlotte contains a wealth of fascinating information concerning the island's social and natural history. Eleven kilometres (7 miles) east of Port Ellen stands the Kildalton Cross. A block of local green stone adorned with Old Testament scenes, it is one of the most impressive 8th-century

Celtic crosses in Britain. Worth a visit for its archaeological and historical interest is the medieval stronghold of the Lords of the Isles, **Finlaggan**, which is under excavation. Islay's superb beaches support a variety of bird life, some of which can be seen at the Royal Society for the Protection of Birds (RSPB) reserve at Gruinart.

🏛 Museum of Islay Life
Port Charlotte. 📞 *(01496) 850358.* 🕐 *Easter– Oct: daily.* 📷 ♿

Kintyre ❻

Argyll & Bute. 🚶 *8,000.* 🚆 *Oban.* 🚌 *Campbeltown.* 🛈 *Campbeltown (01586) 552056.*

A LONG, NARROW PENINSULA stretching far south of Glasgow, Kintyre has superb views across to the islands of Gigha, Islay and Jura. The 14 km (9 mile) Crinan Canal, which opened in 1801, is a

delightful inland waterway and its 15 locks bustle with pleasure craft in the summer. The town of Tarbert (meaning "isthmus" in Gaelic) takes its name from the neck on which it stands, which is narrow enough to drag a boat across, between the waters of Loch Fyne and West Loch Tarbert. This feat was first achieved by the Viking King Magnus Barfud who, in 1198, was granted by treaty as much land as he could sail around.

Travelling further south past Campbeltown, the B842 road ends at the headland known as the Mull of Kintyre, which was made famous when former Beatle Paul McCartney commercialized a traditional pipe tune of the same name. Westward from Kintyre lies the isle of Rathlin. It is here that Robert the Bruce learned patience in his constant struggles against the English by observing a spider weaving an elaborate web in a cave.

Sailing boats moored at Tarbert harbour, Kintyre

Loch Awe 7

Argyll. 🚆 🏠 *Dalmally.* ℹ️ *Inveraray (01499) 302063.*

O NE OF THE longest freshwater lochs in Scotland, Loch Awe stretches 40 km (25 miles) across a glen in the southwestern Highlands. A short drive east from the town of Lochawe are the remains of **Kilchurn Castle**, abandoned after being struck by lightning in the 18th century. Dwarfing the castle is Ben Cruachan. The huge summit of 1,125 m (3,695 ft) can be reached by the narrow Pass of Brander, where Robert the Bruce fought the Clan MacDougal in 1308. Near the village of Taynuilt, the preserved Lorn Furnace at Bonawe is a reminder of the iron-smelting industry that destroyed much of the area's woodland in the last centuries.

On the A816, to the south of the loch, is **Kilmartin House**. The museum here displays artifacts from local prehistoric sites, as well as reconstructions of boats, utensils and jewellery, providing a vivid glimpse of life in prehistoric Scotland.

🏛 **Kilmartin House**
Kilmartin. 📞 *(01546) 510278.*
🕐 *daily.* 🖼 🚻 www.kht.org.uk

McCaig's Tower looming over the houses and fishing boats of Oban

Oban 8

Argyll. 🏘 *8,500.* 🚆 🏠 ⛴
ℹ️ *Argyll Square (01631) 563122.*

K NOWN AS THE "Gateway to the Isles", this bustling port on the Firth of Lorne commands fine views of the Argyll coast. Shops crowd the seafront around the "little bay" which gives Oban its name, and fresh fish is always for sale on the busy pier. Regular ferries leave for Mull, Coll, Tiree, Barra, South Uist, Islay, Colonsay and Lismore, making Oban one of the most visited places on the west coast.

Built on a steep hill, the town is dominated by the immense **McCaig's Tower**, an eccentric Colosseum-like structure built in the 1800s. Other major landmarks are the pink granite cathedral and the 600-year-old ruined keep, **Dunollie Castle**, once the northern outpost of the Dalriadic Scots. Among Oban's other attractions are working centres for glass and pottery, and Oban Distillery, producers of fine malt whisky.

Early in August yachts converge on the town for West Highland Week, while at the end of the month, Oban's Highland Games take place. Nearby Kilmore, Taynuilt and Tobermory, on Mull, also host summer Highland Games.

ENVIRONS: A few miles north of Oban, off the A85, is the 13th-century **Dunstaffnage Castle** where Flora MacDonald was briefly imprisoned for helping Bonnie Prince Charlie escape in 1746. Further north at Barcaldine is **Oban Sealife Centre**, where panoramic aquariums allow you to view all manner of creatures swimming underwater. The **Rare Breeds Park**, situated 3 km (2 miles) south of Oban, has unusual breeds of farm animals such as Soay and Jacobs sheep, as well as shaggy Highland cattle. At Kilninver, **A World in Miniature** houses a collection of over 50 dolls' houses, some with interiors by Charles Rennie Mackintosh *(see p101)*. Further south is **Arduaine Garden**, noted for its spectacular displays and for the diverse varieties of rhododendrons and azaleas that come into bloom in late spring.

⚓ **Dunstaffnage Castle**
Connel. 📞 *(01631) 562465.*
🕐 *daily.* ● *Oct–Mar: Thu pm & Fri.*
🖼 🚻
🐟 **Oban Sealife Centre**
Barcaldine, near Connel. 📞 *(01631) 720386.* 🕐 *daily.* 🖼 🚻
🐟 **Rare Breeds Park**
New Barren. 📞 *(01631) 770608.*
🕐 *Apr–Oct: daily.* 🖼 🚻
🏛 **A World in Miniature**
Kilninver. 📞 *(01852) 316202.*
🕐 *Easter–Sep: daily.* 🖼 🚻
🌷 **Arduaine Garden**
(NTS) Kilmelford. 📞 *(01852) 200366.*
🕐 *daily.* 🖼 🚻 🅿 *by appointment.*

The ruins of Kilchurn Castle on the shore of Loch Awe

The picturesque kaleidoscope of houses in Tobermory, one of Mull's most favoured tourist stops

Mull ❾

Argyll. ⛴ 2,800. ⛴ from Oban, Lochaline and Kilchoan; from Fionnphort, on Mull, to Iona.
🛈 Tobermory (01688) 302182; Craignure (01680) 812377.

THE LARGEST OF the Inner Hebridean islands, Mull features rough moorlands, the rocky peak of Ben More and a splendid beach at Calgary. Most roads follow the coastline, affording wonderful seaviews. From Craignure, the Mull and West Highland Railway offers a short trip to the baronial **Torosay Castle**. The gardens are lined with statues, and inside is a wealth of 19th-century paintings and furniture.

On a promontory to the east lies the 13th-century **Duart Castle**, home of the chief of Clan Maclean. You can visit the Banqueting Hall, State Rooms and the dungeons that once held prisoners from a Spanish Armada galleon, sunk in 1588 by one Donald Maclean. At the northern end of Mull is the town of **Tobermory**, with its brightly coloured buildings along the seafront. Built as a fishing village in 1788, it is now a popular harbour for yachts.

ENVIRONS: The small and very beautiful island of **Iona** is one of the biggest attractions on Scotland's west coast. A restored abbey stands on the site where Irish missionary St Columba began his crusade in 563 and made Iona "the Cradle of Christianity" in Europe. In the abbey graveyard, 48 Scottish kings are said to be buried. During the summer months the abbey has a large influx of visitors.

If the weather is fine, make a trip to **Fingal's Cave** on the Isle of Staffa (see p15). One of Scotland's natural wonders, the cave is surrounded by "organ pipes" of basalt, the inspiration for Mendelssohn's *Hebrides Overture*. Boat trips run there from Fionnphort and Ulva, and to the seven **Treshnish Isles**. These uninhabited isles are a sanctuary for thousands of seabirds, including puffins, razorbills, kittiwakes and skuas. Dutchman's Cap is the most distinctive in shape, but Lunga is the main stop for tour boats.

🏛 **Torosay Castle**
Near Craignure. 【 (01680) 812421.
Castle ⬜ Easter–mid-Oct: daily. 🎫
Gardens ⬜ daily. 🎫 ♿ gardens.
🏛 **Duart Castle**
Off A849, near Craignure. 【 (01680) 812309. ⬜ May–mid-Oct: daily. 🎫
🐦 **Fingal's Cave and Treshnish Isles**
⛴ Easter–Oct. 【 (01688) 400242.
Timetable varies, call for details. 🎫

Coll and Tiree ❿

Argyll. ⛴ 950. ⛴ from Oban.
✈ from Glasgow to Tiree only.
🛈 Oban (01631) 563122.

THESE LOW, FERTILE islands are the most westerly in the Inner Hebrides and, despite frequent notices of winter gale warnings, record higher hours of sunshine than the rest of Britain. Predominantly crofting communities, they offer beautiful beaches and impressive surf. Tiree's soil is 60 per cent shell sand, so no trees can grow. In spring, both islands are ablaze with wild flowers.

Breacachadh Castle, the restored 15th-century home of Clan Maclean until 1750, overlooks a bay in south Coll but is not open to the public. Tiree has two free museums, the **Sandaig Thatched House Museum**, with items from life in the late 19th and early 20th centuries, and the **Skerryvore Lighthouse Museum** in Hynish – the lighthouse stands 20 km (12 miles) offshore.

A traditional croft building on the island of Coll

The Three Sisters, Glencoe, rising majestically in the late autumn sunshine

Glencoe ⑪

Lochaber. **≷** *Fort William.*
🚌 *Glencoe.* **ℹ** *NTS Visitor Centre,*
Ballachulish (01855) 811296.
◯ *Mar–Oct: daily.* 📷 **♿**

R ENOWNED for its awesome scenery and savage history, Glencoe was compared by Dickens to "a burial ground of a race of giants". The precipitous cliffs of Buachaille Etive Mor and the knife-edged ridge of Aonach Eagach present a formidable challenge even to experienced mountaineers.

Against a backdrop of craggy peaks and the tumbling River Coe, the Glen offers superb hill-walking. Stout footwear, waterproofs and attention to safety warnings are essential. Details of routes, ranging from the easy half-hour between the NTS Visitor Centre and Signal Rock (from which the signal was given to commence the massacre) to a stiff 10-km (6-mile) haul up the Devil's Staircase can be had from the Visitor Centre. Guided walks are offered in summer by the NTS Ranger Service. East of

Glencoe lies Rannoch Moor, one of the emptiest areas in Britain. A dramatic way to view it is from the chairlift at the **Glencoe Ski Centre**.

To the southwest, a road leads through steep-sided Glen Etive to the coast near Oban. Winding round the many sea lochs, this road crosses the Appin Peninsula and gives a grand view of Castle Stalker (private).

At the Ballachulish Bridge a side road branches to Kinloch-leven. This village, at the head of a long attractive loch, combines two contrasting images of dramatic mountains and an austere aluminium works.

☒ Glencoe Ski Centre
Kingshouse, Glencoe. **(** *(01855)*
851226. **◯** *daily.* 📷 **♿** *limited.*

Fort William ⑫

Lochaber. **🏠** *11,000.* **≷** **🚌**
ℹ *Cameron Sq (01397) 703781.*

F ORT WILLIAM, one of the major towns on the west coast, is noted not for its looks but for its location at the foot of Ben Nevis. The **Jacobite Steam Train** runs the magical route from here to Mallaig *(see p137),* as do ordinary trains.

🚂 Jacobite Steam Train
≷ *Fort William.* **(** *(01397) 703791.*
Departs 10:20am late-Jun–Sep: Mon–Fri; also Sun late-Jul–early Sep.

THE MASSACRE OF GLENCOE

In 1692, the chief of the Glencoe MacDonalds was five days late in registering an oath of submission to William III, giving the government an excuse to root out a nest of Jacobite supporters. For ten days 130 soldiers, captained by Robert Campbell, were hospitably entertained by the unsuspecting MacDonalds. At dawn on 13 February, in a terrible breach of trust, the soldiers fell on their hosts, killing some 38 MacDonalds. Many more died in their wintry mountain hideouts. The massacre, unsurprisingly, became a political scandal, though there were to be no official reprimands for three years.

Detail of *The* **Massacre of Glencoe by James Hamilton**

Ben Nevis ⓭

Lochaber. 🚊 *Fort William.* 🚌 *Glen Nevis.* 🛈 *Ionad Nibheis Visitor Centre, Glen Nevis (01397) 705922.* ◯ *Easter–Oct: daily.* ♿

WITH ITS SUMMIT in cloud for about nine days out of ten, and capable of developing blizzard conditions at any time of the year, Britain's highest mountain is a mishmash of metamorphic and volcanic rocks. The sheer northeastern face poses a technical challenge to experienced rock climbers. By contrast, thousands of visitors each year make their way to the peak via a relatively gentle, but long and stony, western path. Motorbikes, even cars, have ascended via this path, and runners pound up and down it during the annual Ben Nevis

Ben Nevis as seen from the northwest

Race. On one of the rare fine days, visitors who make their way to the summit will be rewarded with breathtaking views. On a cloudy day, a walk through the lush landscape of

Glen Nevis may be more rewarding than making an ascent, which will reveal little more at the summit than a ruined observatory and memorials testifying to the tragic deaths of walkers and climbers, either from exposure or from falls.

To the north of Ben Nevis, the **Nevis Range Gondola** provides access to a ski centre, restaurant and other tourist facilities, all situated at 650 m (2,130 ft).

🚠 **Nevis Range Gondola**
Off A82, Torlundy. 📞 *(01397) 705825.* ◯ *mid-Dec–mid-Oct: daily.*

CLIMBING BEN NEVIS

The main path up Ben Nevis, called the Old Bridle Path, starts in Glen Nevis. Numerous visitors each year are lulled into a false sense of security by mild weather conditions in the Glen, occasionally with fatal results. You must wear stout footwear (not trainers) and take hat and gloves and enough layers of clothing to allow for sub-zero temperatures at the top, even on a summer day. Also take plenty of food and drink, and an Ordnance Survey map and compass even if you think you won't need them. It is amazingly easy to lose the path in cloudy or snowy conditions, especially when starting the descent.

TIPS FOR WALKERS

Starting Point ①: *Visitor Centre.*
Starting Point ②: *Achintee.*
Starting Point ③: *400 m (440 yds) beyond campsite (very limited parking).*
Length: *16 km (10 miles); 6–8 hours average for round trip.*
Weather Information: *Metcall (0891) 500441.*
Level: *moderate difficulty on a dry day with broken cloud, but prone to rapid weather change; extremely difficult in snow.*

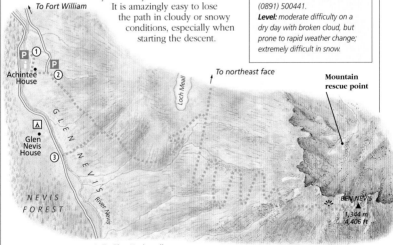

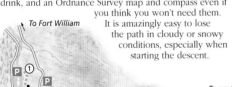

KEY

▪ ▪ Old Bridle Path	☀ Viewpoint
— Minor road	🅿 Parking
△ Camping	🛈 Visitor centre

0 metres   1,000
0 yards   1,000

Road to the Isles Tour ⑭

THIS SCENIC ROUTE goes past vast mountain corridors, breathtaking beaches of white sand and tiny villages to the town of Mallaig, one of the ferry ports for the isles of Skye, Rum, Eigg, Muck and Canna. In addition to stunning scenery, the area is steeped in Jacobite history *(see p147)*.

(see p147)

TIPS FOR DRIVERS

Tour length: 72 km (45 miles).
Stopping-off points: Glenfinnan NTS Visitors' Centre (01397 722-250) explains the Jacobite risings and serves refreshments; the Arisaig House Hotel in Beasdale serves excellent Scottish food.

Mallaig ⑦
The Road to the Isles ends at Mallaig, an active little fishing port with a very good harbour and one of the ferry links to the Isle of Skye *(see pp152–3)*.

Morar ⑥
The road continues through Morar, renowned for its white sands, and Loch Morar, rumoured to be the home of a 12-m (40-ft) monster known as Morag.

Prince's Cairn ⑤
The road crosses the Ardnish Peninsula to Loch Nan Uamh, where a cairn marks the spot from which Bonnie Prince Charlie left for France in 1746.

Ardnamurchan Peninsula ⑮

Argyll. 🚢 *from Fishnish, Tobermory (Mull) to Kilchoan.* 🛈 *Kilchoan (01972) 510222; Fort William (01397) 703781.*

THIS PENINSULA and the adjacent areas of Moidart and Morvern are some of the west coast's best-kept secrets. They are characterized by a sinuous coastline, rocky mountains and beaches. Some of the best beaches are found at the tip of the peninsula, the most westerly point of mainland Britain.

The **Ardnamurchan Point Visitor Centre** at Kilchoan explores the history of lighthouses and light-keeping, and at Glenmore you can visit the award-winning **Ardnamurchan Natural History Centre**. The centre has encouraged wildlife to inhabit its "living building", and wild red deer can even graze on its turf roof. An enchanting wooded road runs from Salen to Strontian, or you can go north to Acharacle.

A view from Roshven, near Arisaig, across to the islands of Eigg and Rum

The **Mingarry Museum** is dedicated to poaching and illicit whisky distilling.

🛈 **Ardnamurchan Point Visitor Centre**
Kilchoan. 📞 *(01972) 510210.* 🅿 *Apr–Oct: daily.* 🆔 ♿
🏛 **Ardnamurchan Natural History Centre**
Glenmore. 📞 *(01972) 500254.* 🅿 *Apr–Oct: daily.* 🆔 *exhibition only.* ♿
🏛 **Mingarry Museum**
Mingarry. 📞 *(01967) 431662.* 🅿 *Easter–Sep: Mon–Sat.* 🆔 ♿ *limited.*

Rum, Eigg, Muck and Canna ⑯

Small Isles. 👥 *150.* 🚢 *from Mallaig or Arisaig.* ♿ *Canna only.* 🛈 *Mallaig (01687) 462170.*

EACH OF THE four "small isles" has an individual character and atmosphere, but shares a sense of tranquillity. Canna is a narrow island surrounded by cliffs and has a scattering of unworked archaeological sites.

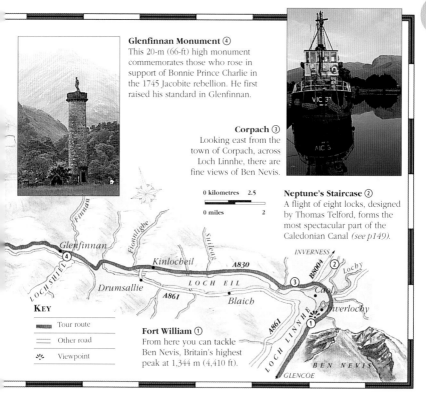

Glenfinnan Monument ④
This 20-m (66-ft) high monument commemorates those who rose in support of Bonnie Prince Charlie in the 1745 Jacobite rebellion. He first raised his standard in Glenfinnan.

Corpach ③
Looking east from the town of Corpach, across Loch Linnhe, there are fine views of Ben Nevis.

Neptune's Staircase ②
A flight of eight locks, designed by Thomas Telford, forms the most spectacular part of the Caledonian Canal *(see p149).*

0 kilometres 2.5
0 miles 2

Fort William ①
From here you can tackle Ben Nevis, Britain's highest peak at 1,344 m (4,410 ft).

KEY

▬▬▬ Tour route

═══ Other road

☀ Viewpoint

Once owned by Gaelic scholar John Lorne Campbell, it now belongs to the National Trust for Scotland. It has few inhabitants and little accommodation.

Eigg is the most varied of the four islands. Dominated by the distinctive sugarloaf hill, the Sgurr of Eigg, it has a glorious beach with "singing sands" that make odd noises when moved by feet or by the wind. Here the islanders symbolize the spirit of community land ownership, having successfully led a high-profile campaign to buy their island from an unpopular landlord.

Muck takes its name from the Gaelic for "pig", which it is said to resemble in shape. The smallest of the islands, but no less charming, it is owned by a family who runs a farm and a hotel. Rum

is the largest and most magnificent island, with scabrous peaks that bear Norse names and are home to an unusual colony of Manx shearwater birds. The island's rough tracks make it best suited to the active visitor. Now owned by Scottish Natural Heritage and a centre for red deer research, it previously belonged to the wealthy Bullough family who built

Colourful fishing boats in Mallaig harbour

Kinloch Castle. Its design and furnishings were revolutionary at the time and it remains a fascinating piece of design history.

⛪ **Kinloch Castle**
🎫 *(01687) 462037.* ⏱ *Apr–Oct: daily; Nov–Mar: call for details.* 📷 ♿ 🎟

Mallaig ⑰

Lochaber. 🚶 *980.* 🚂 🚌 ⛴ *from Ardvasar (Skye).* ℹ *(01687) 462170.*

THE HEART OF Mallaig is its harbour, which has an active fishing fleet and ferries that serve the "small isles" and Skye. The atmosphere is rather more commercial than leisurely, but it is set in an area of outstanding beauty. In the village itself is **Mallaig Marine World**, which incorporates aquariums and a permanent fishery exhibition.

🐟 **Mallaig Marine World**
🎫 *(01687) 462292.* ⏱ *Mar–Oct: daily; Nov–Feb: Mon–Sat.* ⚫ *late Jan.* 📷 ♿ 🎟 *by appointment.*

Killiecrankie Walk ⑱

IN AN AREA famous for its scenery and historical connections, this circular walk offers views that are typical to the Highlands. The route is fairly flat, though ringed by mountains, and meanders through a wooded gorge, passing the Soldier's Leap and a Victorian viaduct.

There are ideal picnic spots along the way, and the shores of man-made Loch Faskally are lined with beautiful trees. Returning along the River Tummel, the route crosses one of Queen Victoria's favourite Highland areas before it doubles back to complete the circuit.

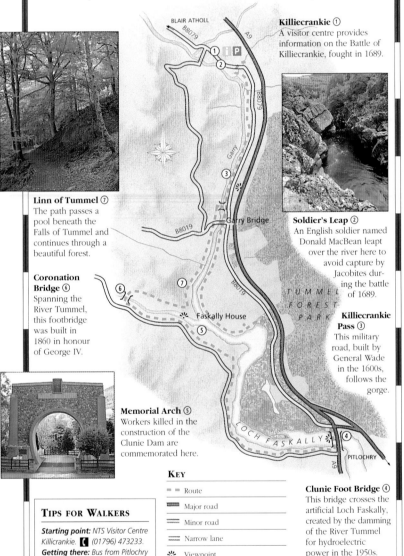

Killiecrankie ①
A visitor centre provides information on the Battle of Killiecrankie, fought in 1689.

Linn of Tummel ⑦
The path passes a pool beneath the Falls of Tummel and continues through a beautiful forest.

Coronation Bridge ⑥
Spanning the River Tummel, this footbridge was built in 1860 in honour of George IV.

Soldier's Leap ②
An English soldier named Donald MacBean leapt over the river here to avoid capture by Jacobites during the battle of 1689.

Killiecrankie Pass ③
This military road, built by General Wade in the 1600s, follows the gorge.

Memorial Arch ⑤
Workers killed in the construction of the Clunie Dam are commemorated here.

Clunie Foot Bridge ④
This bridge crosses the artificial Loch Faskally, created by the damming of the River Tummel for hydroelectric power in the 1950s.

Map labels: BLAIR ATHOLL, B8079, A9, Garry, Garry Bridge, B8019, Faskally House, TUMMEL FOREST PARK, LOCH FASKALLY, PITLOCHRY, A9

KEY

▪ ▪	Route
	Major road
	Minor road
	Narrow lane
⚬	Viewpoint
P	Parking
	Visitor centre

0 kilometres   1
0 miles   0.5

TIPS FOR WALKERS

Starting point: NTS Visitor Centre Killiecrankie. ☎ (01796) 473233.
Getting there: Bus from Pitlochry or Aberfeldy.
Length: 10 km (6 miles).
Level: Very easy.

The distinctive white turrets and façade of the ducal Blair Castle

Blair Castle ⑲

Blair Atholl, Perthshire. 【 *(01796) 481207.* ➡ *Blair Atholl.* ◌ *Apr–Oct: daily.* 🎫 ✓ 👍 *limited.*

Tʜɪs ʀᴀᴍʙʟɪɴɢ, turreted castle has been altered and extended so often in its 700-year history that it now provides a unique insight into the history and changing tastes of aristocratic life in the Highlands.

The elegant 18th-century wing, with its draughty passages hung with antlers, has a display that includes the gloves and pipe of Bonnie Prince Charlie *(see p153),* who spent two days here gathering support for a Jacobite uprising *(see p147).* Family portraits span 300 years, and include paintings by such masters as Johann Zoffany and Sir Peter Lely. Sir Edwin Landseer's *Death of a Hart in Glen Tilt* (1850) was painted nearby and hangs in the ballroom.

Queen Victoria visited the castle in 1844 and conferred on its owners, the Dukes of Atholl, the distinction of being allowed to maintain a private army. The Atholl Highlanders, as the men were christened, are still in existence today.

Pitlochry ⑳

Perthshire. 🚶 *2,500.* ➡ 🚌 ℹ *22 Atholl Rd (01796) 472215.*

Sᴜʀʀᴏᴜɴᴅᴇᴅ ʙʏ the pine-forested hills of the central Highlands, Pitlochry became a famous town after Queen Victoria described it as one of the finest resorts in Europe.

In early summer, wild salmon leap up the ladder built into the Power Station Dam on their way to spawning grounds further up the river. The **Power Station Visitor Centre** outlines the hydro-electric scheme, which harnesses the waters of the River Tummel.

Blair Atholl Distillery is the home of Bell's whisky. Open for guided tours, the distillery gives visitors an insight into whisky making *(see pp30–31).*

One of Scotland's most famous stages, the **Festival Theatre**, is located in Port-na-Craig. It operates a summer season, during which the programme of performances changes daily.

🏭 **Blair Atholl Distillery**
Perth Rd. 【 *(01796) 472234.* ◌ *Easter–Sep: daily (Sun: pm); Oct–Easter: Mon–Fri.* 🎫 ✓ 👍 *limited.*
🎭 **Festival Theatre**
Port-na-Craig. 【 *(01796) 472680.* ◌ *mid-May–Oct: daily.* 🎫 *for plays.* 👍 ✓ www.pitlochry.org.uk
ℹ **Power Station Visitor Centre**
Port-na-Craig. 【 *(01796) 473152.* ◌ *late Mar–Oct: daily.* 🎫 ✓

The ruins of Dunkeld Cathedral

Dunkeld ㉑

Tayside. 🚶 *2,200.* ➡ *Birnam.* 🚌 ℹ *The Cross (01350) 727688.*

Sɪᴛᴜᴀᴛᴇᴅ ʙʏ the River Tay, this ancient and charming village was all but destroyed in the Battle of Dunkeld, a Jacobite defeat, in 1689. The **Little Houses** lining Cathedral Street were the first to be re-built, and remain fine examples of an imaginative restoration.

The sad ruins of the 14th-century **cathedral** enjoy an idyllic setting on shady lawns beside the Tay, against a backdrop of steep and wooded hills. The choir is used as the parish church, and its north wall contains a Leper's Squint (a little hole through which lepers could see the altar during mass). It was while on holiday in the countryside around Dunkeld that the children's author, Beatrix Potter, found the inspiration for her Peter Rabbit stories.

Salmon ladder at the Power Station Dam in Pitlochry

The Cairngorms ❷

Wild goat

Rising to a height of 1,309 m (4,296 ft), the Cairngorm mountains form the highest landmass in Britain. Cairn Gorm itself is the site of one of Britain's first ski centres. A weather station at the mountain's summit provides regular reports, essential in an area known for sudden changes of weather. Walkers should be sure to follow the mountain code without fail. The chairlift that climbs Cairn Gorm affords superb views over the Spey Valley. Many estates in the valley have centres which introduce the visitor to Highland land use.

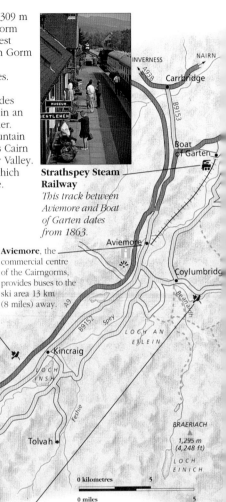

Strathspey Steam Railway
This track between Aviemore and Boat of Garten dates from 1863.

Aviemore, the commercial centre of the Cairngorms, provides buses to the ski area 13 km (8 miles) away.

Kincraig Highland Wildlife Park
Driving through this park, the visitor can see bison alongside bears, wolves and wild boar. All of these animals were once common in the Spey Valley.

INVERNESS   NAIRN
Carrbridge
Boat of Garten
Aviemore
Coylumbridge
LOCH AN EILEIN
Kincraig
LOCH INSH
Kingussie
NEWTONMORE
PERTH
B970
Tolvah
BRAERIACH
1,295 m (4,248 ft)
LOCH EINICH

0 kilometres   5
0 miles   5

The Cairngorms, viewed from Aviemore

Rothiemurchus Estate
Highland cattle can be seen among many other creatures at Rothiemurchus. A visitor centre provides guided walks and illustrates life on a Highland estate.

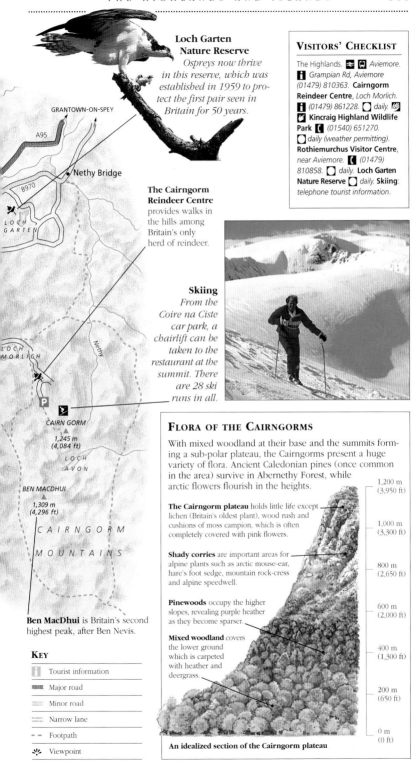

Loch Garten Nature Reserve
Ospreys now thrive in this reserve, which was established in 1959 to protect the first pair seen in Britain for 50 years.

GRANTOWN-ON-SPEY

A95

Nethy Bridge

B970

LOCH GARTEN

Nethy

LOCH MORLICH

P

CAIRN GORM

**1,245 m
(4,084 ft)**

LOCH AVON

BEN MACDHUI

**1,309 m
(4,296 ft)**

C A I R N G O R M

M O U N T A I N S

Ben MacDhui is Britain's second highest peak, after Ben Nevis.

VISITORS' CHECKLIST

The Highlands. 🚂 ✈ *Aviemore.*
ℹ *Grampian Rd, Aviemore
(01479) 810363.* **Cairngorm
Reindeer Centre,** *Loch Morlich.*
ℹ *(01479) 861228.* ⬜ *daily.* 🅿
🚌 **Kincraig Highland Wildlife
Park** 📞 *(01540) 651270.*
⬜ *daily (weather permitting).*
Rothiemurchus Visitor Centre,
near Aviemore. 📞 *(01479)
810858.* ⬜ *daily.* **Loch Garten
Nature Reserve** ⬜ *daily.* **Skiing:**
telephone tourist information.

The Cairngorm Reindeer Centre
provides walks in the hills among Britain's only herd of reindeer.

Skiing
From the Coire na Ciste car park, a chairlift can be taken to the restaurant at the summit. There are 28 ski runs in all.

FLORA OF THE CAIRNGORMS

With mixed woodland at their base and the summits forming a sub-polar plateau, the Cairngorms present a huge variety of flora. Ancient Caledonian pines (once common in the area) survive in Abernethy Forest, while arctic flowers flourish in the heights.

The Cairngorm plateau holds little life except lichen (Britain's oldest plant), wood rush and cushions of moss campion, which is often completely covered with pink flowers.

Shady corries are important areas for alpine plants such as arctic mouse-ear, hare's foot sedge, mountain rock-cress and alpine speedwell.

Pinewoods occupy the higher slopes, revealing purple heather as they become sparser.

Mixed woodland covers the lower ground which is carpeted with heather and deergrass.

1,200 m (3,950 ft)

1,000 m (3,300 ft)

800 m (2,650 ft)

600 m (2,000 ft)

400 m (1,300 ft)

200 m (650 ft)

0 m (0 ft)

An idealized section of the Cairngorm plateau

KEY

ℹ	Tourist information
▰▰	Major road
▱▱	Minor road
═══	Narrow lane
– –	Footpath
☆	Viewpoint

Aberdeen ❷❸

SCOTLAND'S THIRD LARGEST CITY and Europe's offshore oil capital, Aberdeen has prospered since the discovery of oil in the North Sea in the early 1970s. The sea bed has now yielded 50 oilfields. Widely known as the Granite City, its forbidding and rugged outlines are softened by sumptuous year-round floral displays in the public parks and gardens, the Duthie Park Winter Gardens being the largest in Europe. The city harbour, one of Britain's most important fishing ports, is at its best early in the morning during the auctions at Scotland's largest fish market.

The spires of Aberdeen, rising behind the city harbour

Exploring Aberdeen

The city centre flanks the 1.5-km (1-mile) long Union Street, ending to the east at the Mercat Cross. The cross stands by Castlegate, the one-time site of the city castle, and now only a marketplace. From here, the cobbled Shiprow meanders southwest and passes Provost Ross's House on its way to the harbour. A bus can be taken 1.5 km (1 mile) north of the centre to Old Aberdeen, which, with its medieval streets and wynds (narrow, winding lanes), has the peaceful character of a separate village. Driving is restricted in some streets.

🏛 King's College

College Bounds, Old Aberdeen. 🅲 (01224) 273702. ◯ daily. 🅶
Founded in 1495 as the city's first university, the college now has a visitor centre that provides details of its history. The interdenominational chapel, consecutively Catholic and Protestant in the past, has a distinctive lantern tower, rebuilt after a storm in 1633. Douglas Strachan's stained-glass windows add a modern touch to the interior, which contains a 1540 pulpit, later carved with heads of Stuart monarchs.

⛪ St Andrew's Cathedral

King St. 🅲 (01224) 640119. ◯ May–Sep: Mon–Sat. 🅶 🅿 by arrangement.
The Mother Church of the Episcopal Church in the United States, St Andrew's has a memorial to Samuel Seabury, the first Episcopalian bishop in the US, who was consecrated in Aberdeen in 1784. A series of coats of arms adorns the ceiling above the north and south aisles, contrasting colourfully with the white walls and pillars. They represent the American states and the Jacobite families of Aberdeenshire.

The elegant lantern tower of the chapel at King's College

🏛 Art Gallery

Schoolhill. 🅲 (01224) 646333 ◯ daily. 🅶 www.aberdeen.net.uk
Housed in a Neo-Classical building, the Art Gallery has a wide range of exhibitions, with an emphasis on modern works. A collection of Aberdonian silver is included among the decorative arts on the ground floor. A permanent collection of 18th- to 20th-century art features such names as Toulouse-Lautrec, Raeburn and Reynolds. Local granite merchant Alex Macdonald bequeathed a number of the works on display.

⛪ Church of St Nicholas

George St. ◯ May–Sep: daily; Oct–Apr: Mon–Fri (am). 🅶
Founded in the 12th century, St Nicholas is Scotland's largest parish church. Though the present structure dates from 1752, many earlier relics can be seen inside. After damage during the Reformation, the interior was divided into two. A chapel in the East Church holds iron rings used to secure witches in the 17th century, while in the West Church there are embroidered panels attributed to Mary Jameson (1597–1644).

🏛 Maritime Museum

Shiprow. 🅲 (01224) 337700. ◯ daily. 🅶
Overlooking the harbour is the Provost Ross's House, which dates back to 1593 and is one of the oldest residential buildings in town. The Maritime Museum housed here traces the history of Aberdeen's long seafaring tradition. The exhibitions cover numerous topics from shipwrecks, rescues and shipbuilding to models that illustrate the workings of the many oil installations situated off the east coast of Scotland.

⛪ St Machar's Cathedral

The Chanonry. 🅲 (01224) 485988. ◯ daily. 🅶 www.isb.net/stmachar
Dominating Old Aberdeen, the 15th-century St Machar's Cathedral is the oldest granite building in the city. The stonework of one arch dates back to the 14th century. The nave now serves as a parish church and its magnificent oak ceiling is adorned with the coats of arms of 48 popes, emperors and princes of Christendom.

PROVOST SKENE'S HOUSE

Guestrow. 📞 *(01224) 641086.* 🕐 *Mon–Sat.* 📷

Once the home of Sir George Skene, a 17th-century provost (mayor) of Aberdeen, the house was built in 1545 and remains one of the oldest houses in the city. Inside, period rooms span 200 years of design. The Duke of Cumberland stayed here during the weeks preceding the Battle of Culloden *(see p146).*

VISITORS' CHECKLIST

Grampian. 🚶 *220,000.*
✈ *13 km (8 miles) NW Aberdeen.*
🚆 🚌 *Guild St.* ℹ *Broad St*
(01224) 632727. 🗓 *Thu, Fri, Sat.*

The 18th-century Parlour, with its walnut harpsichord and covered fire-side chairs, was the informal room in which the family would have tea.

The Regency Room typifies early 19th-century elegance. A harp dating from 1820 stands by a Grecian-style sofa and a French writing table.

The Painted Gallery has one of Scotland's most important cycles of religious art. The panels are early 17th century, though the artist is unknown.

The 17th-century Great Hall contains heavy oak dining furniture. Provost Skene's wood-carved coat of arms hangs above the fireplace.

The Georgian Dining Room, with its Classical design, was the main formal room in the 16th century and still has its original flagstone floor.

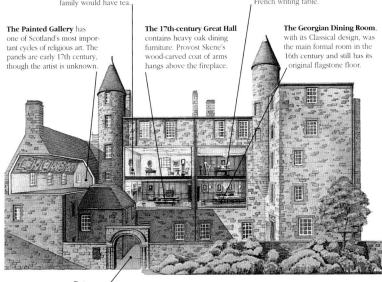

Entrance

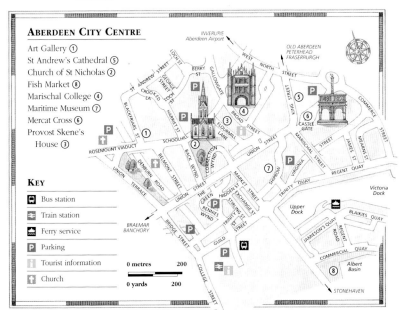

ABERDEEN CITY CENTRE

Art Gallery ①
St Andrew's Cathedral ⑤
Church of St Nicholas ②
Fish Market ⑧
Marischal College ④
Maritime Museum ⑦
Mercat Cross ⑥
Provost Skene's
  House ③

KEY

🚌	Bus station
🚆	Train station
⚓	Ferry service
🅿	Parking
ℹ	Tourist information
✝	Church

0 metres   200
0 yards   200

Royal Deeside Tour ㉔

Since Queen Victoria's purchase of the Balmoral Estate in 1852, Deeside has been best known as the summer home of the British Royal Family, though it has been associated with royalty since the time of Robert the Bruce in the 1300s. This route follows the Dee, one of the world's most prolific salmon rivers, through some magnificent Grampian scenery.

Muir of Dinnet Nature Reserve ④
An information centre on the A97 provides an excellent place from which to explore this beautiful mixed woodland area, formed by the retreating glaciers of the last Ice Age.

Balmoral ⑥
Bought by Queen Victoria for 30,000 guineas in 1852, after its owner choked to death on a fishbone, the castle was rebuilt in the Scottish Baronial style at Prince Albert's request.

Ballater ⑤
The old railway town of Ballater has royal warrants on many of its shop fronts. It grew as a 19th-century spa town, its waters reputedly providing a cure for tuberculosis.

Speyside Malt Whisky Trail ㉕

Grampian. ℹ *Elgin (01343) 542666.*

Such are the climate and geology of the Grampian mountains and glens bordering the River Spey that half of Scotland's whisky distilleries are found on Speyside. They span a large area so a car is required. The signposted "Malt Whisky Trail" takes you to seven distilleries and one cooperage (a place where barrels are made), all with excellent visitor centres and tours of their premises.

There is no secret to whisky distilling *(see pp 30–31):* essentially barley is steeped in water and allowed to grow, a process called "malting"; the grains are then dried with peat smoke, milled, mixed with water and allowed to ferment; the frothy liquid goes through a double process of distillation. The final result is a raw, rough

Oak casks, in which the maturing whisky is stored at the distilleries

whisky that is then stored in old oak sherry casks for 3 to 16 years, during which time it mellows. Worldwide, an average of 30 bottles of Scotch whisky are sold every second.

The visitor centres at each Whisky Trail distillery provide similar, and equally good, guided tours of the workings and audio-visual displays of their individual histories. Their entry charges are usually redeemable against the purchase of a bottle of whisky. One visit to a single distillery can suffice, but a different slant on the process is given at the **Speyside Cooperage**. Here the visitor can learn about the making of the wooden casks that are eventually used to store the whisky.

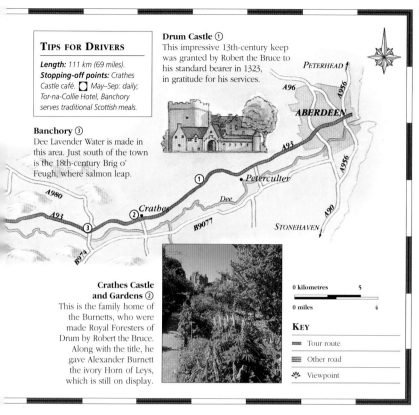

TIPS FOR DRIVERS

Length: 111 km (69 miles).
Stopping-off points: Crathes
Castle café. ◯ May–Sep: daily;
Tor-na-Collie Hotel, Banchory
serves traditional Scottish meals.

Drum Castle ①
This impressive 13th-century keep
was granted by Robert the Bruce to
his standard bearer in 1323,
in gratitude for his services.

Banchory ③
Dee Lavender Water is made in
this area. Just south of the town
is the 18th-century Brig o'
Feugh, where salmon leap.

**Crathes Castle
and Gardens** ②
This is the family home of
the Burnetts, who were
made Royal Foresters of
Drum by Robert the Bruce.
Along with the title, he
gave Alexander Burnett
the ivory Horn of Leys,
which is still on display.

PETERHEAD

ABERDEEN

Peterculter

Dee

STONEHAVEN

0 kilometres   5

0 miles   4

KEY

▬ Tour route

▬ Other road

❋ Viewpoint

⛰ Cardhu Distillery
Knockando. 📞 (01340) 872550.
◯ Jul–Sep: daily; Oct–Jun: Mon–Fri.
📷 ♿

⛰ Dallas Dhu Distillery
Forres. 📞 (01309) 676548.
◯ Apr–Sep: daily; Oct–Mar:
Sat–Thu. 📷 ♿

⛰ Glenfarclas Distillery
Ballindalloch. 📞 (01807) 500245. ◯
Mon–Fri (Jun–Sep: daily). 📷 ♿ ✓

⛰ Glenfiddich Distillery
Dufftown. 📞 (01340) 820373.
◯ Mon–Fri (Easter–mid-Oct: daily).
♿ ✓

⛰ Glen Grant Distillery
Rothes. 📞 (01542) 783303. ◯ mid-
Mar–Oct: daily. 📷 ✓ ♿ limited.

⛰ The Glenlivet Distillery
Glenlivet. 📞 (01542) 783220.
◯ mid-Mar–Oct: daily.
📷 ✓ ♿ limited.

⛰ Speyside Cooperage
Craigellachie. 📞 (01340) 871108.
◯ Mon–Fri (Jun–Sep: Mon–Sat).
📷 ✓ ♿ limited.

⛰ Strathisla Distillery
Keith. 📞 (01542) 783044.
◯ Feb–mid-Mar: Mon–Fri; mid-
Mar–Nov: daily. 📷 ♿ limited.

Elgin ㉖

Grampian. 🏛 25,000. 🚉 🚌 🛈
17 High St (01343) 542666. 🚐 Sat.

WITH ITS COBBLED market-
place and crooked lanes,
the popular town of Elgin still
retains much of its medieval
layout. The 13th-century
cathedral ruins are all that
remain of one of Scotland's
architectural triumphs. Once
known as the Lantern of the
North, the cathedral was
severely damaged in 1390 by
the Wolf of Badenoch (the
son of Robert II) in revenge
for his excommunication by
the Bishop of Moray. Further
damage came in 1576 when
the Regent Moray ordered the
lead roofing to be stripped.
Among the remains is a Pictish
cross-slab in the nave and a
basin where one of the town's
benefactors, Andrew Anderson,
was kept as a baby by his
homeless mother. The **Elgin
Museum** has anthropological

and geological displays, while
the **Moray Motor Museum**
has over 40 cars and motorbikes, dating back to 1904.

🏛 Elgin Museum
1 High St. 📞 (01343) 543675. ◯
Easter–Oct: daily (Sun: pm). 📷 ♿ ✓
🏛 Moray Motor Museum
Bridge St, Bishopmill. 📞 (01343)
544933. ◯ Easter–Oct: daily. 📷 ♿

**Details of the central tower of
the 13th-century Elgin Cathedral**

An aerial picture of Fort George, illustrating its imposing position

Fort George ㉗

Inverness. **[** (01667) 462777. ⚌ 🏛
Inverness, Nairn. ◯ daily. 🖼 📷 ♿

ONE OF THE FINEST examples of European military architecture, Fort George holds a commanding position on a windswept promontory jutting into the Moray Firth, ideally located to suppress the Highlands. Completed in 1769, the fort was built after the Jacobite risings to discourage further rebellion in the Highlands, and has remained a military garrison ever since.

The **Regimental Museum** of the Queen's Own Highlanders is housed in the Fort. Some of the barrack rooms have been reconstructed to show the conditions of the common soldiers stationed here more than 200 years ago. The **Grand Magazine** contains an outstanding collection of arms and military equipment. Fort George's extensive battlements also make an excellent place from which to watch dolphins, which can be seen playing in the waters of the Moray Firth.

Culloden ㉘

(NTS) Inverness. ⚌ 🏛 Inverness.

A DESOLATE STRETCH of moorland, Culloden looks much as it did on 16 April 1746, the date of the last battle to be fought on British soil (see p45). Here the Jacobite cause, with the help of Bonnie Prince

Charlie's leadership (see p153), finally perished under the onslaught of nearly 9,000 Hanoverian troops, led by the Duke of Cumberland. All is explained, with audio-visual displays, in the excellent **NTS Visitor Centre** on the site.

ENVIRONS: Roughly 1.5 km (1 mile) east of Culloden are the outstanding Neolithic burial sites at **Clava Cairns**.

🛈 **NTS Visitor Centre**
On the B9006 east of Inverness.
[(01463) 790607. ◯ daily.
● Jan. 🖼 ♿

Cawdor Castle ㉙

On B9090 (off A96). **[** (01667) 404615. ⚌ Nairn, then bus or taxi. 🚌 from Inverness. ◯ May–mid-Oct: daily. 🖼 ♿ gardens and ground floor only.

WITH ITS TURRETED central tower, moat and drawbridge, Cawdor Castle is one of the most romantic stately homes in the Highlands. Though the castle is famed for being the 11th-century home of Shakespeare's tragic character Macbeth, and the scene of his murder of King Duncan, it is historically unproven that either figure came here.

An ancient holly tree preserved in the vaults is said to be the one under which, in 1372, Thane William's donkey, laden with gold, stopped for a rest during its master's search for a place to build a fortress. According to legend, this was how the site for the castle was chosen. Now, after 600 years of continuous occupation (it is still the home of

the Thanes of Cawdor) the house is a treasury of family history. It contains a number of rare tapestries and portraits by the 18th-century painters Joshua Reynolds (1723–92) and George Romney (1734–1802). Furniture in the Pink Bedroom and Woodcock Room includes work by the 18th-century designers Chippendale and Sheraton. In the Old Kitchen, the huge Victorian cooking range stands as a shrine to below-stairs drudgery. The castle's extensive grounds provide beautiful nature trails, as well as a nine-hole golf course.

The drawbridge on the eastern side of Cawdor Castle

Inverness ㉚

Highland. 🏔 60,000. ⚌ 🏛
🛈 Castle Wynd, (01463) 234353.

IN THE HIGHLANDS, all roads lead to the region's "capital", Inverness, the centre of communication, commerce and administration for six million outlying acres and their scattered populations. Despite being the largest city in the

A contemporary picture, *The Battle of Culloden* (1746), by D Campbell

The red sandstone exterior of Inverness Castle high above the city centre, aglow in the light of the setting sun

north, it is more like a town in its atmosphere, with a compact and easily accessible centre. Although sadly defaced by modern architecture, Inverness earns a worthy reputation for its floral displays in summer, and for the River Ness, which flows through the centre and adds considerable charm. The river is frequented by salmon fishermen during the summer, even where it runs through the city centre. Holding the high ground above the city is **Inverness Castle**, a Victorian building of red sandstone, now used as the court house. Just below the castle, next to the tourist information office, is **Inverness Museum and Art Gallery,** which houses permanent and touring exhibitions and runs workshops for children. The main shopping area fans out in three directions from here and includes a lively pedestrian precinct where pipers and other musicians can be found busking.

Kilt maker with Royal Stuart tartan

Across the river is **Balnain House**, an innovative museum dedicated to Highland music. All aspects of the music are explained using recordings, and live sessions are held. Visitors can even have a shot at playing the bagpipes. Upstream from here, on the banks of the Ness, stands **Eden Court Theatre**, which has a varied programme of local and international performers.

Following the tree-lined banks of the river further upstream leads to the **Island Walks**, accessed by a pedestrian suspension bridge. This is an attractive and peaceful haven with a resident population of ducks. And beyond this, further upstream still, is **Inverness Sports Centre and Aquadome**, which offers swimming pools, spas and a variety of wild, spiralling flumes. Thomas Telford's Caledonian Canal (*see pp148–9*), constructed between 1804 and 1822, is still in constant use and can be viewed at Tomnahurich Bridge. From here, **Jacobite Cruises** runs regular summer cruises along the length of Loch Ness. These cruises are an excellent way to spend a

sunny afternoon. Inverness is an ideal base for touring the rest of the Highlands as it lies within easy reach of most of the region's best-known attractions, including the emotive battlesite of Culloden, 8 km (5 miles) to the east.

🏛 **Inverness Museum and Art Gallery**
Castle Wynd. 🄲 (01463) 237114.
🄾 Mon–Sat. 🗲
🏛 **Balnain House**
40 Huntly St. 🄲 (01463) 715757.
🄾 May–Aug: daily; Sep–Apr: Mon–Sat. 🖾 🗲 limited.
🎭 **Eden Court Theatre**
Bishop's Rd. 🄲 (01463) 234234. 🖾
🄿 🗲 www.edencourt.uk.com.
🏊 **Inverness Sports Centre and Aquadome**
Bught Park. 🄲 (01463) 667500.
🄾 daily. 🖾 🗲
🚢 **Jacobite Cruises**
Tomnahurich Bridge, Glenurquhart.
🄲 (01463) 233999. 🖾 🗲

THE JACOBITE MOVEMENT

The first Jacobites (mainly Catholic Highlanders) were the supporters of James VII of Scotland (James II of England) who was deposed by his Parliament in the "Glorious Revolution" of 1688. With the Protestant William of Orange on the throne, the Jacobites' desire to restore the Stuart monarchy led to the uprisings of 1715 and 1745. The first, in support of James VIII, the "Old Pretender", ended at the Battle of Sherrifmuir (1715). The failure of the second uprising, with the defeat at Culloden, saw the end of Jacobite hopes and led to the demise of the clan system and the suppression of Highland culture for more than a century.

James II, **by Samuel Cooper (1609–72)**

The Great Glen ❸

FOLLOWING THE PATH of a geological fault, the Great Glen forms a scenic route from Inverness on the east coast to Fort William on the west. The glacial rift valley was created when the landmass split and moved 400 million years ago. A series of four lochs includes the famous Loch Ness, home of the elusive monster. The Caledonian Canal, built by Thomas Telford, provides a link between the lochs, and has been a shipping channel as well as a popular tourist route since 1822. Hiring a boat or taking a leisurely drive are ideal ways to view the Glen.

Common redpoll

THE GREAT GLEN

Spean Bridge is home to a Woollen Mill selling traditional knitwear and tweeds. Close to the village is the impressive Commando Memorial, a tribute to the local men who lost their lives in World War II.

Loch Lochy

Lochy is one of the four beautiful lochs of the Great Glen, formed by a fissure in the earth and erosion by glaciers. There are caves nearby where Bonnie Prince Charlie is said to have hidden after the Battle of Culloden.

STAR SIGHTS

★ **Loch Ness**

★ **Caledonian Canal**

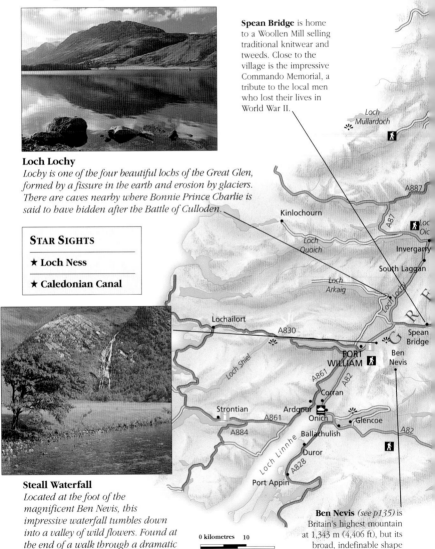

Steall Waterfall

Located at the foot of the magnificent Ben Nevis, this impressive waterfall tumbles down into a valley of wild flowers. Found at the end of a walk through a dramatic gorge, this is the perfect place to picnic.

Loch Mullardoch

Kinlochourn

Loch Quoich

Loch Arkaig

Invergarry

South Laggan

Lochailort

A830

Loch Shiel

FORT WILLIAM

Ben Nevis

Spean Bridge

Corran

Strontian

Ardgour

Onich

Glencoe

A861

A884

Ballachulish

Duror

Port Appin

Loch Linnhe

A828

0 kilometres 10

0 miles 10

Ben Nevis *(see p135)* is Britain's highest mountain at 1,343 m (4,406 ft), but its broad, indefinable shape belies its immense size.

Fort Augustus is a pretty village situated at the southwestern end of Loch Ness. The base for boat cruises around the loch, it is also the site of a Benedictine Abbey.

VISITORS' CHECKLIST

Highland. 🚹 *Castle Wynd, Inverness (01463) 234353; Cameron Sq, Fort William (01397) 703781.* **The Official Loch Ness Exhibition** 📞 *(01456) 450573.* ⬜ *daily.* 🅿 🅱 **Urquhart Castle** 📞 *(01456) 450551.* ⬜ *daily.* 🅿

★ **Loch Ness**
Scotland's most famous loch, the 37 km (23 miles) of Loch Ness provide a beautiful route through the Glen. Urquhart Castle rises imposingly over the water.

Foyers Waterfall
nestles among the trees above Loch Ness; a winding path yields spectacular views.

KEY

▬▬	Main route through the Glen
▬▬	Major road
▭▭	Minor road
🚶	Good walking area
☀	Viewpoint
🚹	Tourist information
⛴	Car ferry
🅱	Boating and watersports centre

THE LOCH NESS MONSTER

First sighted by St Columba in the 6th century, "Nessie" has attracted increasing attention since ambiguous photographs were taken in the 1930s. Though serious investigation is often undermined by hoaxers, sonar techniques continue to yield enigmatic results: plesiosaurs, giant eels and too much whisky are the most popular explanations. The Official Loch Ness Exhibition, at Drumnadrochit, presents the photographic evidence and wide variety of scientific explanations proffered over the years.

★ **Caledonian Canal**
This splendid canal provides a base from which to view the Glen's beautiful surroundings. From Inverness, the canal travels via Fort Augustus to the eight locks at Neptune's Staircase – a feat of engineering.

The shores of the Black Isle in the Moray Firth

Black Isle 🔢

Ross & Cromarty. 🔢 10,600. 🚉
🚌 Inverness. 🛈 North Kessock
(01463) 731505.

THOUGH THE DRILLING plat-
forms in the Cromarty Firth
recall how oil has changed
the local economy, the broad
peninsula of the Black Isle is
still largely composed of farmland and fishing villages.
The town of **Cromarty** was
an important 18th-century port
with thriving rope and lace
industries. Many of its merchant houses still stand. The
award-winning museum in
the **Cromarty Courthouse**
provides heritage tours of
the town. The thatched **Hugh
Miller's Cottage** is a museum
to the theologian and geologist
Hugh Miller (1802–56), who
was born in Cromarty.

Fortrose boasts a ruined
14th-century cathedral, while
a stone on Chanonry Point
commemorates the Brahan
Seer, a 17th-century prophet.
He was burnt alive in a barrel
of tar by the Countess of
Seaforth after he foresaw her
husband's infidelity. For local
archaeology, the **Groam
House Museum** in the town
of Rosemarkie is worth a visit.

🏛 **Cromarty Courthouse**
Church St, Cromarty. 📞 (01381)
600418. 🔲 Apr–Oct: daily; Nov–Mar:
daily (pm). ⬤ 23 Dec–Feb. 🏷
🚻 **Hugh Miller's Cottage**
(NTS) Church St, Cromarty.
📞 (01381) 600245. 🔲 May–Sep:
daily (Sun: pm). 🏷 🔵 limited.
🏛 **Groam House Museum**
High St, Rosemarkie. 📞 (01381)
620961. 🔲 Easter week· pm only;
May–Sep: daily (Sun: pm); Oct–Apr: Sat
& Sun (pm). 🏷 🔵 ground floor only.

THE HIGHLAND CLEARANCES

During the heyday of the clan system *(see pp26–7)*, tenants
paid their land-holding chieftains rent in the form of military
service. However, with the destruction of the clan system
after the Battle of Culloden *(see p146)*, landowners began
to demand a financial rent, which their tenants were unable
to afford, and the land was gradually bought up by Lowland
and English farmers. In what became known as "the year
of the sheep" (1792), thousands of tenants were evicted,
sometimes forcibly,
to make way for live-
stock. Many emigrated
to Australia, America
and Canada. The ruins
of their crofts can still
be seen, especially in
Sutherland and the
Wester Ross.

The Last of the Clan
(1865) by Thomas Faed

Strathpeffer 🔢

Ross & Cromarty. 🔢 1,400.
🚉 Dingwall. 🚌 Inverness. 🛈 North
Kessock (01463) 731505.

STANDING 8 km (5 miles) east
of the Falls of Rogie, the
holiday centre of Strathpeffer
still retains the refined charm
that made it well-known as a
Victorian spa and health resort.
The town's huge hotels and
gracious layout recall the days
when European royalty and
lesser mortals flocked to the
chalybeate- and sulphur-laden
springs, believed to alleviate
tuberculosis. It is still possible
to sample the water at the
unmanned **Water Tasting
Pavilion** in the town centre.

🚻 **Water Tasting Pavilion**
The Square. 🔲 Easter–Oct: daily.

Dornoch 🔢

Sutherland. 🔢 2,200. 🚉 Golspie,
Tain. 🚌 Inverness, Tain. 🛈 The
Square (01862) 810400.

WITH ITS FIRST-CLASS golf
course and extensive
sandy beaches, Dornoch is a
popular holiday resort, but it
has retained a peaceful atmosphere. The medieval cathedral
(now the parish church) was
all but destroyed in a clan
dispute in 1570; it was finally
restored in the 1920s for its
700th anniversary. A stone at
the beach end of River Street
marks the place where Janet
Horne, the last woman to be
tried for witchcraft in Scotland,
was executed in 1722.

ENVIRONS: Nineteen kilometres
(12 miles) northeast of the
resort is the stately, Victorianized pile of **Dunrobin Castle**,
magnificently situated in a
great park with formal gardens
overlooking the sea. Since the
13th century this has been the
seat of the Earls of Sutherland.
Many of its rooms are open to
visitors, and a steam-powered
fire engine is among the mis-
cellany of objects on display.
To the south of Dornoch
stands the peaceful town of
Tain. Though once patronized
by medieval kings as a place
of pilgrimage, it became an

administrative centre for the Highland Clearances, when the tolbooth was used as a jail. All is explained in the heritage centre, **Tain Through Time**.

♠ **Dunrobin Castle**
Near Golspie. 【 *(01408) 633177.*
◯ *Apr–mid-Oct: daily.*
🏛 **Tain Through Time**
Tower St. 【 *(01862) 894089.*
◯ *Apr–Oct: daily; Nov–Mar: by appointment.*

The serene cathedral precinct in the town of Dornoch

Glen Shiel ㉟

Skye & Lochalsh. 🚃 *Kyle of Lochalsh.*
🚌 *Glen Shiel.* 🛈 *Bayfield House, Bayfield Lane (01478) 612137.*

Dominating one of Scotland's most haunting regions, the awesome summits of the Five Sisters of Kintail rear into view at the northern end of Loch Cluanie as the A87 enters Glen Shiel. The **visitor centre**

at Morvich offers ranger-led excursions in the summer. Further west, the road passes the romantic **Eilean Donan Castle**, connected to the land by a causeway. After becoming a Jacobite *(see p147)* stronghold, it was destroyed in 1719 by English warships. In the 19th century it was restored, and it now contains a number of relics of the Jacobite cause.

♠ **Eilean Donan Castle**
Off A87, near Dornie. 【 *(01599) 555202.* ◯ *Apr–Oct: daily.*

Isle of Skye ㊱

See pp152–3.

Wester Ross ㊲

Ross & Cromarty. 🚃 *Achnasheen, Strathcarron.* 🚌 *Gairloch.*
🛈 *Gairloch (01445) 712130.*

Leaving Loch Carron to the south, the A890 suddenly enters the northern Highlands and the great wilderness of Wester Ross. The Torridon Estate, sprawling on either side of Glen Torridon, includes some of the oldest mountains on earth (Torridonian rock is over 600 million years old), and is home to red deer, wild cats and wild goats. Peregrine falcons and golden eagles nest in the towering sandstone mass of Beinn Eighe, above the village of Torridon, with its breathtaking views over Applecross towards Skye. The **Torridon**

Typical Torridonian mountain scenery in the Wester Ross

Countryside Centre offers guided walks in season, and essential information on the natural history of the region.

Further north, the A832 cuts through the **Beinn Eighe National Nature Reserve**, Britain's oldest wildlife sanctuary. Remnants of the ancient Caledonian pine forest still stand on the banks and isles of Loch Maree, providing shelter for pine martens and wildcats. Buzzards and golden eagles nest on the alpine slopes. **Beinn Eighe Visitor Centre** has information on the reserve.

Along the coast, a series of exotic gardens thrive in the warming influence of the Gulf Stream. The most impressive is Inverewe Gardens *(see p156)*.

🏛 **Torridon Countryside Centre**
(NTS) Torridon. 【 *(01445) 791221.*
◯ *May–Sep: daily.*
🌿 **Beinn Eighe Visitor Centre**
Near Kinlochewe, on A832. 【 *(01445) 760258.* ◯ *May–Sep: daily.*

The western side of the Five Sisters of Kintail, seen from a viewpoint above Ratagan

Isle of Skye

Otter in the haven by the coast at Kylerhea

THE LARGEST of the Inner Hebrides, Skye can be reached by the bridge linking Kyle of Lochalsh and Kyleakin. A turbulent geological history has given the island some of Britain's most varied and dramatic scenery. From the rugged volcanic plateau of northern Skye to the ice-sculpted peaks of the Cuillins, the island is divided by numerous sea lochs, leaving the traveller never more than 8 km (5 miles) from the sea. Limestone grasslands predominate in the south, where the hillsides, now the home of sheep and cattle, are scattered with the ruins of crofts abandoned during the Clearances (*see p150*). Historically, Skye is best known for its association with Bonnie Prince Charlie.

Skeabost has the ruins of a chapel which is associated with St Columba. Medieval tombstones can be found in the graveyard.

Grave of Flora MacDonald

Kilmuir

WESTERN ISLES

Uig

L O C H
S N I Z O R T

• Lusta

Milovaig

Dunvegan

Skeabost

0 kilometres   10

0 miles   5

Portnalong

Talisker

The Talisker distillery produces one of the best Highland malts, often described as "the lava of the Cuillins".

C U I L

SGURR
ALASDAIR
993 m
(3,258 ft)

Dunvegan Castle
The seat of the chiefs of the Clan MacLeod since the 11th century, Dunvegan contains the Fairy Flag, a fabled piece of magical silk treasured by the clan for its protection.

Cuillins
Britain's finest mountain range is within three hours' walk from Sligachan, and in summer a boat sails from Elgol to the desolate inner sanctuary of Loch Coruisk. As he fled across the surrounding moorland, Bonnie Prince Charlie is said to have claimed: "even the Devil shall not follow me here!"

KEY

	Tourist information
	Major road
	Minor road
	Narrow lane
☀	Viewpoint

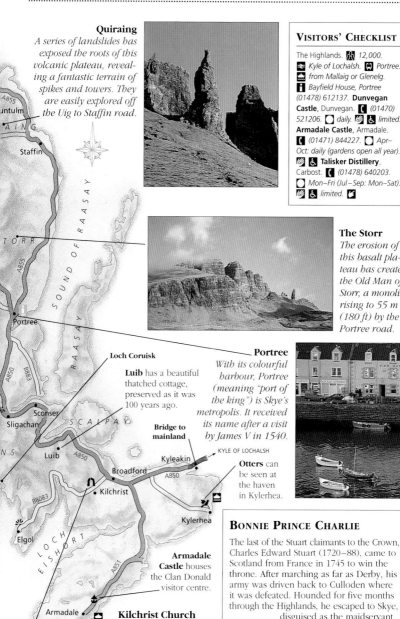

Quiraing

A series of landslides has exposed the roots of this volcanic plateau, revealing a fantastic terrain of spikes and towers. They are easily explored off the Uig to Staffin road.

The Storr

The erosion of this basalt plateau has created the Old Man of Storr, a monolith rising to 55 m (180 ft) by the Portree road.

Loch Coruisk

Luib has a beautiful thatched cottage, preserved as it was 100 years ago.

Portree

With its colourful harbour, Portree (meaning "port of the king") is Skye's metropolis. It received its name after a visit by James V in 1540.

Bridge to mainland

Otters can be seen at the haven in Kylerhea.

Armadale Castle houses the Clan Donald visitor centre.

Kilchrist Church

This ruined pre-Reformation church once served Skye's most populated areas, though the surrounding moors are now deserted. Its last service was held in 1843, after a new church was built in Broadford.

BONNIE PRINCE CHARLIE

The last of the Stuart claimants to the Crown, Charles Edward Stuart (1720–88), came to Scotland from France in 1745 to win the throne. After marching as far as Derby, his army was driven back to Culloden where it was defeated. Hounded for five months through the Highlands, he escaped to Skye, disguised as the maidservant of a woman called Flora MacDonald, from Uist. From the mainland, he sailed to France in September 1746, and died in Rome. Flora was buried in 1790 at Kilmuir, on Skye, wrapped in a sheet taken from the

The prince, disguised as a maidservant bed of the "bonnie" (handsome) prince.

Dawn over the desolate tablelands of northern Skye, viewed from the Quiraing ▷

Inverewe Gardens ❸

On A832, near Poolewe, Highland. 🛈 *(01445) 781200.* ⏱ *mid-Mar–Oct: daily.* ♿ 🅿 ⬇

INVEREWE GARDENS attract over 130,000 visitors a year for the simple reason that they are considered a national treasure. The gardens contain an extra-ordinary variety of trees, shrubs and flowers from around the world, despite being at a latitude of 57.8º north.

Inverewe was started in 1862 by the 20-year-old Osgood Mackenzie after being given an estate of 4,860 ha (12,000 acres) of exposed, barren land next to his family's holding. At that time there was just one dwarf willow growing there. Mackenzie began by planting shelter trees and then went on to create a walled garden using imported soil. He found that the west coast's climate, warmed by the North Atlantic Drift from the Gulf Stream *(see p21),* encouraged the growth of exotic species.

By 1922, the gardens had achieved international recognition as one of the great plant collections. In 1952 they were donated to the National Trust for Scotland. At Inverewe today you can find Blue Nile

Some of the many unusual plants cultivated at Inverewe Gardens

lilies, the tallest Australian gum trees growing in Britain and fragrant rhododendrons from China. Planting is designed to provide colour all year, but the gardens are at their best between spring and autumn.

Ullapool ❹

Highland. 🚶 *1,800.* 🚉 *Inverness.* 🚌 🚢 🛈 *Argyle St (01854) 612135.*

WITH ITS WIDE streets, white-washed houses, palm trees and street signs in Gaelic, Ullapool is one of the prettiest villages on the west coast. Planned and built as a fishing station in 1788, it occupies a peninsula jutting into Loch Broom. Fishing is no longer important, except when East European "klondyker" factory ships moor in the loch in the winter. The major activity is now the ferry to Stornoway on Lewis *(see table, p213).* The **Ullapool Museum** offers an insight into local history.

🏛 **Ullapool Museum**
7–8 Argyle St. 🛈 *(01854) 612987.* ⏱ *Mon–Sat.* ♿ ⬇

ENVIRONS: The natural wonders of this area include the rugged Assynt Mountains, a short drive north, and, to the south, the deep and precipitous Corrieshalloch Gorge.

At **Achiltibuie**, it is worth visiting the **Hydroponicum**, a "Garden of the Future", where flowers grow without soil. The town also has a **Smokehouse** where the process of curing salmon can be viewed. Tour boats run from here, and from Ullapool, to the **Summer Isles** – a small, sparsely populated group, once the home of noted environmentalist, Fraser Darling. Achiltibuie is worth a visit for the scenic drive alone.

♣ **Hydroponicum**
Achiltibuie. 🛈 *(01854) 622202.* ⏱ *Easter–end Sep: daily.* ♿ ⬇ *limited.*
🌿 **Smokehouse**
Achiltibuie. 🛈 *(01854) 622353.* ⏱ *Easter–end Sep: Mon–Sat.*

A tranquil, late-evening view of Ullapool and Loch Broom on the northwestern coast of Scotland

Majestic cliffs on Handa Island, a welcome refuge for seabirds

Handa Island 🔟

Highland. 🚢 *from Tarbet, near Scourie, Apr–Aug.* ℹ️ *Scottish Wildlife Trust, Edinburgh (0131) 312 7765.*

LOCATED JUST offshore from Scourie on the west coast, this small island is an important breeding sanctuary for many species of seabirds.

In past centuries it was inhabited by a hardy people, who had their own queen and parliament. The last 60 inhabitants were evacuated in 1847 when their potato crop failed. The island was also used as a burial ground as it was safe from the wolves that inhabited the mainland.

The island is now managed by the Scottish Wildlife Trust. A walk takes visitors to the 100-m (328-ft) high northern cliffs. On the way you are liable to experience the intimidating antics of great and Arctic skuas (large migratory birds) swooping low over your head. Early in the year 11,000 pairs of razorbills can be found on Handa, and 66,000 pairs of guillemots, the largest breeding colony of this species in Britain.

ENVIRONS: The highest waterfall in Britain is **Eas Coul Aulin**, at 180 m (590 ft). It is best seen after rainfall, from a tour boat based at Kylesku, 24 km (15 miles) to the south of Handa.

Cape Wrath and the North Coast 🔢

Highland. 🚗 🚢 *May–Sep (01971) 511376.* ℹ️ *John O'Groats (01955) 611373; Wick (01955) 602596.*

THE NORTHERN edge of mainland Scotland spans the full variety of Highland geography, from mountainous moorlands and dazzlingly white beaches to flat, green farmland.

Cape Wrath is alluring not only for its name but for its cliffs, constantly pounded by the Atlantic. There are many stacks rising out of the sea that swarm with seabirds. The lighthouse was among the last in Scotland to be automated in 1998. In summer, a minibus serves the 13-km (8-mile) road leading to Cape Wrath. In order to reach the bus, you must take the connecting passenger boat from the pier by the Cape Wrath Hotel, as the cape is cut off by the Kyle of Durness. At Durness is **Smoo Cave**, an awesome cavern hollowed out of limestone. **Smoo Innercave Tours** run trips there. Just outside Durness, a community of artists has established the **Balnakeil Craft Village**, displaying pottery, enamelwork, wood carving, printmaking and paintings. Astonishingly white beaches follow one after the other along the coast, and the road then loops round Loch Eriboll – the

A nesting kittiwake

deepest of the sea lochs and a base for Atlantic and Russian convoys during World War II.

The **Strathnaver Museum** in Bettyhill explains the notorious Sutherland "Clearances", the forced evictions of 15,000 people to make way for sheep. At Rossal, 16 km (10 miles) south of Bettyhill, is an archaeological walk around an excavated village, which provides important information on life in pre-Clearance days.

A gigantic white dome at **Dounreay** marks the nuclear reprocessing plant, where you can tour the works and visit the free exhibition centre in summer. The main town on the coast here is Thurso, a village of solid stone buildings. Once famous for its locally quarried stone slabs, Thurso's industry died with the advent of cement. Each September, Thurso hosts "Northlands", the Scottish Nordic Music Festival.

John O'Groats is probably the most famous name on the map here, said to be the very northerly tip of the mainland, although this is in fact nearby **Dunnet Head**. Apart from a quaint harbour where day trips leave for Orkney, John O'Groats is a tourist trap. More rewarding are the cliffs at **Duncansby Head**, where you can enjoy the natural ferocity of the Pentland Firth.

🚢 **Smoo Innercave Tours**
38 Sango Mor, Durness. 📞 *(01971) 511259.* ⭕ *Apr–Sep: daily.* 🅿️
🏛 **Strathnaver Museum**
Clachan, Bettyhill. 📞 *(01641) 521418.* ⭕ *Apr–Oct: Mon–Sat.* 🅿️ ♿ *limited.*

Duncansby Head, Caithness, at the far northeast corner of Scotland

Orkney Islands ❷

I T IS SAID THAT THE DIFFERENCE between Orkney and Shetland is that Shetlanders are fishermen with farms while Orcadians are farmers with boats. Orkney's geology is radically different from its neighbour and so is its character – flat and gently undulating islands with rich soil that makes the grass lush green and nurtures summer crops of grain. The 70 islands contain the densest concentration of archaeological sites in Britain, testifying to their long history of settlement. Orcadians are warm and easy-going, except during the fierce Christmas and New Year football matches, known as the *Ba'*, in Kirkwall.

VISITORS' CHECKLIST

Orkney. 🏠 *19,800.* ✈ ⛴ *from Scrabster (Caithness), Aberdeen and Lerwick on mainland Shetland, and from John O'Groats (May–Sep only).* ℹ *Kirkwall (01856) 872856.* www.orkney.com

The Old Man of Hoy, a majestic stone column off the coast of Hoy

Kirkwall

A charming town with flag-stoned streets and a small, busy harbour, Kirkwall is mainland Orkney's administrative centre. **St Magnus Cathedral** is an 860-year-old architectural masterpiece made of yellow and red stone. Each June it is host to a week-long festival of classical music. Opposite the cathedral is the ruin of **Earl's Palace**, a once splendid example of Renaissance architecture. Boats run to the island of Shapinsay where the stylish **Balfour Castle**, with its original furnishings, has stood since 1840.

🏛 **Earl's Palace**
ℹ *(0131) 668 8800.* ◯ *Apr–Sep.* 💷
♣ **Balfour Castle**
◖ *(01856) 711282.* ◯ *May–Sep: Wed, Sun.* 💷 ✔ ♿ *ground floor only.*

Mainland Orkney

Five miles from the town of Stromness is **Maes Howe**, the finest chambered tomb in Western Europe, built before 2,700 BC to align with the winter solstice. Vikings plundered the tomb around 1150, and their graffiti is itself a treasure of ancient linguistic inscriptions. Nearby are the huge Standing Stones of Stenness and the famous Ring of Brodgar, consisting of 36 standing stones.

Even better known, however, is the astonishing prehistoric village of **Skara Brae**, inhabited from about 3,100 BC for 500 years until buried by shifting sands. A storm uncovered the remains in 1850. On display are Stone Age beds, dressers and kitchens. To the south of Kirkwall, the road runs over the Churchill Barriers, great causeways built by Italian prisoners of war to protect the British fleet stationed in the bay of Scapa Flow. They also built the Italian Chapel, which lies close to the road and is worth visiting.

⋔ **Maes Howe and Skara Brae**
ℹ *(0131) 668 8800.* ◯ *daily.* 💷 ♿

Other Islands

The **Lyness Visitor Centre** on the island of **Hoy** has an exceptional exhibition, graphically reviving the events of Scapa Flow on 16 June 1919, when the surrendered German Fleet was scuttled by its crews, and 74 ships were sunk.

The Old Man of Hoy, a stack at the west end of the island measuring 137 m (450 ft), is well worth the 6 km (4 mile) walk to reach it. **Rousay** has so many archaeological sites it is known as the "Egypt of the North", while **Sanday**, as its name suggests, consists largely of sandy beaches.

ℹ **Lyness Visitor Centre**
◖ *(01856) 791300.* ◯ *May–Sep: daily; Oct–Apr: Mon–Fri.* 💷 ♿

The colourful stone exterior of St Magnus Cathedral

SEABIRDS OF THE ORKNEY AND SHETLAND ISLANDS

As seabirds spend most of their time away from land, nesting is a vulnerable period in their lives. Inaccessible cliffs such as those at Herma Ness on Unst in the Shetland Islands and St John's Head on the Orkney island of Hoy provide security for thousands of migrant and local birds.

Herring gull

Fulmar

Shetland Islands ⑬

THIS GROUP OF OVER A HUNDRED cliff-edged islands forms the most northerly domain of Scotland. Shetlanders are a friendly people, with a distinctive dialect derived from their long connection with Norway. Nowhere in Shetland is further than 5 km (3 miles) from the sea, and fishing and salmon farming still provide a major contribution to the economy. In recent times, North Sea oil has brought important revenue and employment. In winter Shetland suffers severe storms, but in summer the sun can shine for 19 hours. The islands are famous for their profusion of fiddle music and annual Viking festivals.

VISITORS' CHECKLIST

Shetland. 🏠 23,000. ✈
🚢 from Aberdeen and from
Stromness on mainland Orkney.
🛈 Lerwick (01595) 693434.
www.shetland-tourism.co.uk

The prehistoric settlement of Jarlshof, with its Norse and Viking remains

Lerwick

Mainland Shetland's chief town is attractive, with flag-stoned wynds (narrow lanes), grey stone buildings and old "lodberries" (houses with a private pier). The **Shetland Museum** contains artifacts from shipwrecks and the whaling era, and replicas of the St Ninian's Isle Treasure. The Clickimin *broch* (prehistoric fort) is easy to get to, but the one at Mousa is its superior. Tour boats run from the harbour to the gannet colony at **Noss**. Lerwick's *Up Helly Aa* Viking fire festival takes place in late January, and there are numerous folk music festivals in April and October.

🏛 **Shetland Museum**
☎ (01595) 695057. ◯ Mon–Sat.
● local public hols. ♿

Mainland Shetland

Fine beaches and pretty inlets provide the visitor with lengths of striking coastline. **Jarlshof Prehistoric and Norse Settlement**, in the extreme south, is the archaeological site of a settlement that spanned 3,000 years from Neolithic to Viking times. The nearby cliffs of Sumburgh Head are worth a visit, and on the west coast, the sand isthmus at St Ninian's Isle offers an interesting walk. The ornate **Mousa Broch**, on the island of Mousa, is the best-preserved of its kind in Britain.

🏠 **Jarlshof Prehistoric and Norse Settlement**
☎ (01950) 460112. ◯ Apr–Sep: daily. 🅿 🛈 limited. 🎫 by request.
🏠 **Mousa Broch**
☎ (01950) 431367. ◯ Apr–Sep.

Other Islands

All islands in Shetland have regular ferry connections, though the outlying ones are weather-dependent. It is worth visiting **Hermaness National Nature Reserve** on Unst, not only to see the startling numbers of birds, but also to look out over the most northerly tip of Scotland, to the lighthouse islets of Muckle Flugga. **Unst Heritage Centre and Boat Haven** has a museum.

Fair Isle is famed for its seabirds and brightly patterned sweaters, and **Foula** (where Christmas is celebrated on 6 January) has the most dramatic 365-m (1,200-ft) cliffs. Every island has its own character, and many, such as the islands of Out Skerries, hold community dances where traditional Shetland dances are still performed with enthusiasm.

🦅 **Hermaness National Nature Reserve**
☎ (01957) 711278. ◯ Apr–Sep: daily.
🛈 **Unst Heritage Centre and Boat Haven**
☎ (01957) 711528. ◯ May–Sep: daily (pm only). 🎫 donation. ♿

The dramatic Viking fire festival of *Up Helly Aa*, a major Shetland event

Puffin

Great skua

Razorbills

Black guillemot

Western Isles ⑭

WESTERN SCOTLAND ENDS with this remote chain of islands, made of some of the oldest rock on earth. Almost treeless landscapes are divided by countless waterways, while the western, windward coasts are edged by miles of white sandy beaches. For centuries, the eastern shores, composed largely of peat bogs, have provided islanders with fuel. Man has been here for 6,000 years, living off the sea and the thin turf, though abandoned monuments including a Norwegian whaling station on Harris attest to the difficulties faced in commercializing the islanders' traditional skills. Gaelic, part of an enduring culture, is widely spoken.

The interior of a croft house, on show in the Black House Museum

The monumental Standing Stones of Callanish in nothern Lewis

Lewis and Harris

Forming the largest landmass of the Western Isles, Lewis and Harris are a single island, though Gaelic dialects differ between the two areas. From the administrative centre of **Stornoway**, with its bustling harbour and colourful house fronts, the ancient **Standing Stones of Callanish** are only 26 km (16 miles) to the west. Just off the road on the way to Callanish are the ruins of **Carloway Broch**, a Pictish *(see p41)* tower over 2,000 years old. The more recent past can be explored at Arnol's **Black House Museum** – a showcase of crofting life as it was until 50 years ago.

South of the rolling peat moors of Lewis, a range of mountains marks the border with Harris, which is entered by passing Aline Lodge at the head of Loch Seaforth. Only a little less spectacular than the peaks of the mainland and the Isle of Skye, the mountains of Harris are a paradise for the hillwalker. From their summits on a clear day, the distant isle of St Kilda can be seen 80 km (50 miles) to the west. The ferry port of Tarbert stands on a slim isthmus separating North and South Harris. The tourist office provides addresses for local weavers of the tough Harris Tweed. Some weavers still use indigenous plants to create the various dyes.

From Leverburgh, on Harris' southern tip, a ferry sails to Berneray and North Uist.

🏛 **Black House Museum**
[(01851) 710395. ⏱ Apr–Sep:
Mon–Sat; Oct–Mar: Mon–Thu & Sat.

The Uists and Benbecula

After the dramatic scenery of Harris, the lower-lying, largely waterlogged southern isles may seem an anticlimax, though they nurture secrets well worth discovering. Long, white, sandy beaches fringe the Atlantic coast, edged with one of Scotland's natural treasures: the lime-rich soil known as *machair*. During the summer months, the soil is covered with wild flowers, the unique fragrance of which can be detected far out to sea.

From **Lochmaddy**, North Uist's main village, the A867 crosses 5 km (3 miles) of causeway to **Benbecula**, the isle from which the brave Flora MacDonald smuggled Bonnie Prince Charlie to Skye *(see p153)*. Benbecula is a flat island covered by a mosaic of small lochs. Like its neighbours, it is known for good trout fishing. Here, and to the north, the Protestant religion holds sway, while Catholicism prevails in the southern islands. Benbecula's chief source of employment is the Army Rocket Range, which

The harbour at Stornoway, the principal town on Lewis and Harris

has its headquarters in the main village of Bailivanich. Another causeway leads to South Uist, with its golden beaches, which are renowned as a National Scenic Area.

Eriskay

One of the smallest and most enchanting of the Western Isles, Eriskay epitomizes their peace and beauty. The island is best known for the wrecking of the *SS Politician* in 1941, which inspired the book and film *Whisky Galore*. A bottle from its cargo and other relics can be seen in Eriskay's only bar. It was at the beautiful beach of Coilleag A'Phrionnsa (Prince's beach) that Bonnie Prince Charlie first set foot on Scotland at the start of his 1745 campaign. As a result, a rare convolvulus flower that grows here has become associated with him.

Blue waters off the coast of Barra, looking east to the Isle of Rum

Barra

The dramatic way to arrive on Barra is by plane – the airstrip is a beach and the timetable depends on the tide. Barra is a pretty island, with its central core of hills and circular road. The western side is almost all beaches. Over 1,000 species of flowers have been recorded.

The view over Castlebay from the Madonna and Child statue, on the top of Heaval hill, is particularly fine. The romantic **Kisimul Castle**, set on an island, is the 15th seat of the Clan MacNeil. It is currently being restored. Other attractions are the **Barra Heritage Centre** and also a golf course.

♣ **Kisimul Castle**
🏰 *(01871) 810336.* ◯ *May–Sep: Mon, Wed, Sat.* 🎟

🄸 **Barra Heritage Centre**
🏰 *(01871) 810336.* ◯ *May–Sep: Mon–Sat.* 🅷

A group of St Kildan men with their catch of fulmar seabirds

St Kilda

These "Islands on the Edge of the World" were the most isolated habitation in Scotland until the ageing population requested to be evacuated in 1930. The St Kildans developed a unique lifestyle based on harvesting seabirds. The largest gannetry in the world (40,000 pairs) is now to be found here. There are three islands and three stacks of awesome beauty, each with soaring cliffs

rising sheer to 425 m (1,400 ft) at their highest. Such is their isolation that separate sub-species of mouse and wren have evolved. Tours are run by **Western Edge** and **Murdo Macdonald**. Volunteers can also pay to join summer work parties on the island, run by the **National Trust of Scotland,** which owns St Kilda.

🄸 **Western Edge**
51 York St, Aberdeen. 🄲 *(01224) 210564.*
🄸 **Murdo Macdonald**
1 Erista, Uig, Isle of Lewis.
🄲 *(01851) 672381.*
🄸 **National Trust of Scotland**
Albany Chambers, Albany St, Oban, Argyll. 🄲 *(01631) 570000.*

CROFTING

Crofts are small parcels of agricultural land, worked in conjunction with another source of income as they are generally too small to provide total subsistence. They originated in the early 1800s when landlords made available units of poor land on the coast, clearing the people from the more fertile areas, and making them dependent on wages from either fishing or collecting kelp (seaweed used to make commercial alkali). When these sources of income diminished, crofters endured over 50 years of extreme hardship through famine, high rents, eviction and lack of security. Not until 1886 was an Act passed which gave crofters security and allowed families the right of inheritance (but not ownership). Today there are 17,000 registered crofts, almost all in the Highlands and islands. Governed by special regulations prohibiting the creation of new crofts, the crofters are eligible for special grants. Most crofters raise sheep, but recent trends are tree planting and providing habitats for rare birds. The future of crofting is uncertain, but it remains a vital part of Highland communities.

A traditional, thatched crofter's house on the island of North Uist

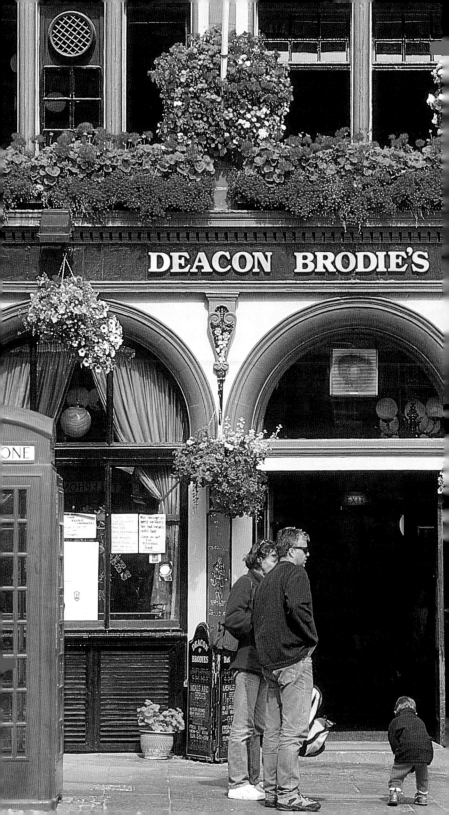

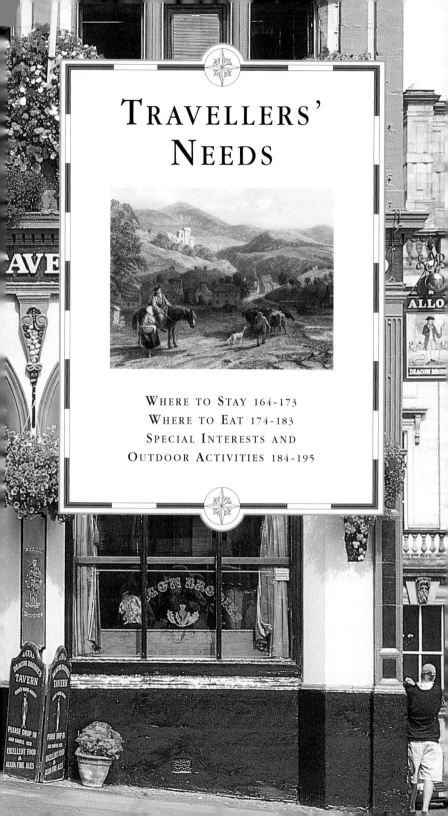

TRAVELLERS' NEEDS

WHERE TO STAY

THE RANGE OF HOTELS and other accommodation available in Scotland is extensive, and whatever your budget, you should be able to find something to suit your needs. Different types of accommodation are described below, and the hotel listings section on pages 166–173 includes over 90 of the best places to stay, from luxurious country-house hotels and castles, to cosy bed-and-breakfasts, to basic campsites. Many offer non-smoking rooms.

Malmaison Hotel's distinctive sign

This selection represents both excellence and good value. Self-catering holidays are also growing in popularity. This type of accommodation is particularly well suited to those on a tight budget or families with young children, who may find hotels to be a little formal and inflexible. We have also added some useful introductory information on the campsites and caravan parks in Scotland, which provide an adventurous, reasonably priced alternative to hotels and guest houses.

Stately interior of Kildrummy Castle Hotel (see p172) in the Grampians

HOTEL CLASSIFICATIONS

THE SCOTTISH TOURIST board's Quality Assurance Scheme is a useful guide when choosing holiday accommodation. Hotels, bed-and-breakfasts and self-catering are all covered in the scheme. A grade from "de luxe" to "approved" is awarded along with a classification of "five crowns" to "listed", indicating the facilities available.

PRICES, HIDDEN EXTRAS AND BOOKING

HOTEL RATES ARE normally quoted per room and include VAT (value-added tax) and service charge. Top-of-the-range hotels can cost over £200 and an average hotel in Edinburgh or Glasgow about £70–£150 for two people, including breakfast. Outside the city, expect to pay £50–£90 for a similar standard, or £12.50–£30 for bed-and-breakfast.

Tipping is not expected other than in very exclusive hotels. High rates are charged for telephone calls made from your room, so it may be worth buying a phonecard and using the lobby telephone instead.

Some hotels require a non-refundable deposit. If you cancel a room early on, you should not have to pay the full price. Tourist Information Centres offer a Book-a-Bed-Ahead scheme and, for a small fee, they will reserve a room.

COUNTRY HOUSE HOTELS AND CASTLES

THE TERM "country house hotel" has been applied liberally by some hoteliers who think gas log-fires and reproduction furniture are sufficient to warrant the name on their brochures. The genuine article is not hard to spot, however, as the buildings are invariably of architectural value, filled with antiques and fine furnishings, and situated in extensive grounds. Converted castles offer visitors the chance to live and dine like a lord. The atmosphere is intimate yet refined, with cordon bleu cooking and a well-stocked wine cellar. Although the room tariffs are high, the height of comfort and luxury is guaranteed.

COACHING INNS AND SHOOTING LODGES

COACHING INNS can be found throughout Scotland. In former times they were staging points for people journeying by horse and carriage, where horses could rest and travellers could find food and lodging.

Generally attractive, historic buildings, inns are often the town's focal point. Some are cottage style with a thatched roof, others are Georgian or Victorian with sash windows and doorways framed with pillars and porticoes. They nearly always have traditional decor, and usually a reliable restaurant serving regional, home-cooked food in a friendly and informal atmosphere.

The authentic dining area at Dalhousie Castle

◁ **A colourful display of flowers outside Deacon Brodie's Tavern on the Royal Mile in Edinburgh**

In the more rural areas of Scotland, there are shooting lodges which also provide accommodation. These are often part of a large estate, and the property of a local landowner. They are comfortably furnished without being overly luxurious, which helps to keep down the price of a room. It is not obligatory to go shooting while staying at these lodges, but that may be a facility on offer, and fresh game will be served in the restaurant.

A traditional croft cottage, one of many self-catering properties in Scotland

The majestic Malmaison Hotel (*see p167*) on the quayside in Leith

BED-AND-BREAKFASTS AND GUESTHOUSES

F OR INEXPENSIVE accommodation and a chance to meet local Scottish people, bed-and-breakfast is the ideal choice. Often family-owned, they are basic, no-frills establishments with a choice of a full, cooked breakfast or cereal and toast included in the price.

B & Bs, as they are commonly known, dominate the lower price range, and in the remote areas of Scotland can be the only form of accommodation available. The buildings are often cosy farmhouses with homely decor, and you are likely to receive a more personal, friendly welcome than at the larger, busier hotels.

Guesthouses also offer reasonably priced, basic accommodation. They usually contain a number of bedrooms, as well as a communal sitting or dining area. The Scottish Tourist Board (STB) publishes the "Scotland: Bed-and-Breakfast" guide, which lists over 1,500 B & Bs and guesthouses.

SELF-CATERING

T HE FREEDOM OF self-catering accommodation (efficiency units) will appeal to those who prefer to stay in one place and be independent, or those with young children and a limited budget. There are many places all over Scotland, ranging from luxury apartments in the cities to converted barns or cottages in the country. Local tourist offices have the most comprehensive and up-to-date lists, and provide a booking service.

CAMPING AND CARAVANNING

A CHOICE OF campsites and caravan (recreational vehicle) parks, normally open from Easter to October, can be found all over Scotland. During the summer months parks fill up quickly, so book ahead. Road signs indicate where to find the campsites and caravan parks off the main roads.

Two clubs, the **Caravan Club** (01342 326944) and the **Camping and Caravanning Club** (01203 694995), publish guides listing their parks, and it may be worthwhile becoming a member. Both clubs operate their own grading system. A typical camping or caravan pitch (site) costs from £6–£10 per night, making it an economical way to see Scotland.

YOUTH HOSTELS

T HERE ARE AROUND 80 youth hostels in Scotland, owned by the **Scottish Youth Hostels Association** or **SYHA** (01786 891400). Most hostels offer central heating, hot showers and cheap evening meals. Accommodation is usually in the form of single-sex dormitories, but occasionally there are separate family rooms. You must be a member of the SYHA in order to stay in one of their youth hostels; anyone over the age of 5 can join upon arrival.

Invercoe campsite in the Highlands – basic facilities but wonderful views

Choosing a Hotel

HOTELS in this guide have been selected across a wide price range for their excellent facilities and locations. Many also have a recommended restaurant. The chart lists hotels by region; colour-coded thumb tabs indicate the regions covered on each page. Map references pertain to the inside back cover. For restaurant listings, see pages 176–83.

	CREDIT CARDS	RESTAURANT	CHILDREN WELCOME	GARDEN/TERRACE	NUMBER OF ROOMS
EDINBURGH					
OLD TOWN: *Ibis Hotel* ££ 6 Hunter Square. ☎ (0131) 240 7000. FAX (0131) 240 7007. An attractive hotel that blends into the fabric of the Old Town, ideally situated close to the Royal Mile and Princes Street. 🖥 TV 📶 ⚡ P ♿	AE DC MC V		●		97
OLD TOWN: *Jury's Edinburgh Inn* ££ 43 Jeffrey Street. ☎ (0131) 200 3300. FAX (0131) 200 0400. With great views to Calton Hill, this hotel is conveniently situated close to the Royal Mile, Princes Street and Waverley Station. 🖥 TV 📶 ⚡ ♿	AE DC MC V	●	●		186
OLD TOWN: *Point Hotel* ££ 34 Bread Street. ☎ (0131) 221 5555. FAX (0131) 221 9929. This striking, stylish conversion, with colour-themed floors, is only a few minutes' walk from Edinburgh Castle and the Grassmarket. 🖥 TV 📶 ⚡ ♿	AE DC MC V	●	●		94
OLD TOWN: *Apex Hotel* £££ 31-35 Grassmarket. ☎ (0131) 300 3456. FAX (0131) 220 5345. A comfortable modern building in the historic Grassmarket, amid shops and eating places. Some bedrooms overlook the castle. 🖥 TV 📶 ⚡ P ♿	AE DC MC V	●	●	●	175
OLD TOWN: *Bank Hotel* £££ 1 South Bridge. ☎ (0131) 556 9043. FAX (0131) 558 1362. An imaginative new conversion of a former bank, situated at the heart of the Old Town, close to the Royal Mile. Each of the bedrooms is individually designed to commemorate a famous Scot. 🖥 TV ⚡ P	AE MC V		●		9
NEW TOWN: *Sibbet House* ££ 26 Northumberland Street. ☎ (0131) 556 1078. FAX (0131) 557 9445. A friendly guesthouse in a tastefully decorated Georgian building, furnished with antiques. The breakfasts are especially noteworthy. 🖥 TV 24 ⚡ P	MC V		●		8
NEW TOWN: *Stuart House* ££ 12 East Claremont Street. ☎ (0131) 557 9030. FAX (0131) 557 0563 This attractive, family-run hotel, in the northeastern part of the New Town, is set in a residential area just 15 minutes' walk from Princes Street. 🖥 TV ⚡	AE DC MC V		●		7
NEW TOWN: *Drummond House* £££ 17 Drummond Place. ☎ (0131) 557 9189. FAX (0131) 557 9189. A charming Georgian house close to the centre of Edinburgh with elegant decor and furnishings. ● Christmas week. 🖥 ⚡ entire establishment.	MC V				4
NEW TOWN: *Parliament House* £££ 15 Calton Hill. ☎ (0131) 478 4000. FAX (0131) 478 4001. An original Georgian town house, with an impressive, convenient location next to Calton Hill. Continental breakfast served in your room. 🖥 TV 📶 ♿	AE DC MC V	●	●		53
NEW TOWN: *Albany* ££££ 39 Albany Street. ☎ (0131) 556 0397. FAX (0131) 557 6633. An elegant and luxurious hotel incorporating three historically listed Georgian terraced houses, situated in the eastern part of the New Town. The Haldanes restaurant in the basement is very good. 🖥 TV	AE MC V	●	●		21
NEW TOWN: *Channings* ££££ South Learmonth Gardens. ☎ (0131) 315 2226. FAX (0131) 332 9631. Close to the city centre, this hotel consists of five converted Edwardian houses. Smart and very well kept, but still homely. 🖥 TV 📶 24	AE MC V	●	●		53
NEW TOWN: *Howard* ££££ 32–36 Great King Street. ☎ (0131) 557 3500. FAX (0131) 557 6515. A stylish and urbane small hotel, converted from three adjoining Georgian houses. Superb facilities and exemplary service. 🖥 TV 📶 24 P ♿	AE DC MC V	●	●	●	15

	Price categories				

Price categories for a standard double room per night, inclusive of breakfast, service charges and any additional taxes such as VAT:
£ under £50
££ £50–£100
£££ £100–£150
££££ £150–£200
£££££ over £200.

RESTAURANT
Hotel restaurant or dining room usually open to non-residents unless otherwise stated.

CHILDREN WELCOME
Child cots and a baby-sitting service available. Some hotel restaurants have children's portions and high chairs.

GARDEN/TERRACE
Hotels with a garden, courtyard or terrace.

CREDIT CARDS
Indicates which credit cards are accepted: *AE* American Express; *DC* Diners Club; *MC* MasterCard/Access; *V* VISA

	CREDIT CARDS	RESTAURANT	CHILDREN WELCOME	GARDEN/TERRACE	NUMBER OF ROOMS
NEW TOWN: *Caledonian* **£££££** Princes Street. **(** *(0131) 459 9988.* **FAX** *(0131) 225 6632.* This hotel is an institution in Edinburgh. Centrally located, it is a popular place to meet. Excellent restaurant – La Pompadour.	AE DC MC V	■	●	■	249
FURTHER AFIELD: *Hawes Inn* **££** Newhalls Road, South Queensferry. **(** *(0131) 331 1990.* **FAX** *(0131) 319 1120.* Located close to the magnificent Forth Railway Bridge, facing the shore, this historic building featured in RL Stevenson's novel, *Kidnapped.*	AE DC MC V	■	●	■	8
FURTHER AFIELD: *Old Aberlady Inn* **££** Main Street, Aberlady, East Lothian. **(** *(01875) 870503.* **FAX** *(01875) 870209.* Situated close to Aberlady Bay nature reserve and beaches, the inn has attractive rooms and a bistro with good traditional cooking.	MC V				6
FURTHER AFIELD: *The Malmaison Hotel* **£££** Tower Place, Leith. **(** *(0131) 555 6868.* **FAX** *(0131) 468 5002.* A converted sailor's home situated on the historic Leith quayside. Individual and stylishly designed rooms overlook the harbour.	AE DC MC V	■	●	■	62
FURTHER AFIELD: *Greywalls Hotel* **£££££** Gullane, East Lothian. **(** *(01620) 842144.* **FAX** *(01620) 842241.* An outstanding Lutyens country house set in walled gardens designed by Gertrude Jekyll. Adjacent to the Muirfield golf course.	AE DC MC V	■	●	■	23

SOUTHERN SCOTLAND

	CREDIT CARDS	RESTAURANT	CHILDREN WELCOME	GARDEN/TERRACE	NUMBER OF ROOMS
AUCHENCAIRN: *Balcary Bay* **£££** Auchencairn, Castle Douglas, D & G. **Map** D5. **(** *(01556) 640217.* **FAX** *(01556) 640272.* A family-run hotel in an excellent position on the shores of Balcary Bay. Quality of service is evident as many visitors return year after year to this friendly, traditional establishment. ● *mid-Nov–Feb.*	AE MC V	■	●	■	17
DRYBURGH: *Dryburgh Abbey Hotel* **££** Dryburgh, Roxburghshire. **Map** E5. **(** *(01835) 822261.* **FAX** *(01835) 823945.* This country house hotel, set in secluded grounds next to the ruins of Dryburgh Abbey and the River Tweed, is ideal for fishing.	AE MC V	■	●	■	38
JEDBURGH: *Hundalee House* **£** Jedburgh, Roxburgh, Borders. **Map** E5. **(** & **FAX** *(01835) 863011.* A well-presented bed-and-breakfast, in an attractive 18th-century house set in large gardens. Guests are assured privacy and seclusion.				■	5
KELSO: *Roxburgh Hotel* **££££** Kelso, Roxburghshire. **Map** E5. **(** *(01573) 450331.* **FAX** *(01573) 450611.* A delightful country house hotel, owned by the Duke of Roxburgh. Elegant and relaxed, it is set in large grounds running down to the River Teviot. Golf, tennis, fishing and shooting are available to residents.	MC V	■	●	■	22
KIRKCUDBRIGHT: *Gladstone House* **££** 48 High Street, Kirkcudbright, D & G. **Map** D6. **(** & **FAX** *(01557) 331734.* Exceptional bed-and-breakfast hotel in this appealing town. Decorated with taste, it is an attractive and civilized place to stay.	MC V			■	3
MOFFAT: *Beechwood Country House Hotel* **££** Harthope Place, Moffat, D & G. **Map** D5. **(** *(01683) 220210.* **FAX** *(01683) 220889.* Friendly and efficient family-run hotel, perched on a hill and surrounded by trees. Simple décor and a carefree atmosphere. ● *Jan–mid-Feb.*	AE MC V	■	●	■	7
PEEBLES: *Cringletie House* **£££** Peebles, Borders. **Map** D5. **(** *(01721) 730233.* **FAX** *(01721) 730244.* Comfortable and peaceful country house hotel set in beautiful grounds. Run by the same family for years, it has a relaxed atmosphere.	AE MC V	■	●	■	13

For key to symbols see back flap

Price categories for a standard double room per night, inclusive of breakfast, service charges and any additional taxes such as VAT:
£ under £50
££ £50–£100
£££ £100–£150
££££ £150–£200
£££££ over £200.

RESTAURANT
Hotel restaurant or dining room usually open to non-residents unless otherwise stated.

CHILDREN WELCOME
Child cots and a baby-sitting service available. Some hotel restaurants have children's portions and high chairs.

GARDEN/TERRACE
Hotels with a garden, courtyard or terrace.

CREDIT CARDS
Indicates which credit cards are accepted: *AE* American Express; *DC* Diners Club; *MC* MasterCard/Access; *V* VISA.

	CREDIT CARDS	RESTAURANT	CHILDREN WELCOME	GARDEN/TERRACE	NUMBER OF ROOMS
PORTPATRICK: *Crown* ££ North Crescent, Portpatrick, Stranraer. **Map** C6. ((01776) 810261. FAX (01776) 810551. A popular pub-hotel overlooking the harbour, with bedrooms that are spotless, bright and neat. Food is served in the traditional-style bar and the smarter conservatory restaurant. ⌂ TV P	AE DC MC V	▓	●	▓	12
WALKERBURN: *Tweed Valley* ££ Walkerburn, nr Peebles, Borders. **Map** D5. ((01896) 870636. FAX (01896) 870639. A family hotel with an emphasis on relaxation and comfort, close to the River Tweed. A lovely location, reflecting the warm service. ⌂ TV 24 P	AE MC V	▓	●	▓	20

GLASGOW

	CREDIT CARDS	RESTAURANT	CHILDREN WELCOME	GARDEN/TERRACE	NUMBER OF ROOMS
CITY CENTRE: *Babbity Bowster* ££ 16–18 Blackfriars Street. ((0141) 552 5055. FAX (0141) 552 7774. An unusual hotel with immense character. Behind the finely restored Adam façade are a few simple, neat bedrooms. ⌂ P	AE DC MC V	▓	●	▓	7
CITY CENTRE: *The Brunswick* ££ 106-108 Brunswick Street. ((0141) 552 0001. FAX (0141) 552 1551. Situated in the restored "Merchant City" area, this hotel has an individual, contemporary style. It is compact but comfortable. ⌂ TV ⟰ 24 ⟷ &	AE DC MC V	▓	●		21
CITY CENTRE: *Cathedral House* ££ 28-32 Cathedral Square. ((0141) 552 3519. FAX (0141) 552 2444. Located within the original historic core, close to the cathedral, the hotel is a refurbished older building, with comfortable bedrooms. ⌂ TV ⟷ P	AE DC MC V	▓	●		8
CITY CENTRE: *Malmaison* ££ 274 West George Street. ((0141) 572 1000. FAX (0141) 572 1002. Beautifully decorated rooms, with satellite TV and CD player, provide a stylish stay. The brasserie serves Mediterranean cuisine. ⌂ TV ⟰ 24 ⟷ &	AE DC MC V	▓	●		72
CITY CENTRE: *The Copthorne* £££ 50 George Square. ((0141) 332 6711. FAX (0141) 332 4264. The Copthorne is a large hotel facing George Square, with traditional comforts and an attractive conservatory for breakfast, drinks or simply to watch the world go by. ⌂ TV ⟰ 24 ⟷	AE DC MC V	▓	●	▓	140
CITY CENTRE: *Hilton* £££ 1 William Street. ((0141) 204 5555. FAX (0141) 204 5004. Large city-centre hotel that is both smart and stylish. Predominantly catering for the business market. ⌂ TV ⟰ 24 P ⌸ &	AE DC MC V	▓	●		319
WEST END: *Hillhead Hotel* ££ 32 Cecil Street. ((0141) 339 7733. FAX (0141) 339 1770. Set in a quiet residential location, this hotel is close to Kelvingrove Gallery, the Botanic Gardens and a number of restaurants and bars. ⌂ TV ⟷ P	AE MC V		●		11
WEST END: *Town House* ££ 4 Hughenden Terrace. ((0141) 357 0862. FAX (0141) 339 9605. An expertly restored Victorian house, where you are assured a friendly welcome. The bedrooms have grand proportions. ⌂ TV 24 ⟷ P	AE MC V		●	▓	10
WEST END: *Wickets Hotel* ££ 52 Fortrose Street. (& FAX (0141) 334 9334. This family-run hotel is close to the Scottish Exhibition Centre and Kelvingrove Art Gallery. ● 24–26 Dec, 31 Dec–2 Jan. ⌂ TV 24 P	AE MC V	▓	●	▓	11
WEST END: *Nairn's* £££ 13 Woodside Crescent. ((0141) 353 0707. FAX (0141) 331 1684. Gracious terraced house converted to a stylish, contemporary design suited to elegant living and dining. Close to Kelvingrove Art Gallery. ⌂ TV P	AE DC MC V	▓	●		4

WEST END: *One Devonshire Gardens* £££££   AE · DC · MC · V · 27
1 Devonshire Gardens. ((0141) 339 2001. FAX (0141) 337 1663.
The ultimate smart town-hotel. Lavish furnishings and stylish decor.
First class service and an excellent restaurant. 🖥 TV 24 🛎 P

CENTRAL SCOTLAND

ARRAN: *Kilmichael House Hotel* £££   MC · V · 9
Glen Cloy, Brodick, Isle of Arran. **Map** C5. ((01770) 302219. FAX (01770) 302068.
This small hotel provides a warm welcome and every comfort in elegant
surroundings. It also affords some of the best food in Arran. 🖥 TV 24 P ₺

AUCHTERARDER: *Auchterarder House* ££££   AE · DC · MC · V · 15
Auchterarder. **Map** D4. ((01764) 663646. FAX (01764) 662939.
A fine Victorian baronial-style house, the rooms have regal proportions but
the ambience is relaxed and cosy, and the food is very good. 🖥 TV 24 P

AUCHTERARDER: *Gleneagles* ££££££   AE · DC · MC · V · 229
Auchterarder. **Map** D4. ((01764) 662231. FAX (01764) 662134.
Originally built by the Caledonian Railway Company in 1924, this
magnificent hotel is internationally renowned. 🖥 TV 🛏 24 🛎 P 🏊 ₺

BALQUHIDDER: *Monachyle Mohr Farmhouse* ££   MC · V · 11
Balquhidder, Perthshire. **Map** C4. ((01877) 384622. FAX (01877) 384305.
Set in extensive grounds overlooking Loch Voil, this hotel combines warmth
with high standards, and has an excellent restaurant and bar. 🖥 🛎 P ₺

BLAIRGOWRIE: *Kinloch House* £££   AE · DC · MC · V · 21
Near Blairgowrie, Perthshire. **Map** D3. ((01250) 884237. FAX (01250) 884333.
A handsome baronial house, this hotel's emphasis is on country pursuits.
Wonderful, relaxed surroundings and a superb restaurant. 🖥 TV 🛎 P ₺

CALLANDER: *Roman Camp Country House* ££   AE · DC · MC · V · 14
Callander. **Map** D4. ((01877) 330003. FAX (01877) 331533.
Set in extensive gardens, this peaceful, charming retreat has a unique atmos-
phere. The excellent menu offers traditional Scottish fare. 🖥 TV 🛎 P ₺

GLAMIS: *Castleton House* £££   MC · V · 6
Eassie, nr Glamis, Forfar. **Map** D3. ((01307) 840340. FAX (01307) 840506.
Reasonably close to Dundee and Glamis Castle, this family-run, country
house hotel is set in peaceful, attractive countryside. Good food. 🖥 TV 🛎 P

HAWKCRAIG POINT: *Hawkcraig House* £   · 2
Hawkcraig Point, Aberdour, Fife. **Map** D4. ((01383) 860335.
Staying in this small, whitewashed, old ferryman's house is a pleasant
experience. Lovely setting and friendly owners. ⬤ Oct–Apr. 🖥 TV P

LARGS: *Brisbane House* £££   AE · DC · MC · V · 23
14 Greenock Rd, Esplanade, Largs. **Map** C4. ((01475) 687200. FAX (01475) 676295.
Attractive 18th-century house which has been modernized to make it smart
and stylish. Some bedrooms overlook the Firth of Clyde. 🖥 TV 24 P

MARKINCH: *Balbirnie House* ££££   AE · DC · MC · V · 30
Balbirnie Park, Markinch, Fife. **Map** D4. ((01592) 610066. FAX (01592) 610529.
Surrounded by extensive parkland, the setting for this Georgian mansion
is outstanding. It is unashamedly luxurious, but the atmosphere remains
informal and unstuffy. 🖥 TV 24 🛎 P ₺

ST ANDREWS: *Old Course Hotel* £££££   AE · DC · MC · V · 125
St Andrews. **Map** E4. ((01334) 474371. FAX (01334) 477668.
Not a very beautiful hotel outside but no expense has been spared
inside – the result is tasteful luxury. 🖥 TV 🛏 24 🛎 P 🏊 ₺

SCONE: *Murrayshall House Country House Hotel* £££   AE · DC · MC · V · 27
Scone, Perthshire. **Map** D4. ((01738) 551171. FAX (01738) 552595.
A turreted, baronial hall with its own golf course. The rooms are rather
formal and starchy, but still luxuriously comfortable. Excellent food is
served in the restaurant. 🖥 TV P ₺

STEWARTON: *Chapeltoun House* £££   MC · V · 8
Irvinge Rd, Stewarton, Kilmarnock & Loudoun, Ayrshire. **Map** C5.
((01560) 482696. FAX (01560) 485100.
A country house hotel in peaceful surroundings, decorated with understated
elegance. The owners are friendly and hospitable. 🖥 TV 🛎 P ₺

For key to symbols see back flap

<table>
<tr><td>

Price categories for a standard double room per night, inclusive of breakfast, service charges and any additional taxes such as VAT:
£ under £50
££ £50–£100
£££ £100–£150
££££ £150–£200
£££££ over £200.

</td><td>

RESTAURANT
Hotel restaurant or dining room usually open to non-residents unless otherwise stated.
CHILDREN WELCOME
Child cots and a baby-sitting service available. Some hotel restaurants have children's portions and high chairs.
GARDEN/TERRACE
Hotels with a garden, courtyard or terrace.
CREDIT CARDS
Indicates which credit cards are accepted: *AE* American Express; *DC* Diners Club; *MC* MasterCard/Access; *V* VISA.

</td></tr>
</table>

	CREDIT CARDS	RESTAURANT	CHILDREN WELCOME	GARDEN/TERRACE	NUMBER OF ROOMS
STRACHUR: *Creggans Inn* **££** Strachur, Argyll, Strathclyde. **Map** C4. ☎ *(01369) 860279.* **FAX** *(01369) 860637.* Convivial inn with pretty bedrooms, in a superb spot overlooking Loch Fyne. The food is excellent, both in the formal restaurant and at the bar, and the service is superb throughout the whole establishment. 🔒 TV P ♿	AE DC MC V	▥	●	▥	17
TROON: *Piersland House* **£££** Craigend Rd, Troon, Ayrshire. **Map** C5. ☎ *(01292) 314747.* **FAX** *(01292) 315613.* An appealing mock-Tudor house close to the championship golf course. A cottage annexe has been added in which each suite has its own sitting room. Good food is available. 🔒 TV 24 P ♿	AE DC MC V	▥	●	▥	28
TURNBERRY: *Turnberry* **£££££** Turnberry, Ayrshire. **Map** C5. ☎ *(01655) 331000.* **FAX** *(01655) 331706.* Huge Edwardian hotel and health spa refurbished to luxurious standards. What the Turnberry perhaps lacks in atmosphere it more than makes up for in comfort. 🔒 TV ⬆ 24 P ≋ ♿	AE DC MC V	▥	●	▥	132

THE HIGHLANDS AND ISLANDS

	CREDIT CARDS	RESTAURANT	CHILDREN WELCOME	GARDEN/TERRACE	NUMBER OF ROOMS
ABERDEEN: *Udny Arms* **££** Main Street, Newburgh, Aberdeen. **Map** E3. ☎ *(01358) 789444.* **FAX** *(01358) 789012.* A village pub with character and comfortable rooms. Close to a golf course and the Ythan estuary nature reserve and known for its good food. ● *24–27 Dec.* 🔒 TV ✂ P ♿ *limited.*	AE DC MC V	▥	●	▥	26
ABERDEEN: *Maryculter House Hotel* **£££** South Deeside Road, Maryculter, Aberdeen. **Map** E3. ☎ *(01224) 732124.* **FAX** *(01224) 733510.* A historic hotel with Templar connections set in quiet, rural surroundings on the banks of the River Dee, with riverside walks close by. 🔒 TV 24 ✂ P ♿	AE DC MC V	▥	●	▥	23
ACHILTIBUIE: *Summer Isles* **££** Achiltibuie, near Ullapool, Ross & Cromarty, Highlands. **Map** C2. ☎ *(01854) 622282.* **FAX** *(01854) 622251.* A special hotel that meets all expectations, with well-appointed rooms and a superb restaurant. There are breathtaking views to the Summer Isles. 🔒 P	MC V	▥	●		13
ARDUAINE: *Loch Melfort Hotel* **££** Arduaine, by Oban, Argyll. **Map** C4. ☎ *(01852) 200233.* **FAX** *(01852) 200214.* Comfortable accommodation here, with the best views on the west coast. The panoramic restaurant, looking to Scarba and Jura, serves local seafood. Arduaine Garden *(see p132)* lies adjacent to the grounds. ● *Jan.* 🔒 TV P ♿	AE MC V	▥	●	▥	26
ARISAIG: *Arisaig House* **£££££** Arisaig, Highlands. **Map** B3. ☎ *(01687) 450622.* **FAX** *(01687) 450626.* A dour exterior gives no indication of the bright, cheerful interior and the charming, courteous staff. Smart, stylish public rooms and pleasant bedrooms; pretty gardens and a wonderful restaurant. 🔒 TV P	MC V	▥		▥	12
BALLATER: *Balgonie Country House* **££** Braemar Place, Ballater, Aberdeenshire. **Map** D3. ☎ & **FAX** *(013397) 55482.* Family-run country house hotel on the outskirts of Ballater. The excellent fare features Scottish cuisine, and the wonderful hospitality favours any guest who likes home-from-home comforts. 🔒 TV P	AE DC MC V	▥		▥	9
BALLINDALLOCH: *Delnashaugh Inn* **££** Ballindalloch, Banffshire, Grampian. **Map** D2. ☎ *(01807) 500255.* **FAX** *(01807) 500389.* Overlooking the River Avon in the Spey Valley, this hotel makes a perfect base for exploring the area, and is lovely to return to after a day's sight-seeing. The food is especially good. ● *Nov–Mar.* 🔒 TV P ♿	AE DC MC V	▥	●		9

BARRA: *Castlebay Hotel* £££
Castlebay, Isle of Barra, Western Isles. **Map** A3.
((01871) 810223. FAX (01871) 810455.
A friendly, family-owned hotel overlooking the bay, where you can take a boat to Mingulay and Eriskay. The food is highly recommended. 🏠 TV P
MC V — 14

COLONSAY: *Isle of Colonsay Hotel* £££
Isle of Colonsay, Argyll. **Map** B4. ((01951) 200316. FAX (01951) 200353.
A friendly, comfortable hotel on this remote and unspoiled island that has superb wildlife and beaches. The chef uses all local produce. 🏠 TV P &
MC V — 11

CRINAN: *Crinan Hotel* £££
Crinan, Lochgilphead, Argyll. **Map** C4. ((01546) 830261. FAX (01546) 830292.
This hotel is in a superb position by the harbour, where the Sound of Jura meets the Atlantic Ocean. The service is excellent, but a visit is worthwhile for the stunning views alone. 🏠 TV 🛁 ✂ P &
AE MC V — 22

CROMARTY: *Royal* ££
Marine Terrace, Cromarty, Highlands. **Map** D2. ((01381) 600217. FAX (01381) 600813.
With beautiful views overlooking the Firth of Cromarty, this friendly, unpretentious hotel has a traditional feel. The well-decorated bedrooms are comfortable and spotless. 🏠 TV P
AE MC V — 10

DORNOCH: *Dornoch Castle Hotel* ££
Castle Street, Dornoch, Sutherland. **Map** D2. ((01862) 810216. FAX (01862) 810981.
An interesting, historic building dating from the late 15th, early 16th centuries, and formerly part of the Bishop's Palace. There is a secluded garden and the food is very good. ● *Nov–Mar.* 🏠 TV 🛁 P
AE MC V — 17

DULNAIN BRIDGE: *Auchendean Lodge* £
Dulnain Bridge, by Grantown on Spey, Inverness-shire. **Map** D2. (& FAX (01479) 851347.
Set in spectacular scenery near Aviemore and Cairngorm, this welcoming hotel is an Edwardian shooting lodge. Conveniently situated for exploring the Speyside distilleries and the alluring countryside. 🏠 TV P
AE DC MC V — 7

DUNKELD: *Kinnaird* £££££
Kinnaird Estate, near Dunkeld, Tayside. **Map** D3. ((01796) 482440. FAX (01796) 482289.
Surrounded by a vast, beautiful country estate, this 18th-century house has been converted into a sumptuous, luxurious hotel where no expense has been spared. 🏠 TV 🛁 P &
AE MC V — 9

HARRIS (WESTERN ISLES): *Ardvourlie Castle* £££
Aird Amhulaidh, Isle of Harris, W Isles. **Map** B2. ((01859) 502307. FAX (01859) 502348.
Victorian shooting lodge on the shores of Loch Seaforth. Original features include working gas and oil lamps. The highly praised restaurant offers local fare; dinner is included in the price of your room. 🏠 P &
— 4

HARRIS (WESTERN ISLES): *Scarista House* £££
Scarista, Isle of Harris, W Isles. **Map** B2. ((01859) 550238. FAX (01859) 550277.
Scarista House, a Georgian manse, provides an extremely agreeable retreat in the Western Isles. Set in a remote spot overlooking a beach, the hotel is famed for its delicious food. 🏠 P ✂
MC V — 5

IONA (NEAR MULL): *Argyll Hotel* ££
Isle of Iona, Argyll. **Map** B4. ((01681) 700334. FAX (01681) 700510.
An unpretentious, friendly hotel on this very special island. The style is simple and unfussy. Ask for a bedroom facing the sea for the most wonderful views. ● *Nov–Mar.* 🏠
MC V — 15

INVERNESS: *Dunain Park* ££££
Inverness, Inverness-shire. **Map** D2. ((01463) 230512. FAX (01463) 224532.
Surrounded by a large garden, and close to Inverness, this hotel provides a convenient and peaceful base for touring the area. The staff are pleasant and the standards comfortably high. 🏠 TV ✂ P 🏊 &
AE MC V — 11

ISLE ORNSAY (SKYE): *Eilean Iarmain* £££
Sleat, Isle of Skye, Highlands. **Map** B3. ((01471) 833332. FAX (01471) 833275.
Traditional 19th-century seaside inn with a Gaelic feel. Wonderful views from the comfy bedrooms and public rooms. 🏠 TV ✂ P
AE DC MC V — 12

KENTALLEN OF APPIN: *Ardsheal House* ££
Kentallen of Appin, Argyll. **Map** C3. ((01631) 740227. FAX (01631) 740342.
Set above the shores of Loch Linnhe, with stunning views, this hotel is very hospitable. The bedrooms and public rooms are well furnished. 🏠 P
AE MC V — 9

Price categories for a standard double room per night, inclusive of breakfast, service charges and any additional taxes such as VAT:
£ under £50
££ £50–£100
£££ £100–£150
££££ £150–£200
£££££ over £200.

RESTAURANT
Hotel restaurant or dining room usually open to non-residents unless otherwise stated.

CHILDREN WELCOME
Child cots and a baby-sitting service available. Some hotel restaurants have children's portions and high chairs.

GARDEN/TERRACE
Hotels with a garden, courtyard or terrace.

CREDIT CARDS
Indicates which credit cards are accepted: *AE* American Express; *DC* Diners Club; *MC* MasterCard/Access; *V* VISA.

	CREDIT CARDS	RESTAURANT	CHILDREN WELCOME	GARDEN/TERRACE	NUMBER OF ROOMS
KILDRUMMY: *Kildrummy Castle* £££ Kildrummy, near Alford, Gordon, Grampian. (*(01975) 571288.* **Map** E3. **FAX** *(01975) 571345.* Large, rather stately, Victorian castellated building, set in lovely gardens overlooking a 13th-century castle ruin. The superb interior decoration is every bit as beautiful as the surroundings. ● *Jan.* ▭ TV P	AE MC V	■	●	■	16
KILLIECRANKIE: *Killiecrankie Hotel* £££ Killiecrankie, by Pitlochry, Perthshire. **Map** D3. (*(01796) 473220.* **FAX** *(01796) 472451.* Smart country house hotel in a scenic setting. The excellent meals, which are chosen from a menu of hearty fare, may be taken in the enjoyable surroundings of the conservatory. ▭ TV ⚡ P ⚹	MC V	■	●	■	10
KYLESKU, BY LAIRG: *Kylesku Hotel* ££ Kylesku, by Lairg, Sutherland. **Map** D2. (*(01971) 502231.* **FAX** *(01971) 502313.* A family-run hotel with a welcoming atmosphere, situated on the shore of Loch Glencoul. The restaurant specializes in local seafood. ● *Nov–Mar.* ▭ TV ⚡ P	MC V	■	●		8
LEDAIG: *Isle of Eriska* £££££ Ledaig, near Oban, Argyll. **Map** C3. (*(01631) 720 371.* **FAX** *(01631) 720 531.* Situated on its very own island, this grand, 19th-century baronial hall has charming rooms. Service in the dining room is formal in the evenings, and guests are expected to change for dinner; an air of comforting tradition pervades. ● *Jan–mid-Feb.* ▭ TV 24 P ⊞ ⚹	AE MC V	■	●	■	17
LEWIS, TIMSGARRY: *Baile Na Cille* £ Timsgarry, Isle of Lewis, Highlands. **Map** B1. (*(01851) 672242.* **FAX** *(01851) 672241.* A very easy-going, friendly hotel in an amazing location at the end of a long beach. A perfect place to get away from it all. ● *mid-Sep–Mar.* ▭ ⚡ P	AE DC MC V	■	●	■	9
MARNOCH: *Old Manse of Marnoch* ££ Bridge of Marnoch, near Huntly, Gordon, Aberdeenshire. **Map** E2. (& **FAX** *(01466) 780873.* A very attractive part-Georgian, part-Edwardian house, situated on the River Deveron, and decorated with flair and style. The bedrooms are very comfortable and the food is imaginative, using local produce. ▭ TV P	MC V	■		■	5
MUIR OF ORD: *Dower House* ££ Highfield, Muir of Ord, Ross-shire, Highlands. **Map** C2. (& **FAX** *(01463) 870090.* An extremely agreeable small hotel that is attractively decorated. Pleasing bedrooms and a first-rate restaurant. ▭ TV 24 ⚡ P ⚹	MC V	■	●	■	5
MULL, BUNESSAN: *Ardfenaig House* ££££ Nr Bunessan, Isle of Mull, Strathclyde. **Map** B4. (*(01681) 700210.* **FAX** *(01681) 700210.* In a superb position at the head of Loch Caol in the southwest of the island, this hotel has comfortable rooms with great views. Many different types of sports can be enjoyed here, and a charming atmosphere of relaxation ensures a good post-exertion recovery. ● *Nov–Mar.* ▭ P	MC V	■		■	5
MULL, TOBERMORY: *Western Isles Hotel* £££ Tobermory, Isle of Mull, Strathclyde. **Map** B3. (*(01688) 302012.* **FAX** *(01688) 302297.* A grand, traditional establishment, with views over Tobermory Bay and the Sound of Mull. Very welcoming and comfortable, with log fires in winter. There is a choice of three restaurants, including a conservatory which is particularly delightful. ● *17–27 Dec.* ▭ TV P	AE MC V	■	●	■	25
NAIRN: *Clifton House* £££ Nairn, Highlands. **Map** D2. (*(01667) 453119.* **FAX** *(01667) 452836.* An individual town-hotel, decorated and furnished with flair and unremitting good taste. The restaurant comes highly recommended. ● *Dec–Jan.* ▭ P	AE DC MC V	■	●	■	12

ONICH: *Cuilcheanna House* £ | MC V | | | | 7
Onich, by Fort William, Inverness-shire. **Map** C3. *(01855) 821226.*
Expect exceptional home cooking by chef Linda Scott at this country
house hotel overlooking the beautiful Loch Linnhe. The four-course
dinners change daily and are outstanding value, although they are
available only to residents of the hotel. ☐ **P** ☐

ORKNEY: *Foveran* ££ | MC V | | ● | | 8
St Ola, Kirkwall, Orkney. *(01856) 872389.* FAX *(01856) 876430.*
A modern hotel with great views over Scapa Flow and the South Isles.
Comfortable rooms and a good restaurant. ● *Jan.* ☐ TV ☐ **P**

PORT APPIN: *Airds* ££££ | MC V | | ● | | 12
Port Appin, Appin, Argyll. **Map** C3. *(01631) 730236.* FAX *(01631) 730535.*
A former ferry inn with a modest whitewashed exterior, inside it is smart
and comfortable with a very good restaurant. ☐ TV **P**

SHETLAND, BUSTA: *Busta House* ££ | AE DC MC V | | ● | | 20
Busta, Brae, Shetland. *(01806) 522506.* FAX *(01806) 522588.*
A civilized, family-run hotel beside its own little harbour. This early 18th-
century house is relaxed and comfortable. ● *22 Dec–3 Jan.* ☐ TV **P** ☐

SHETLAND, WALLS: *Burrastow House* £££ | AE DC MC V | | ● | | 5
Walls, Shetland. *(01595) 809307.* FAX *(01595) 809213.*
In a very remote part of western Shetland, this is a wonderful place to
escape to for absolute calm and tranquillity. Comfort is not sacrificed
here, and the food is delicious. ☐ **P** ☐

SHIELDAIG: *Tigh-an-Eilean* £££ | MC V | | ● | | 11
Shieldaig, near Strathcarron, Ross & Cromarty, Highlands. **Map** C2.
(01520) 755251. FAX *(01520) 755321.*
On the bank of Loch Shieldaig, this is one of the best small hotels in
Scotland. Very comfortable, with charming owners and a high standard of
both food and service. ● *mid-Oct–Easter.* ☐ **P**

SKYE, DUNVEGAN: *Harlosh House* £££ | MC V | | ● | | 6
Near Dunvegan, Isle of Skye, Highlands. **Map** B2. *& FAX (01470) 521367.*
This small hotel provides a friendly, peaceful base for exploring the
island of Skye. The food is excellent, and the hotel is situated in a
superb location on the shore of Loch Bracadale. ● *Oct–Mar.* ☐ ☐ **P**

SKYE, PORTREE: *Viewfield House* £ | MC V | | ● | | 11
Portree, Isle of Skye, Highlands. **Map** B2. *(01478) 612217.* FAX *(01478) 613517.*
A rambling building that has been a family house for 200 years. Guests are
made very welcome and everyone dines together. ● *mid-Oct–mid-Apr.* ☐ **P**

SKYE, STAFFIN: *Flodigarry Hotel* ££ | MC V | | ● | | 19
Flodigarry, Staffin, Isle of Skye. **Map** B2. *(01470) 552203.* FAX *(01470) 552301.*
Set on the spectacular Trotternish Peninsula with magnificent views, the
building was originally associated with Flora Macdonald. The hotel has a
conservatory and offers friendly, traditional hospitality. ☐ ☐ **P** ☐

THURSO: *Forss House* ££ | AE MC V | | ● | | 11
Thurso, Caithness, Highlands. **Map** D1. *(01847) 861201.* FAX *(01847) 861301.*
A welcoming hotel on the wilds of the northern coast. Imposing on the
outside, but inside it is comfortable and cheerful. ☐ TV ☐ **P** ☐

ULLAPOOL: *Ceilidh Place* ££ | AE DC MC V | | ● | | 13
14 West Argyle St, Ullapool, Wester-Ross, Highlands. **Map** C2.
(01854) 612103. FAX *(01854) 612886.*
Lots going on here – musical evenings and exhibitions, a café and
bookshop. Residents can escape the hurly-burly to their own peaceful
sitting room. ☐ ☐ **P** ☐ *limited.*

ULLAPOOL: *Altnaharrie Inn* £££££ | AE MC V | | | | 8
Ullapool, Ross & Cromarty, Highlands. **Map** C2. *(01854) 633230.*
Reached by boat from Ullapool, this hotel will guarantee you tranquil,
panoramic views. Staying here is a special, but somewhat expensive,
experience. Good food is on offer. ☐ ☐ *entire establishment.* **P**

WHITEBRIDGE: *Knockie Lodge* £££ | AE DC MC V | | | | 10
Whitebridge, Highlands. **Map** C3. *(01456) 486276.* FAX *(01456) 486389.*
An outstanding, peaceful setting for this former hunting lodge above Loch
Nan Lann allows you to enjoy the good food undisturbed. ● *Nov–Apr.* ☐ **P**

For key to symbols see back flap

WHERE TO EAT

SCOTTISH FOOD NEED strike no terror in the visiting gourmet's heart; Scotland's restaurant scene has moved far from its once dismal reputation. This is partly due to an influx of foreign chefs and cooking styles. You can now sample a wide range of international cuisine throughout Scotland, with the greatest choice in Edinburgh and Glasgow. Home-grown restaurateurs have also risen to the challenge of re-deeming Scottish food, and the indigenous cooking has improved beyond all

Ryan's Bar in Edinburgh

recognition in the last decade. You can now eat extremely well in Scotland regardless of your budget, and at most times of the day in the major towns and cities, although the more rural establishments are less flexible. Affordable, well-prepared but less elaborate food is making a mark in all types of brasseries, restaurants and cafés throughout the country. The restaurant listings on pages 176–83 feature some of the best places to eat, as well as those with a consistently good track record.

The vast selection of beer and whisky available in a typical Scottish pub

PRICES AND BOOKING

ALL RESTAURANTS are required by law to display their current prices outside the door. These amounts include VAT (value-added tax) at 17.5 per cent, and any service or cover charge should also be specified. This should give a rough idea of what the meal will cost before you enter the restaurant.

Wine can be pricey when dining out in Scotland, and extras like coffee and bottled water may be disproportionately expensive compared to the cost of the food. Service charges (usually between 10 and 15 per cent) are sometimes added automatically to the bill. If service charge has not been included, you are expected to leave a tip – the amount will depend on the level of service that you have received. The majority of restaurants accept cheques with a cheque guarantee card, or credit cards. Pubs

usually prefer cash to cards. It is advisable to book a table before making a special journey to a restaurant. City restaurants are very busy, and some of the more renowned establishments can be fully booked up to a month in advance. If you cannot keep a reservation, cancel it by telephone.

TASTE OF SCOTLAND SCHEME

EVERY YEAR, some 500 eating establishments across the country, ranging from traditional farmhouse restaurants to those in luxury, five-star hotels, are thoroughly inspected.

Once a meal has been sampled, the inspectors decide whether the restaurant meets, and sometimes even exceeds, their criteria of the highest levels of quality and service. Those that do are included in the *A Taste of Scotland* guide, which is rigorously updated

once a year. The compilers of the guide are always eager to hear of their readers' experiences, good or bad, as this may influence their decision as to which establishments to include. They also pass on the comments to the relevant establishments for analysis.

BREAKFAST, LUNCH AND DINNER

TRADITIONALLY, breakfast in Scotland begins with cereal and milk, followed by bacon, eggs and tomato, and usually black pudding (blood sausage) too. It finishes with toast and marmalade, and a pot of tea. The alternative is a continental breakfast of black coffee, fruit juice and a croissant or two.

The most popular lunchtime foods are sandwiches, salads, baked potatoes and ploughman's lunches (a roll, hunk of cheese or ham and relishes), found mainly in pubs. A traditional Sunday lunch of roast meat and vegetables is served in some pubs and restaurants. Grand hotels can offer five or six courses for dinner, but usually there are only three.

One of Glasgow's many new and fashionable Italian restaurants

Fast food in Edinburgh: a fish and chip shop on the Portobello promenade

Dessert is often followed by cheese and oatcakes. Outside the larger towns and cities, dinner is usually eaten between 6pm and 9pm, and no later. In Scotland lunch is sometimes called "dinner" and the evening meal may be called "tea".

AFTERNOON TEA

NO VISITOR SHOULD miss the experience of a proper British afternoon tea, which can rival breakfast as the most enjoyable meal of the day. There are hundreds of tearooms all over Scotland, offering a choice of delicious sandwiches and cakes. Dundee Cake and shortbread are particular favourites and are wonderful eaten with a cup of tea. Scotch pancakes swimming in butter are another appetizing speciality.

The Mitre pub on Edinburgh's Royal Mile

CHILDREN

MANY PLACES now welcome junior diners *(see the listings for details)* and some actively encourage families, at least during the day or early evening. They may offer a separate children's menu, or simply adapt the portions to suit a child's appetite. Some also provide highchairs. Italian, Spanish, Indian and fast-food restaurants nearly always welcome children, and even pubs are relaxing their rules and may provide special play areas.

VEGETARIAN FOOD

BRITAIN IS AHEAD of many of its European counterparts in providing vegetarian alternatives to meat dishes, and Scotland is no exception. A few of the establishments listed in this guide serve only vegetarian meals, and most cater for non-meat-eaters *(see the listings for an indication of restaurants serving vegetarian dishes).* Edinburgh and Glasgow have the widest choice, but smaller towns and villages are also beginning to experiment with meat-free dishes. Vegetarians wishing to find a wider choice than is offered by Scottish and English food should try South Indian, Chinese and other ethnic restaurants as they have a tradition of good vegetarian cuisine.

FAST FOOD

SCOTLAND IS RIGHTLY famed for its "fish suppers" (fish and chips) and there are many seaside fish bars selling wonderfully fresh fish and chips (French fries). Most also offer chicken suppers. Away from the coast the fish may not be as amazingly fresh, but there are plenty of good places from which to choose.

Visitors will find the usual fast food chains, such as Pizza Hut, McDonald's, Burger King and KFC, as well as sandwich bars and "greasy spoon" cafés that serve mainly fried food.

Taking afternoon tea in Scotland – an elegant and enjoyable pastime

PUBS AND WINE BARS

SCOTTISH ALCOHOL licensing laws are different from the rest of Britain, most apparent in the later closing times of pubs and bars. Whereas in England and Wales most places close at 11pm, many in Scotland, particularly in the towns and cities, stay open until midnight or even 1 or 2am. During the Festival in August *(see pp78–9),* Edinburgh's drinking holes often do not close until 3am.

While the old-fashioned, dark and occasionally slightly shabby pubs still exist, a new breed of bar has become popular in Scotland in recent years. In the towns and cities, wine bars have become two-a-penny. Unlike the traditional pubs, the choice of drink is not limited to a few beers. Wine bars tend to be noisy, with a predominantly young clientele. Here, the emphasis is on variety, with lively happy hours and interesting cocktails.

Choosing a Restaurant

THE RESTAURANTS in this guide have been selected across a wide price range for their good value, exceptional food and interesting location. Many are in recommended hotels. The chart lists the restaurants by region starting with Edinburgh; colour-coded thumb tabs indicate the regions covered on each page. For hotel listings, see pp166–73.

	CREDIT CARDS	CHILDREN WELCOME	FIXED-PRICE MENU	VEGETARIAN	TRADITIONAL SCOTTISH
EDINBURGH					
OLD TOWN: *Café Florentin* £ 8 St Giles Street. ☏ *(0131) 225 6267.* A cosmopolitan, informal café serving a full range of coffees, teas and light meals. French breads and pastries are the speciality here. Other Edinburgh branches are on Grindlay Street and in Stockbridge. ● *25 Dec.* ✂		●	■	●	
OLD TOWN: *Black Bo's* ££ 57 Blackfriars St. ☏ *(0131) 557 6136.* Small vegetarian restaurant in the Old Town which really cares about food. Imaginative and well flavoured dishes form the menu. ● *1 Jan, 25–6 Dec.* ▮	AE MC V	●		●	
OLD TOWN: *The Grain Store* ££ 30 Victoria Street. ☏ *(0131) 225 7635.* On the upper floor of an unusual building, in a cobbled street with interesting shops, this restaurant is close to the Castle, Grassmarket and St Giles. Good food in an informal atmosphere. ● *first two weeks Jan, 25–6 Dec.* ▮	AE MC V	●	■	●	■
OLD TOWN: *The Witchery and the Secret Garden Restaurant* £££ Castlehill, Royal Mile. ☏ *(0131) 225 5613.* Situated a few feet away from the entrance to Edinburgh Castle at the top of the Royal Mile, this stylish restaurant specializes in contemporary Scottish cuisine. The wine list is excellent. ● *25 Dec.* ♿ *The Witchery only.* ▮	AE DC MC V	●	■	●	■
OLD TOWN: *The Atrium and the Blue Bar Café* ££££ 10 Cambridge Street. ☏ *(0131) 228 8882.* Stylish interior by the Traverse Theatre reflects the light, simple dishes in The Atrium – the cutting edge of modern Scottish food. For light lunches or dinners, try the Blue Bar upstairs. ● *Sat lunch, Sun.* ♿ *Atrium only.* ▮	AE DC MC V	●		●	
SOUTH SIDE: *Howie's* ££ 63 Dalry Road. ☏ *(0131) 313 3334.* This eclectic bistro, which presents Scottish food with a French twist, has a daily changing menu that ensures its lasting appeal. Customers may bring their own wine. ● *Mon lunch, 1–2 Jan, 25–6 Dec.* ♿ ▮	AE DC MC V	●		●	■
SOUTH SIDE: *The Marque* ££ 19–21 Causewayside. ☏ *(0131) 466 6660.* Stylish restaurant serving outstanding, modern, sophisticated food from chefs with an impeccable Edinburgh reputation. ● *Mon, 1–8 Jan, 25–7 Dec.* ♿ ▮	MC V	●	■	●	
SOUTH SIDE: *Sweet Melinda's* £££ 11 Roseneath Street, Marchmont. ☏ *(0131) 229 7953.* With ingredients from nearby Eddie's Chinese fish market, this is seriously good seafood with a Pacific Rim accent. ● *Sun, Mon, 1–2 Jan, 25–6 Dec.* ♿ ▮	MC V	●		●	
NEW TOWN: *Queen Street Café* £ Scottish National Portrait Gallery, 1 Queen Street. ☏ *(0131) 557 2844.* A delightful coffee shop providing delicious and imaginative home cooking in interesting surroundings. (There is also a good café in the Scottish National Gallery of Modern Art.) ● *25–6 Dec.* ♿ ✂ *entire premises.*		●		●	
NEW TOWN: *The Lost Sock Diner* ££ 11 East London Street. ☏ *(0131) 557 6097.* Adjacent to a launderette, this quirkily titled restaurant is one of the best in the area. The interesting menu includes New York tortilla "wraps". Breakfast is served until 4pm. ● *Sun, Mon dinner, 1 Jan, 25–6 Dec.* ♿ ✂ ▮	AE MC V	●		●	■
NEW TOWN: *Restaurant 36 (Howard Hotel)* ££ 36 Great King Street. ☏ *(0131) 556 3636.* Modern to the point of minimalist, offering Scottish dishes with an international flavour. ● *Sat lunch, 26–7 Dec.* ♿ ✂ *entire premises.* ▮	AE DC MC V	●	■	●	

Price categories include a three-course meal for one, half a bottle of house wine, and all unavoidable extra costs such as cover charge and VAT:
£ under £15
££ £15–£25
£££ £25–£35
££££ £35–£50
£££££ over £50.

CHILDREN WELCOME
Restaurants offering smaller portions and high chairs for children. Special menus sometimes available.
FIXED-PRICE MENU
A good value fixed-price meal, at lunch, dinner or both, usually consisting of three courses.
VEGETARIAN
Vegetarian specialities are included on the menu.
TRADITIONAL SCOTTISH
Several, if not all, of the items on the menu are traditional Scottish recipes, using fresh local produce.

	Credit Cards	Children Welcome	Fixed-Price Menu	Vegetarian	Traditional Scottish
NEW TOWN: *Scalini's Ristorante* ££ 10 Melville Place, Queensferry St. (0131) 220 2999. This Italian restaurant offers authentic cooking, courteous service and a relaxing atmosphere. ● *Sun, 1–2 Jan, 25–6 Dec.*	AE DC MC V	●	■	●	
NEW TOWN: *The Dome* £££ 14 George Street. (0131) 624 8624. In a magnificent building, constructed for the Royal College of Physicians in 1775, the restaurant has a sophisticated menu. Coffee, light lunches and afternoon tea are served al fresco in the courtyard. ● *1–2 Jan, 25–6 Dec.*	AE MC V	●		●	
NEW TOWN: *Haldane's* £££ 39A Albany Street. (0131) 556 8407. Elegant, tranquil restaurant in the Albany Hotel with charming staff and stylish, flavourful contemporary food. ● *Sat & Sun lunch.* entire premises.	AE MC V	●	■	●	■
NEW TOWN: *Indigo Yard* £££ 7 Charlotte Lane. (0131) 220 5603. An informal café/bistro, with outdoor tables, combining restaurant and bar services. Popular in the evenings. Great atmosphere. ● *25 Dec.*	AE MC V	●		●	
NEW TOWN: *Martin's* ££££ 70 Rose Street, North Lane. (0131) 225 3106. A city centre premises provides the location for this excellent restaurant offering a range of imaginative, contemporary Scottish cuisine. The superb Celtic cheeseboard is highly recommended. ● *Sun, Mon.*	AE DC MC V	●	■	●	
NEW TOWN: *Number One Princes Street* ££££ 1 Princes Street. (0131) 556 2414. The restaurant of Edinburgh's finest hotel enjoys a well-deserved reputation for excellence. Also a brasserie offering light meals. ● *2–10 Jan.*	AE DC MC V	●	■	●	
FURTHER AFIELD: *Daniel's* ££ 88 Commercial Street, Leith. (0131) 553 5933. One of the best of the new conservatory restaurants opposite the Scottish Office and piazza. The restaurant serves hearty Alsace food with French charm, and lighter snacks in the café at the back. ● *1 Jan, 25 Dec.*	MC V	●	■	●	■
FURTHER AFIELD: *The Waterfront* ££ 1C Dock Place, Leith. (0131) 554 7427. The restaurant combines small, cosy rooms and a conservatory facing the dock, with outside terraces and a pontoon. The menu reflects the best of Scottish ingredients available, especially fish. ● *25–6 Dec.*	AE MC V	●		●	■
FURTHER AFIELD: *Whitekirk Golf Club and Restaurant* ££ Whitekirk, near North Berwick, East Lothian. (01620) 870300. This restaurant has a rural setting, with lovely views. It offers good value and a friendly atmosphere. ● *Mon–Thu dinner, Nov–Feb.*	MC V	●		●	■
FURTHER AFIELD: *Garden Café* £££ Lennoxlove House, Haddington, East Lothian. (01620) 822156. Masterminded by television cook Clarissa Dickson-Wright, this lovely garden restaurant provides fantastic, stylish fare. ● *Mon.* entire premises.	MC V	●	■	●	■
FURTHER AFIELD: *La Potinière* £££ Main Street, Gullane, East Lothian. (01620) 843214. Run by a husband and wife, this popular restaurant serves mostly French food. Book ahead. ● *Sun–Tue & Thu dinner, Wed, Fri & Sat lunch.* entire premises.			■		
FURTHER AFIELD: *The Rock Restaurant* £££ 78 Commercial Street, Leith. (0131) 555 2225. Stylish restaurant in the centre of Leith. Gourmet menu plus an excellent selection of burgers and steaks. ● *Sun, Mon, 1–2 Jan, 25–6 Dec.*	AE DC MC V	●	■	●	■

Price categories include a three-course meal for one, half a bottle of house wine, and all unavoidable extra costs such as cover charge and VAT:
£ under £15
££ £15–£25
£££ £25–£35
££££ £35–£50
£££££ over £50.

CHILDREN WELCOME
Restaurants offering smaller portions and high chairs for children. Special menus sometimes available.
FIXED-PRICE MENU
A good value fixed-price meal, at lunch, dinner or both, usually consisting of three courses.
VEGETARIAN
Vegetarian specialities are included on the menu.
TRADITIONAL SCOTTISH
Several, if not all, of the items on the menu are traditional Scottish recipes, using fresh local produce.

	CREDIT CARDS	CHILDREN WELCOME	FIXED-PRICE MENU	VEGETARIAN	TRADITIONAL SCOTTISH
FURTHER AFIELD: *Skippers Bistro* £££ 1A Dock Place, Leith. (0131) 554 1018. An intimate, relaxing place in which to dine. The menu, specializing in fish, changes daily. ● *Sun, last week Feb, first two weeks Sep, 25 Dec–4 Jan.* ⚙ ♟	AE DC MC V	●	▪		
FURTHER AFIELD: *(Fitz)Henry* ££££ 19 Shore Place, Leith. (0131) 555 6625. Stylish, slightly eccentric conversion of a warehouse in historic Leith. Sophisticated food served with panache and charm. ● *Sun, 1 Jan, 25 Dec.* ⚙ ♟	AE MC V	●		●	

SOUTHERN SCOTLAND

	CREDIT CARDS	CHILDREN WELCOME	FIXED-PRICE MENU	VEGETARIAN	TRADITIONAL SCOTTISH
ABBEY ST BATHANS: *The Riverside Restaurant* £ Abbey St Bathans, near Duns, Berwickshire. (01361) 840312. Situated off the Gifford to Preston road, this small, friendly restaurant is in a delightful setting near the river, and serves tasty home-made lunches, including local game, and afternoon tea. Riverside walks nearby. ● *Mon.* ⚙	MC V	●		●	
JEDBURGH: *Simply Scottish* ££ High Street, Jedburgh, the Borders. **Map** E5. (01835) 864696. This combined restaurant, café and craft shop, located in the centre of Jedburgh, offers simple, contemporary Scottish cooking with style. ⚙	AE DC MC V	●		●	
KELSO: *Floors Garden Centre Coffee Shop* £ Floors Castle Garden Centre, Kelso, Roxburghshire. **Map** E5. (01573) 225714. Friendly coffee shop attached to attractive garden centre, serving coffee, lunches and afternoon teas. High quality home-made cooking, including estate game, preserves and baking. ● *24 Dec–2 Jan.* ⚙ ⚡	AE MC V	●		●	▪
KIPPFORD: *The Anchor Hotel* ££ Kippford, Dalbeattie, Kirkcudbrightshire. **Map** D6. (01556) 620205. Situated on the waterfront, with views of the boating activity, this friendly pub offers good bar food. Some outside tables. ● *25 Dec.* ⚙ ⚡ ♟	MC V	●		●	
MELROSE: *Burts Hotel* £££ Market Square, Melrose. **Map** E5. (01896) 822285. The restaurant of this townhouse hotel presents the best Scottish game and fish with imagination and flair. ● *25 Dec dinner, 26 Dec.* ⚙ ⚡ *entire premises.*	AE DC MC V		▪	●	▪
PEEBLES: *Kailzie Gardens Restaurant* £££ Kailzie Gardens, near Peebles, Peeblesshire. **Map** D5. (01721) 722807. A delightful courtyard setting on the Peebles to Traquair road, with excellent home-cooked lunches and afternoon teas. ⚙ ⚡ *entire premises.* ♟	MC V	●	▪		▪
PORTPATRICK: *Knockinaam Lodge* ££££ Off A77 near Portpatrick, Dumfries & Galloway. **Map** C6. (01776) 810471. This converted 19th-century hunting lodge is set in an idyllic location overlooking the sea. The cuisine on offer is smart, modern and French. ⚙ ⚡ *entire premises.* ♟	AE DC MC V		▪	●	
TWEEDSMUIR: *The Crook Inn* ££ Tweedsmuir, near Moffat, Peeblesshire. **Map** D5. (01899) 880272. Situated a short way north of Tweedsmuir, on the Moffat to Edinburgh road, this historic inn has interesting 1930s interior features with a cosy atmosphere and log fires. Bar food only. ● *25 Dec.* ⚡ ♟	MC V	●	▪	●	▪

GLASGOW

	CREDIT CARDS	CHILDREN WELCOME	FIXED-PRICE MENU	VEGETARIAN	TRADITIONAL SCOTTISH
CITY CENTRE: *Bouzy Rouge* £ 111 West Regent Street. (0141) 221 8804. This fashionable, busy restaurant concentrates on contemporary Scottish cuisine with an international influence. Bookings are essential. There is also a branch in the Edinburgh West End. ● *1 Jan.* ⚙	AE DC MC V	●	▪	●	▪

City Centre: *Willow Tea Room* (£)
217 Sauchiehall Street. ☏ *(0141) 332 0521.*
Tucked away above a jeweller's shop, this reconstruction of a Mackintosh tearoom *(see p100)* has an impressive range of light lunches and afternoon teas in an Art Nouveau setting. ● *1–2 Jan, 25–6 Dec.*

City Centre: *Café Gandolfi* (£)(£) MC V
64 Albion Street. ☏ *(0141) 552 6813.*
A stunning interior, with stained glass windows and individual pieces of Tim Stead furniture, creates a stylish and stimulating atmosphere for a drink, snack or meal. ● *1–2 Jan, 24 Dec dinner, 25–6 Dec.*

City Centre: *The Fire Station* (£)(£) AE MC V
33 Ingram Street. ☏ *(0141) 552 2929.*
1900s fire station converted into a restaurant with a great atmosphere. Excellent and moderately priced menu, with half-price pasta happy hours between 5 and 7pm, for really good value. ● *1 Jan, 25–6 Dec.*

City Centre: *Fratelli Sarti* (£)(£) AE DC MC V
121 Bath Street. ☏ *(0141) 204 0440.*
This excellent Italian restaurant offers mouth-watering *dolci, gelati* and also very probably the best pizza to be found in Glasgow. There is another branch situated at 133 Wellington Street. ● *1 Jan, 25 Dec.*

City Centre: *Crème de la Crème* (£)(£)(£) AE DC MC V
1071 Argyle Street. ☏ *(0141) 221 3222.*
Extravagantly decorated, bustling Indian restaurant on Glasgow's famous shopping street. Try the adventurous Goanese menu. ● *Sun lunch.*

City Centre: *The Puppet Theatre* (£)(£)(£) AE DC MC V
11 Ruthven Lane. ☏ *(0141) 339 8444.*
In a converted mews off Byres Road, the reputation of The Puppet Theatre continues to grow. Scottish ingredients are presented with flair and imagination. Reservations are essential. ● *Mon, Sat lunch, 1–2 Jan, 25–6 Dec.*

City Centre:: *78 St Vincent Street* (£)(£)(£) AE DC MC V
78 St Vincent Street. ☏ *(0141) 221 7710.*
Decorated with a mural by Glaswegian artist Donald McLeod, this restaurant offers French cuisine with a Scottish touch. ● *Sun lunch, 1 Jan, 25 Dec.*

City Centre: *Thai Fountain* (£)(£)(£) AE MC V
2 Woodside Crescent. ☏ *(0141) 332 2599.*
The Charing Cross area is the location of the finest of Glasgow's few Thai restaurants. Prawn and fish dishes abound, and a great vegetarian menu is also available. ● *Sun.*

City Centre: *The Buttery* (£)(£)(£)(£) AE MC V
652 Argyle Street. ☏ *(0141) 221 8188.*
A converted tenement is the unusual location for one of Glasgow's finest restaurants, where traditional Scottish food is dished up with creative flair. Simpler food served downstairs in the Belfry. ● *Sat lunch, Sun, 1 Jan, 25 Dec.*

City Centre: *Rogano* (£)(£)(£)(£) AE DC MC V
11 Royal Exchange Place. ☏ *(0141) 248 4055.*
This spacious restaurant has been fashionable in Glasgow since the 1930s. Seafood is a speciality. A lighter menu is available downstairs.
● *1 Jan, 25 Dec.*

West End: *Antipasti* (£) MC V
337 Byres Road. ☏ *(0141) 337 2737.*
A good value restaurant with a great atmosphere. Cheerful staff serve hearty portions of pasta and all the trimmings with great efficiency. Worth the wait at busy times; there are some outside tables. ● *1 Jan, 25 Dec.*

West End: *Stravaigin* (£)(£) AE MC V
28 Gibson Street, West End. ☏ *(0141) 334 2665.*
This award-winning restaurant, popular with locals and students, offers a Scottish menu with Eastern influences. ● *Mon, 1–2 Jan, 25–6 Dec.*

West End: *Nairn's* (£)(£)(£) AE DC MC V
13 Woodside Crescent. ☏ *(0141) 353 0707.*
Nick Nairn's restaurant is stylish and elegant and his food contemporary and imaginative, with good flavours. The establishment also has four bedrooms available. ● *1 Jan, 25 Dec.*

Price categories include a three-course meal for one, half a bottle of house wine, and all unavoidable extra costs such as cover charge and VAT:
£ under £15
££ £15–£25
£££ £25–£35
££££ £35–£50
£££££ over £50

CHILDREN WELCOME
Restaurants offering smaller portions and high chairs for children. Special menus sometimes available.
FIXED-PRICE MENU
A good value fixed-price meal, at lunch, dinner or both, usually consisting of three courses.
VEGETARIAN
Vegetarian specialities are included on the menu.
TRADITIONAL SCOTTISH
Several, if not all, of the items on the menu are traditional Scottish recipes, using fresh local produce.

Restaurant	Price	Credit Cards	Children Welcome	Fixed-Price Menu	Vegetarian	Traditional Scottish
WEST END: *Two Fat Ladies* 88 Dumbarton Road. (0141) 339 1944. This informal restaurant features quality fresh fish and Callum Mathieson's thoughtful and creative cooking, to provide Glasgow with one of its best fish restaurants. ● Sun, Mon, 1–15 Jan, public hols.	£££	MC V	●	▥	●	
WEST END: *The Ubiquitous Chip* 12 Ashton Lane, West End. (0141) 334 5007. Located in a cobbled mews off Byres Road, this restaurant is famous not only for its innovative Scottish recipes, but also its outstanding wine list. There is a less expensive, less formal restaurant upstairs. ● 1 Jan, 25 Dec, 31 Dec.	££££	AE DC MC V	●	▥	●	▥
FURTHER AFIELD: *The Top Deck Café* Clyde Valley Garden Centre, Lanark Road, Garrion Bridge, Clyde Valley. (01698) 888880. This inexpensive restaurant with a large, raised terrace offers great views. Convenient for New Lanark and the Falls of Clyde. ● 1 Jan, 25–6 Dec.	£	MC V	●		●	
FURTHER AFIELD: *La Fiorentina* 2 Paisley Road, South Side. (0141) 420 1585. A traditional Italian restaurant, situated close to Kingston Bridge. Great atmosphere with characterful waiters. ● Sun, 1 Jan.	££	AE DC MC V	●	▥	●	
FURTHER AFIELD: *Gingerhill* Hillhead Street, Milngavie. (0141) 956 6515. Situated in the town centre, at the start of the West Highland Way, this cheerful restaurant specializes in Scottish seafood. No alcohol supplied, but you can bring your own wine – no corkage charge. ● Sun, 1 Jan, 26 Dec.	££	MC V	●		●	

CENTRAL SCOTLAND

Restaurant	Price	Credit Cards	Children Welcome	Fixed-Price Menu	Vegetarian	Traditional Scottish
ABERFOYLE: *Braeval* On A81 near Aberfoyle, Stirling. Map C4. (01877) 382711. At the foot of the Trossachs, this outstanding restaurant has a daily changing menu that presents the best of modern cooking. ● Mon–Tue.	£££	AE DC MC V	●	▥	●	
ANSTRUTHER: *The Cellar* 24 East Green, Anstruther, Fife. Map E4. (01333) 310378. Behind the fisheries museum at the east end of the harbour, this is one of the finest fish restaurants in Scotland. ● Sun–Mon (Nov–Easter), 24 Dec–4 Jan.	££££	AE DC MC V		▥		
ARRAN, BRODICK: *Creelers Restaurant* The Home Farm, Brodick, Isle of Arran. Map C5. (01770) 302810. Located outside Brodick, near the castle. A friendly and relaxed restaurant offering a menu of great fish and shellfish, fresh from the boats. ● Mon (except Aug), Nov–mid-March.	£££	MC V	●	▥	●	
BALLOCH: *Georgian Room, Cameron House Hotel* Loch Lomond, Dumbarton & Clydebank. Map C4. (01389) 755565. Fine contemporary cooking is offered by the restaurant of this luxurious hotel on the very pretty southern bank of Loch Lomond. entire premises.	££££	AE DC MC V		▥	●	
CUPAR: *The Peat Inn* Peat Inn, near Cupar, Fife. Map D4. (01334) 840206. Located in the middle of rural Fife, David Wilson has led the revival of great Scottish restaurants. Dining here is a real gastronomic experience. The inn also has eight bedrooms. ● Sun–Mon, 25 Dec. entire premises.	££££	AE MC V	●	▥	●	
DRYMEN: *The Pottery* The Square, Drymen, Stirlingshire. Map C4. (01360) 660458. Friendly restaurant and coffee shop alongside a pottery, serving good home-cooked food all day and delicious afternoon teas. Roaring fires in winter and a delightful terrace in summer. ● 1 Jan, 25 Dec. entire premises.	£	AE DC MC V	●		●	

DUNDEE: *The Royal Oak* ££
167 Brook Street, Dundee. **Map** D4. ((01382) 229440.
A traditional pub with a warm and friendly atmosphere. The bar and dining room provide good value, home-made meals including imaginative Indian dishes. Children welcome until 7:30pm. ● *Sun, 1–2 Jan, 25–6 Dec.* & ♥

MC
V

FAIRLIE: *Fins Restaurant* £££
Fencefoot Farm, Fairlie, near Largs. **Map** C4. ((01475) 568989.
Delightful, small seafood bistro in a converted stone barn, using produce from own fishery and smokehouse, as well as other local supplies. Friendly welcome and cheerful staff. ● *Sun dinner, Mon.* & ⚡ *entire premises.* ♥

AE
DC
MC
V

GIRVAN: *Wildings* £££
Montgomerie Street, Girvan, Ayrshire. **Map** C5. ((01465) 713481.
This comfortable and friendly family-run restaurant offers a varied menu with seafood specialities that vie with the best on the west coast. Expect superb flavours at reasonable prices. ● *Sun dinner, Mon–Tue, Oct, 25 Dec–22 Jan.* & ⚡ *entire premises.*

INVERARAY: *Loch Fyne Oyster Bar* ££
Cairndow, near Inveraray, Argyll. **Map** C4. ((01499) 600264.
The Oyster Bar on the banks of this famous fishing loch enjoys an excellent reputation for its fresh seafood. Booking is advised. ● *1 Jan, 25 Dec.* & ♥

AE
DC
MC
V

KINCARDINE ON FORTH: *The Unicorn Inn* ££
15 Excise Street, Kincardine, Clackmannanshire. **Map** D4. ((01259) 730704.
Surprisingly unassuming location in the heart of this historic village on the River Forth. The restaurant offers excellent seafood and a welcoming and informal atmosphere. ● *Sun, Mon, 1–3 Jan, 25–6 Dec.* & ♥

AE
MC
V

KINCLAVEN: *Ballathie House Hotel* £££
Kinclaven, near Perth & Kinross. **Map** D4. ((01250) 883268.
Scottish dishes of the highest quality in the restaurant of this Victorian country house hotel overlooking the River Tay. ⚡ *entire premises.* & ♥

AE
DC
MC
V

PERTH: *Let's Eat* £££
77-79 Kinnoull Street, Perth. **Map** D4. ((01738) 643377.
A high-quality restaurant in the former Theatre Royal. Good value, imaginative dishes. ● *Sun–Mon, two weeks mid-July, last two weeks Jan* & ⚡ ♥

AE
MC
V

ST ANDREWS: *The Grange Inn* ££
Grange Road, St Andrews, Fife. **Map** E4. ((01334) 472670.
This country inn with views over the famous golfing town is excellent, and offers modern and traditional Scottish fare. ● *Mon–Tue (Nov–Apr).* ⚡ ♥

AE
DC
MC
V

STIRLING: *Scholars Stirling Highland Hotel* £££
Spittal Street, Stirling. **Map** D4. ((01786) 475444.
Set in the old town of Stirling, at the foot of the entrance to the castle, this hotel's restaurant serves fine Scottish fare. ● *Sat lunch.* & ⚡ *entire premises.*

AE
DC
MC
V

THE HIGHLANDS AND ISLANDS

ABERDEEN: *Restaurant on the Terrace* £££
Union Terrace, Aberdeen. **Map** E3. ((01224) 640233.
This traditional hotel, located in the heart of the city, offers European cuisine and also more traditional Scottish cuisine. ● *Sat lunch, Sun lunch.* & ⚡ *entire premises.* ♥

AE
DC
MC
V

ABERDEEN: *The Silver Darling* £££
Pocra Quay, Footdee, North Pier, Aberdeen. **Map** E3. ((01224) 576229.
Well worth finding on the north side of Aberdeen Harbour, this restaurant provides superb seafood which varies according to the daily catch. Great puddings. ● *Sat lunch, Sun (except dinner Easter– Sep), 1–3 Jan, 25–8 Dec.* ♥

AE
DC
MC
V

ACHILTIBUIE: *Summer Isles Hotel* ££££
Achiltibuie, near Ullapool, Ross and Cromarty. **Map** C2. ((01854) 622282.
An idyllic setting overlooking the Summer Isles. The Michelin starred restaurant offers exceptionally fine dinners, and superb seafood lunches and suppers in the adjacent bar. ● *mid-Oct–Easter.* ⚡ *entire premises.* ♥

MC
V

ARCHIESTOWN: *Archiestown Hotel* £££
Archiestown, near Aberlour, Aberdeenshire. **Map** D2. ((01340) 810218.
West of Craigellachie, in the heart of Speyside whisky country, this informal bistro is noted for its warm and inviting atmosphere and good Scottish fare. ● *1 Oct–10 Feb.* ♥

MC
V

For key to symbols see back flap

Price categories include a three-course meal for one, half a bottle of house wine, and all unavoidable extra costs such as cover charge and VAT:
£ under £15
££ £15–£25
£££ £25–£35
££££ £35–£50
£££££ over £50.

CHILDREN WELCOME
Restaurants offering smaller portions and high chairs for children. Special menus sometimes available.

FIXED-PRICE MENU
A good value fixed-price meal, at lunch, dinner or both, usually consisting of three courses.

VEGETARIAN
Vegetarian specialities are included on the menu.

TRADITIONAL SCOTTISH
Several, if not all, of the items on the menu are traditional Scottish recipes, using fresh local produce.

	CREDIT CARDS	CHILDREN WELCOME	FIXED-PRICE MENU	VEGETARIAN	TRADITIONAL SCOTTISH
AUCHMITHIE: *The But'n'Ben* ££ Auchmithie, near Arbroath. **Map** E3. ((01241) 877223. Converted cottages create a cosy setting for this village restaurant. Fresh seafood with a Scottish emphasis. Reasonably priced lunches, high teas and evening meals. ● *Sun dinner, Tue, 1–2 Jan, 25–6 Dec.*	MC V	●		●	●
AVIEMORE: *Corrour House Hotel* ££ Inverdruie near Aviemore, Inverness-shire. **Map** D3. ((01479) 810220. Family-run Victorian house with superb views of the Cairngorm Mountains. Traditional Scottish fare in a pretty setting. ● *mid-Nov–Dec.* entire premises.	DC MC V	●	●	●	●
BALLATER: *Darroch Learg* ££££ Braemar Road, Ballater, Aberdeenshire. **Map** D3. ((013397) 55443. Victorian lodge with views of the Cairngorms. Modern Scottish cooking with delicately flavoured ingredients. ● *10 Jan–1 Feb.* entire premises.	AE DC MC V	●	●	●	
CRINAN: *Lock 16, Crinan Hotel* ££££ Crinan Hotel, Crinan, by Lochgilphead, Argyll. **Map** C4. ((01546) 830261. The third floor restaurant has great views of Jura and Scarba, to complement fabulously fresh seafood. Excellent ground floor restaurant and good lunches in the bar. Coffee shop on the quayside. ● *Sun, Mon dinner, Oct–Mar.*	AE MC V	●	●		
HARRIS (WESTERN ISLES): *Scarista House* £££ Scarista, Isle of Harris, Western Isles. **Map** B2. ((01859) 550238. In an idyllic, west-facing position above the white sand beaches and adjacent to the golf course, this restaurant has superb views and excellent food. Rooms are also available. ● *Oct–Apr.*	MC V		●	●	●
INVERKIRKAIG: *Achin's Bookshop Tea Room* £ Inverkirkaig, near Lochinver, Sutherland. **Map** C1. ((01571) 844262. Near the start of a footpath up the Kirkaig River (Suilven), and attached to one of Britain's most remote bookshops. ● *Oct–Easter.* entire premises.	AE DC MC V	●		●	●
INVERNESS: *Café One* ££ 75 Castle Street, Inverness. **Map** D2. ((01463) 226200. Attractive restaurant in the town centre, using good ingredients cooked in a modern Scottish style. ● *Sun, 1 Jan, 25–6 Dec.*	MC V	●		●	●
INVERNESS: *Adam's Dining Room (Culloden House)* ££££ Off A96 at Culloden, Inverness. **Map** D2. ((01463) 790461. The food is country house style at this historic hotel, with sauces, jellies, sorbets, mousses, and fresh meat, game and fish dishes. entire premises.	AE DC MC V		●	●	●
KIRKTON OF GLENISLA: *Glenisla Hotel* ££ Kirkton of Glenisla, near Alyth, Perthshire. **Map** D3. ((01575) 582223. Tranquil setting and an ideal base for skiing, walking and fishing. Traditional inn with log fires, hearty food and a range of malts. ● *25 Dec.*	MC V	●		●	●
KYLE OF LOCHALSH: *Seagreen Restaurant and Bookshop* ££ Plockton Road, Kyle of Lochalsh, Highlands. **Map** C2. ((01599) 534388. The delicious menu in this café/restaurant offers fresh, local ingredients. Specialities are fish and seafood. ● *1 Jan, 6 Jan–Easter, 25–6 Dec.*	MC V	●		●	
LAGGAN BRIDGE: *Caoldair Kiln Room Coffee Shop* £ Laggan Bridge, near Dalwhinnie, Inverness-shire. **Map** D3. ((01528) 544231. Delicious home-made light lunches and baking, as well as quality crafts, are available here. Some outside tables. ● *Nov–Easter.* entire premises.		●		●	
LOCHINVER: *Lochinver Larder* £££ Main Street, Lochinver, Sutherland. **Map** C1. ((01571) 844356. Family run bistro/coffee shop with beautiful views out to the River Inver and Lochinver Bay. Good value home-cooked local produce with an emphasis on seafood. Home baking to take away. ● *Nov–Mar.* entire premises.	MC V	●		●	●

MULL: *Dovecote Restaurant* ££
Calgary, Isle of Mull, Argyll. **Map** B3. 📞 *(01688) 400256.*
West of Dervaig, close to a fabulous shell beach, is this restaurant in a converted dovecote. Interesting menu based on fresh local produce. Rooms available at the Calgary Farmhouse. ● *Nov–Easter.* ⚬ ⚬ *entire premises.*
MC V

ORKNEY: *The Creel Restaurant* £££
Front Rd, St Margaret's Hope, South Ronaldsay, Orkney. 📞 *(01856) 831311.*
Cosy gastronomic haven in a remote part of the island. Fresh local ingredients, especially seafood. ● *Jan, Feb, two weeks mid-Oct.* ⚬ ⚬ *entire premises.*
MC V

PITLOCHRY: *Moulin Hotel* ££
11 Kirkmichael Road, Moulin, Pitlochry, Perthshire. **Map** D3. 📞 *(01796) 472196.*
Historic inn situated at the foot of Ben Vrackie, on the Pitlochry to Glenisla road. The roaring fires and warm welcome make the Moulin a great venue for lunches, afternoon teas or evening meals. ⚬ ⚬ *entire premises.* 🍷
MC V

PORT APPIN: *The Pier House* £££
Port Appin, Argyll. **Map** C3. 📞 *(01631) 730302.*
A stunning position on the quayside, facing west over Lismore, provides one of the best locations on the west coast. Conservatory dining room with glorious views serves superb seafood. ● *25 Dec.* ⚬ ⚬ *entire premises.* 🍷
MC V

SHETLAND: *Burrastow House* £££
Walls, Shetland. 📞 *(01595) 809307.*
Georgian house in remote, peaceful location on the west coast of the island. Excellent home cooking complements the use of local ingredients. ● *Sun dinner, Mon, Jan, Feb, 14–28 Oct, 25 Dec.* ⚬ ⚬ *entire premises.* 🍷
AE MC V

SKYE, COLBOST: *The Three Chimneys* £££
Colbost, near Dunvegan, Isle of Skye. **Map** B2. 📞 *(01470) 511258.*
This award-winning restaurant offers lovingly prepared local ingredients for an epicurean treat in delightful surroundings. Accommodation is also available. ● *Jan, Feb.* ⚬ ⚬ *entire premises.* 🍷
MC V

SKYE, SLEAT: *Kinloch Lodge* ££££
Sleat, Isle of Skye. **Map** B3. 📞 *(01471) 833214.*
This is the home of the High Chief of the Clan Donald and his wife Lady Claire, a renowned cook who is responsible for the wonderful traditional Scottish cuisine. ⚬ ⚬ *entire premises.* 🍷
AE MC V

STONEHAVEN: *The Tolbooth Restaurant* £££
The Old Pier, The Harbour, Stonehaven, Aberdeen. **Map** E3. 📞 *(01569) 762287.*
Set in an imaginatively converted historic building on the quay. Charming, courteous staff present an interesting contemporary menu, specializing in local fresh seafood. ● *Mon, 1–15 Jan, 25 Dec.* 🍷
MC V

TARBET: *Seafood Café* ££
Tarbet, near Scourie, Sutherland. **Map** C1. 📞 *(01971) 502251.*
Situated in a remote crofting settlement, where boats cross to the nearby bird reserve on Handa Island. The proprietors catch and cook your dinner. Self-catering accommodation is also available. ● *Sun, Sep–Easter.*

THURSO: *Forss Country House Hotel* £££
Near Thurso, Caithness, Highlands. **Map** D1. 📞 *(01847) 861201.*
Peaceful Highland hotel set in 20 acres of woodland. Fresh local produce used in traditional Scottish dishes. ● *24 Dec–4 Jan.* ⚬ *entire premises.* 🍷
AE MC V

TONGUE: *Ben Loyal Hotel* £££
Tongue, Sutherland, Highlands. **Map** D1. 📞 *(01847) 611216.*
A comfortable, family-run restaurant on the north coast, with views of the sea and spectacular Ben Loyal. The well-balanced menu uses quality local ingredients. ● *1–3 Jan, 25–6 Dec.* ⚬
MC V

ULLAPOOL: *Morefield Mariners Restaurant* ££
North Road, Ullapool, Highlands. **Map** C2. 📞 *(01854) 612161.*
Popular, inexpensive restaurant specializing in seafood, with excellent meat and vegetarian dishes. Bar meals served in winter. ● *mid-Oct–Easter.* ⚬ ⚬
MC V

ULLAPOOL: *The Ceilidh Place* £££
14 West Argyle Street, Ullapool, Highlands. **Map** C2. 📞 *(01854) 612103.*
An interesting building with great atmosphere, incorporating a formal restaurant, self-service restaurant, bars and bookshop, as well as rooms above. Imaginative menus at various prices. ⚬ ⚬ *entire premises.* 🍷
AE DC MC V

For key to symbols see back flap

SPECIAL INTERESTS AND OUTDOOR ACTIVITIES

SCOTLAND MAY NOT be able to guarantee sunshine or offer beach culture, but its popularity as a holiday destination is due in no small part to its opportunities for outdoor activities, as well as cultural pursuits. Over the years, the tourist industry has matured to occupy an important role in the Scottish economy, and local businesses have become adept at providing visitors with

A lone piper of the Highlands

what they are looking for. That could be playing golf by the sea, fishing on the Tweed, cruising to see whales off the west coast during the summer, skiing in the Cairngorms in winter, eating fresh oysters at a lochside restaurant or searching for information on ancestors who left the country 200 years ago. Facilities for all kinds of activities have never been better, and this section outlines some of the best.

Searching for records of ancestors, Edinburgh

TRACING GENEALOGY

FROM THE TIME of the infamous Clearances of the 18th century onwards *(see p150)*, Scots have emigrated to Australia, Canada, New Zealand, South Africa, the US and elsewhere in search of an easier life. There are now millions of foreign nationals who can trace their heritage back to Scotland, and uncovering family history is a popular reason for visiting the country.

Professional genealogists can be commissioned, but those interested in conducting investigations themselves should try the **General Register Office for Scotland** (which has records of births, deaths and marriages dating from the 1500s), the **Scottish Genealogy Society** or the **Scottish Record Office**, all found in Edinburgh.

GAELIC STUDIES

THE NORTHWEST of Scotland is the heartland for the Gaelic language. Historically, this was a Celtic language that spread

from mainland Europe to Ireland in the 4th century BC, and later into Scotland where it became the national language. By the 18th century, however, under English rule, Gaelic had become identified with a rebellious clan system that was persecuted after the Jacobite rising of 1745 *(see p45)*. It was marginalized and suffered a decline.

A recent renaissance aims to revive this once-dominant culture with Gaelic broadcasts and by teaching it to children. **An Comunn Gaidhealach**, Scotland's official Gaelic society, organizes the annual Royal National Mod *(see p38)*, a performing arts competition. Other Gaelic societies are **Comunn An Luchd Ionnsachaidh**

and **Comunn na Gàidhlig**. **Sabhal Mor Ostaig**, a college on the Isle of Skye, runs short Gaelic courses for visitors.

FOOD AND DRINK TOURS

SCOTLAND HAS a justified reputation for fine produce, and recent years have seen an upsurge in the number of noteworthy restaurants in Edinburgh and Glasgow. Indeed, Edinburgh has established itself as the number two city for eating out in the British Isles, after London.

One way of sampling Scottish cuisine is to book a holiday through **Connoisseurs Scotland**, which arranges stays at country house hotels with a reputation for top-class cooking, such as the Crinan Hotel in Argyll, or Gleneagles.

The **Scotch Malt Whisky Society** has information for lovers of this spirit. Distilleries are a popular attraction *(see pp30–31 and p144)*, with

Learning about whisky, the "water of life", at a Speyside distillery

names such as **Glenfiddich Distillery** operating tours.

The production of cask-conditioned beers is explained at Edinburgh's **Caledonian Brewery**. An exhibition at **Inverawe Smokehouses**, near Taynuilt in the Highlands, shows the techniques used in smoking fish such as salmon.

VIEWING WILDLIFE

IN COMPARISON with much of the rest of the British Isles, Scotland still has large areas of moor and mountain wilderness and a long, relatively undeveloped coastline that supports a range of animals

Sighting a porpoise as it breaks the calm surface of a sea loch

Walkers on the lookout for red deer and birds of prey at Glen Coe

(see pp16–17). In the mountains near Aviemore, rangers from the **Cairngorm Reindeer Centre** take parties of people on to the mountain to walk among a herd of reindeer.

A convenient way to see the abundant sealife is on a boat trip run by **Maid of the Forth Cruises**, which operates from South Queensferry on the Forth near Edinburgh – dolphins and common seals are resident in these waters. More adventurous are the trips in search of whales offered by **Sea Life Cruises** from the Isle of Mull, but even a casual tourist in the Highlands can spot birds of

prey, otters in the lochs and herds of red deer on the mountainsides. With a large share of Britain's resident and visiting birds, Scotland is also home to a number of important bird sanctuaries, the most celebrated being Handa Island off Scourie on the far northwest coast *(see p157)*. St Abb's Head *(see p84)* east of Edinburgh and Baron's Haugh near Motherwell (on the outskirts of Glasgow) are nearer the cities.

Many wildlife tours are small-scale private businesses that operate according to seasonal and daily demand, so always check the details with the local tourist information offices.

DIRECTORY

TRACING GENEALOGY

General Register Office for Scotland
New Register House,
3 West Register St,
Edinburgh,
EH1 3YT.
(*(0131) 334 0380.*
www.origins.net

Scottish Genealogy Society
15 Victoria Terrace,
Edinburgh, EH1 2JL.
(*(0131) 220 3677.*

Scottish Record Office
General Register House,
2 Princes St,
Edinburgh,
EH1 3YY.
(*(0131) 535 1314.*

GAELIC STUDIES

An Comunn Gaidhealach
109 Church St,
Inverness, IV1 1EY.
(*(01463) 231226.*

Comunn An Luchd Ionnsachaidh
62 High St,
Invergordon, IV18 0DH.
(*(01349) 854848.*

Comunn na Gàidhlig
5 Mitchell's Lane,
Inverness, IV2 3HQ.
(*(01463) 234138.*

Sabhal Mor Ostaig
Teangue, Sleat,
Isle of Skye,
IV44 8RQ.
(*(01471) 844373.*

FOOD AND DRINK TOURS

Caledonian Brewery
42 Slateford Rd,
Edinburgh, EH11 1PH.
(*(0131) 337 1286.*

Connoisseurs Scotland
54 Manor Place,
Edinburgh, EH3 7EH.
(Contact by letter only.)

Glenfiddich Distillery
Dufftown,
Keith, Banffshire,
AB55 4DH.
(*(01340) 820373.*

Inverawe Smokehouses
Taynuilt,
Argyll, PA35 1HU.
(*(01866) 822446.*

Scotch Malt Whisky Society
The Vaults,
87 Giles St,
Edinburgh, EH6 6BZ.
(*(0131) 554 3451.*
www.smws.co.uk

VIEWING WILDLIFE

Cairngorm Reindeer Centre
Aviemore,
PH22 1QU.
(*(01479) 861228.*

Maid of the Forth Cruises
Hawes Pier,
South Queensferry, EH30.
(*(0131) 331 4857.*

Sea Life Cruises
Tobermory,
Isle of Mull, PA75 6QA.
(*(01688) 302787.*

Outdoor Activities at a Glance

O NLY A HANDFUL OF INLAND LOCHS and coastal waters have been exploited by commercial boating and watersports companies, though it is possible to use private vessels on many minor lochs in wilderness areas. Likewise, organized skiing is confined to just five centres. Of the country's several hundred golf courses, most are concentrated in Central and Southern Scotland. This map plots the main centres for various popular activities. For further information about particular sports across Scotland, see pages 188–95.

Handa Island, off the far northwest coast, is one of a number of seabird reserves.

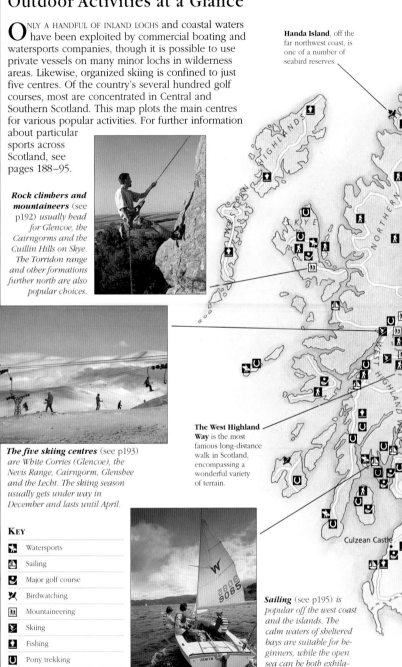

Rock climbers and mountaineers (see p192) *usually head for Glencoe, the Cairngorms and the Cuillin Hills on Skye. The Torridon range and other formations further north are also popular choices.*

The five skiing centres (see p193) *are White Corries (Glencoe), the Nevis Range, Cairngorm, Glenshee and the Lecht. The skiing season usually gets under way in December and lasts until April.*

The West Highland Way is the most famous long-distance walk in Scotland, encompassing a wonderful variety of terrain.

Culzean Castle

KEY

🏄	Watersports
⛵	Sailing
⛳	Major golf course
🦅	Birdwatching
🧗	Mountaineering
🎿	Skiing
🎣	Fishing
🐴	Pony trekking
🚶	Major walking area
▪ ▪	Long-distance walk route

Sailing (see p195) *is popular off the west coast and the islands. The calm waters of sheltered bays are suitable for beginners, while the open sea can be both exhilarating and treacherous. Inland, Loch Ness offers sailing opportunities.*

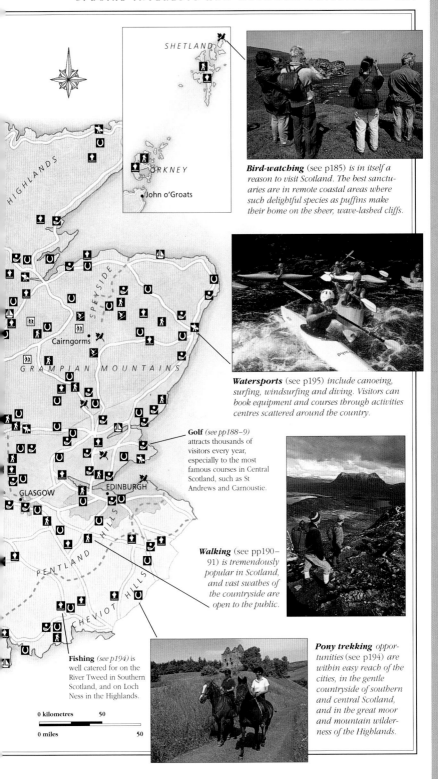

Bird-watching (see p185) *is in itself a reason to visit Scotland. The best sanctuaries are in remote coastal areas where such delightful species as puffins make their home on the sheer, wave-lashed cliffs.*

Watersports (see p195) *include canoeing, surfing, windsurfing and diving. Visitors can book equipment and courses through activities centres scattered around the country.*

Golf *(see pp188–9)* attracts thousands of visitors every year, especially to the most famous courses in Central Scotland, such as St Andrews and Carnoustie.

Walking *(see pp190– 91) is tremendously popular in Scotland, and vast swathes of the countryside are open to the public.*

Fishing *(see p194)* is well catered for on the River Tweed in Southern Scotland, and on Loch Ness in the Highlands.

Pony trekking *opportunities (see p194) are within easy reach of the cities, in the gentle countryside of southern and central Scotland, and in the great moor and mountain wilderness of the Highlands.*

SHETLAND

ORKNEY

• John o'Groats

HIGHLANDS

SPEYSIDE

Cairngorms •

GRAMPIAN MOUNTAINS

GLASGOW

EDINBURGH

PENTLAND HILLS

CHEVIOT HILLS

0 kilometres   50

0 miles   50

Golf in Scotland

THE ANCIENT GAME OF GOLF is synonymous with Scotland and has been played here for hundreds of years. One of the most popular sports in the country, it is enjoyed by people of all ages and capabilities. Wherever you choose to stay, there will always be a golf course within easy reach, from the legendary championship courses

British-made golf tees

to the smaller, intimate locations set amid dramatic countryside or along the coast. Few other countries can rival Scotland in the number, quality and variety of courses. Golf, it is believed by the Scots, is a game for everyone to enjoy.

EARLY HISTORY

VARIATIONS ON the game of golf as we know it today were being played across Europe as long ago as the 14th century, and possibly even in Roman times. Yet it is the Scottish who must be credited with establishing the official game, and encouraging its development across the world. It was in

Duncan Forbes

Scotland that the passion for golf was born. By the middle of the 16th century, the game had become a popular pastime at the highest levels of society – James VI himself was a keen player, as was his mother, Mary, Queen of Scots.

In the late 1800s, wealthy middle-class Englishmen began to follow the example of the Royal Family by taking their holidays in Scotland.

The expansion of the railway system at this time allowed people to get to the seaside links, and the English were so infatuated with the game of golf that they took it home with them. In 1744 the Gentlemen Golfers of Leith, led by Duncan Forbes, drew up the first *Articles & Laws in Playing at Golf*. Although later revised and updated, these original rules, set down by the Scottish professionals of the time, formed the framework for the modern game of golf.

TOOLS OF THE TRADE

THE SCOTTISH influence on golf was not to end there. Many of the professionals playing at the time were also skilled carpenters, instrumental in developing the clubs and balls used in the game. Willie Park Senior was a master clubmaker, and winner of the first Scottish Open in 1860, and Old Tom Morris became a legend in the game for both his playing and craftsmanship. In the days before machinery, the wooden clubs were made entirely by hand.

A scenic view of Gleneagles, one of Scotland's championship courses

The earliest irons were also fashioned by hand, followed by aluminium-headed clubs that differ very little from clubs today. The "guttie" ball was invented in 1848, replacing the expensive and easily damaged "feathery", thus making the game more affordable. The modern, rubber-core ball in use today appeared at the beginning of the 20th century.

THE COURSES

MANY OF Scotland's courses are steeped in history and tradition, such as the championship courses of St Andrews and Carnoustie. But an increasing number of newer courses now offer the same standard of play and variety of landscape. There is something for everyone, and if your purse does not stretch to a round at a top professional course like Gleneagles, there are plenty of smaller, more affordable options, each with their own character, often with stunning views of the coastline.

Some clubs offer accommodation but, if not, there are always hotels and bed-and-breakfasts nearby. Caddy cars (golf carts) and catering facilities are common in all clubs. Nearly all the courses are 18-hole, and are open to visitors, but be aware of occasional restrictions (Royal Troon does not allow ladies to play on the championship courses, for example). The chart shows some of the many courses available. Map references pertain to the map on the inside back cover.

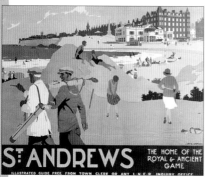

St ANDREWS

THE HOME OF THE ROYAL & ANCIENT GAME

ILLUSTRATED GUIDE FREE FROM TOWN CLERK OR ANY L·N·E·R INQUIRY OFFICE

An old railway poster illustrating the lure of St Andrews as a paradise for golfing enthusiasts

Price categories based on the cost of a round of golf on a weekday (weekends may be more expensive):

£ £10–£15
££ £15–£20
£££ £20–£30
££££ £30–£45
£££££ over £45.

PAY PER ROUND
It is possible to pay for a single round.

PAY PER DAY
It is possible to pay for a whole day's golf. Prices shown represent day rates only if no round rate is available.

ENTRY RESTRICTIONS
There are either restrictions on playing at certain times or special entry requirements – telephone ahead for details.

COASTAL VIEW
The course is situated on the coast with views of the sea.

Course	Price	Pay Per Round	Pay Per Day	Entry Restrictions	Coastal View
ABERDOUR: *Aberdour Golf Club* Seaside Place, Aberdour, Fife. **Map** D4. (01383) 860256.	££	●	■	●	■
ARBROATH: *Arbroath Artisan Golf Club* Elliot, Near Arbroath, Angus. **Map** E3. (01241) 875837.	££	●	■	●	■
AUCHTERARDER: *Gleneagles Hotel Golf Courses* The Gleneagles Hotel, Auchterarder, Perthshire. **Map** D4. (01764) 663543.	£££££	●	■		
CARNOUSTIE: *Carnoustie Golf Club* 3 Links Parade, Carnoustie, Angus. **Map** E4. (01241) 852480.	£££££	●	■	●	■
CRAIGSTON: *Cochrane Castle Golf Club* Craigston, Johnstone, Renfrewshire. **Map** C4. (01505) 320146.	££	●	■	●	
CRUDEN BAY: *Cruden Bay Golf Club* Aulton Road, Cruden Bay, Aberdeenshire. **Map** E2. (01779) 812285.	££££	●	■	●	■
DORNOCH: *Royal Dornoch Golf Club* Golf Road, Dornoch, Sutherland. **Map** D2. (01862) 810219.	£££££	●		●	■
DUNFERMLINE: *Pitreavie Golf Club* Queensferry Road, Dunfermline, Fife. **Map** D4. (01383) 722591.	££	●	■		
EDINBURGH: *Merchants of Edinburgh Golf Club* 10 Craighill Gardens, Edinburgh. **Map** D4. (0131) 447 1219.	££	●	■	●	
GLASGOW: *Haggs Castle Golf Club* 70 Dumbreck Road, Glasgow. **Map** D4. (0141) 427 1157.	£££	●	■	●	
KINROSS: *Green Hotel Golf Courses* Green Hotel, Kinross, Kinross-shire. **Map** D4. (01577) 863407.	££	●	■		
KIRKCALDY: *Kirkcaldy Golf Club* Balwearie Road, Kirkcaldy, Fife. **Map** D4. (01592) 203258.	££	●	■		■
LAMLASH: *Lamlash Golf Club* Lamlash, Isle of Arran. **Map** C5. (01770) 600196.	££		■		■
LARGS: *Largs Golf Club* Irvine Road, Largs, Ayrshire. **Map** C4. (01475) 673594.	£££	●	■		■
MILLPORT: *Millport Golf Club* Golf Road, Millport, Isle of Cumbrae. **Map** C4. (01475) 530311.	££	●	■		■
NAIRN: *Nairn Golf Club* Seabank Road, Nairn, Nairnshire. **Map** D2. (01667) 453208.	£££££	●		●	■
NEWMACHAR: *Newmachar Golf Club* Swailend, Newmachar, Aberdeenshire. **Map** E2. (01651) 863002.	£££	●	■	●	
ST ANDREWS: *St Andrews Links* Pilmour Cottage, St Andrews, Fife. **Map** E4. (01334) 466666.	£££££	●		●	■
SCONE: *Murrayshall Golf Club* Murrayshall Hotel & Golf Course, Scone, Perthshire. **Map** D4. (01738) 551171.	£££	●	■		
SKEABOST: *Skeabost Golf Club* Skeabost House Hotel, Skeabost Bridge, Isle of Skye. **Map** B2. (01470) 532215.	£		■		■
STONEHAVEN: *Stonehaven Golf Club* Cowie, Stonehaven, Kincardineshire. **Map** E3. (01569) 762124.	££		■		■
TROON: *Royal Troon Golf Club Old Course* Craigend Road, Troon, Ayrshire. **Map** C5. (01292) 311555.	£££££		■	●	■

Walking in Scotland

Thermos flask

IT CAN TRULY BE SAID that Scotland is a paradise for walkers. The scenery is superb without being overwhelming, and the variety of terrain encompasses everything from craggy mountains to gentle river valleys, not to mention a magnificent coastline. In recent years there has been an increase in the number of walks available to the public. The local tourist information centre is always a good first port of call if you are looking for advice or suggested routes. Whether you wish to walk for an hour or spend a day on the trail, you will find that Scotland can satisfy all of your walking needs.

Walking boots

not on rough ground where you may need ankle support. Lightweight walking boots are suitable for most seasons.

WALKING OPPORTUNITIES

THIS SECTION deals with low-level walking; mountain activities are covered on pages 192–3, and you can also obtain information from the **Mountaineering Council of Scotland**.

In recent years, greatly improved path networks have been developed, some through the national **Paths for All Partnership**. The networks provide excellent, safe walking opportunities for visitors. Some of the best networks are in the Borders and around Galloway, in Perthshire (around Dunkeld and Pitlochry), in Aberdeenshire (around Huntly), at Braemar and on the island of Bute.

Local authorities and other agencies have created paths and published walking guides for remote areas, such as Wester Ross, the Western Isles, Orkney and Shetland. Some of these walks tie in with ferry services. Most have a cultural or natural history theme, or incorporate a castle, waterfall or other place of interest. The walks are generally from 6 to 12 km (4 to 7 miles) in length.

Long-distance trail signpost for walkers in the Spey river valley

RIGHTS OF WAY

IN SCOTLAND there are public rights of way, but they are not always well defined and some may not be marked on the Ordnance Survey maps. Rights of way maps are held by local councils and also by the **Scottish Rights of Way Society**, based in Edinburgh.

Generally speaking, the advice given in local guidebooks can be relied upon. These books will direct you to easily walkable routes, many of which are signposted. Even if they are not formal rights of way, and thus not marked on any maps, they will have been negotiated with the farmer or landowner. Guidebooks and maps are available from **The Stationery Office** in Edinburgh and **John Smith and Sons** in Glasgow.

Access in some areas may be limited during the stalking season (August to October), but on any areas owned by the **National Trust for Scotland** there is open access all year.

CLOTHING AND EQUIPMENT

THE WEATHER in Scotland is fickle. It can snow in June or be balmy in February, and conditions are liable to change rapidly. This makes selecting the right clothing and equipment tricky. Even in summer, you should take a waterproof jacket if venturing far from shelter. When going on a day walk, take waterproof trousers and a fleece or warm sweater.

The art of being comfortable is to make your clothing adaptable; several thin layers are better than one thick one. Head covering is worth considering – a cap for sunny days or a warmer hat for cold days.

For any walk of more than a couple of hours' duration, take a drink and snack. If you are going to be out all day, take energy foods and liquids.

Good footwear is essential. Countryside walks generally demand strong shoes or boots. Sturdy trainers can be worn on roads or firm tracks, but

Summer walking in Glen Etive

Above the clouds in Knoydart, looking to the Cuillin Hills on Skye

Tourist information centres are good starting places for more details, or you can contact the **Scottish Tourist Board** to obtain their *Walk Scotland* brochure, which describes walks in all parts of Scotland. Their brochure also lists walking festivals. These events, that last up to a week, offer a wide range of guided walks along with a programme of evening entertainment. The first such festival, held in the Borders, started in 1995. Others are now held in the Highlands, Deeside and Perthshire, with more starting up each year.

Compass of the type commonly used by walkers

For information on organized walks, contact the **Ramblers Association Scotland**. There are also hundreds of miles of forest trails and walks across the country. The **Forestry Commission** can provide you with general information.

Longer low-level routes being developed include the Fife Coastal Path, the Clyde Walkway and the Speyside Way extension to Aviemore. All of these can easily be sampled as day walks.

Spring and autumn are especially lovely times of the year for walking in Scotland. The colouring is superb, and there is often a wider choice of accommodation available.

LONG-DISTANCE WALKS

SCOTLAND HAS relatively few formal long-distance routes, though the potential for making up your own is limitless. The three "official" routes are the 152-km (95-mile) West Highland Way from Glasgow to Fort William, the 340-km (211-mile) Southern Upland Way from Portpatrick to Cockburnspath, and the 84-km (52-mile) Speyside Way from Spey Bay to Tomintoul.

Other routes developed by local authorities include the 100-km (62-mile) St Cuthbert's Way from Melrose to Lindisfarne, and the Fife Coastal Path from Inverkeithing to Crail (plans are underway for it to extend to Dundee).

The three principal routes are shown on the activities map *(see pp186–7)*. For information about them, and others being developed, contact **Scottish Natural Heritage** and local tourist information centres.

Surveying the scenery on a wintry day in the Cairngorms

Activities in the Mountains

Detailed area maps

ALTHOUGH SCOTLAND'S highest mountains rise to little over 1,200 m (4,000 ft), they offer a true challenge to the hill walker and rock climber alike. Noted worldwide for their beauty of form and variety of character, the mountains of Scotland command respect among all mountaineers, not least because the climate is so variable. During the winter, conditions can be arctic. Long days in the hills offer a sense of satisfaction and refreshment that is highly valued as a contrast to the hectic pace of modern life.

Hard hats and safety ropes – vital equipment for rock climbing

SAFETY IN THE MOUNTAINS

THE MOUNTAINS of Scotland demand respect at any time of the year, and this means being properly prepared. You should always take with you full waterproofs, warm clothes (including hat and gloves), and food and drink. Take a map and compass and know how to use them. Good boots are essential. Winter mountaineering demands knowledge of ice-axe and crampon techniques. **Glenmore Lodge** in Aviemore is a good centre offering courses in skiing, hill craft and mountaineering.

MOUNTAINEERING IN SCOTLAND

RECREATION IN the mountains takes several forms. Many people aim for the higher hills, known as "Munros" and "Corbetts". These vary in character from the rounded heathery domes of the Monadhliath or the Southern Uplands to the steep, craggy eminences of the west, many of which command superb sea views. Narrow ridges such as the Aonach Eagach above Glencoe, and the peerless Cuillins of Skye, offer exhilarating sport and a special challenge. Given the right conditions, most hills can be climbed in a day, but more remote peaks may demand an overnight camp, or a stay in one of the simple huts known as a "bothy". Winter mountaineering needs extra skills but it also reaps the fantastic reward of the most breathtaking scenery.

Rock and ice climbing in Scotland has a long and distinguished history stretching back over a century. The main climbing areas, including Glencoe, the Cairngorms and Skye, have provided tough training grounds for many climbers who later gained world renown. All year the huge northern faces of Ben Nevis *(see p135)* offer a multitude of climbs at all levels. New areas, including the far northwest and the islands, have been developed more recently, as have particular disciplines such as sea-stack climbing. Techniques are being continually extended and skills refined, so that ever tougher routes can be completed. Ice climbs on the hills

A rucksack for carrying provisions

of Scotland are some of the most demanding in Europe. In recent years, however, the sustained hard frosts needed for good ice climbing have been rare. Nonetheless, winter climbing still thrives, and the only "closed season" on Scotland's mountains is the short period between mid-August and late October, when restrictions apply in certain areas during the stag shooting season. *Heading for the Scottish Hills*, published jointly by the **Mountaineering Council of Scotland** and the Scottish Landowners Federation, gives estate maps and telephone numbers to call for local advice. See the Directory opposite for details of the **Hillphones** message system.

MUNROS AND CORBETTS

SCOTTISH MOUNTAINS rising just above 900 m (3,000 ft) are often called "Munros" after Sir Hugh Munro, first president of the Scottish Mountaineering Club (SMC). In 1891 Munro published the first comprehensive list of mountains fulfilling

Rock climbers ascending Polldubh, Glen Nevis

Enjoying a superb mountain panorama in the northern Highlands

this criterion. The list has been maintained by the SMC ever since, and the hills are now officially classed as Munros. Normally, the principal summits on a hill are Munros; the lesser summits are called "Tops". Revised several times, the list now totals 284 Munros.

The first known Munroist was the Rev AE Robertson in 1901. He finished his tour of the Munros on Meall Dearg, above Glencoe, and it is recorded that he kissed the cairn before kissing his wife, such was his enthusiasm as the first of many dedicated Munroists.

In the 1920s, J Rooke Corbett published a list of the summits that measured 760–915 m (2,500–3,000 ft). These 221 "Corbetts", as they became known, have a clearer definition than the Munros – they must be single summits.

A third list is available, of summits of 610–760 m (2,000–2,500 ft) called "Grahams". All summits in Scotland over 610 m have now been categorized and published. The hills are described, with ascent routes, in the SMC guide *The Munros and the Corbetts, and other Scottish Hills*, and in *The Munros Almanac* and *The Corbetts Almanac*. The third set is listed in a publication called *The Grahams*.

SKIING IN SCOTLAND

THERE ARE FIVE ski centres in Scotland: **White Corries** at Glencoe, **Nevis Range** *(see pp135)*, **The Lecht**, **Cairngorm** *(see pp140–41)* and **Glenshee**. The Lecht tends to have the gentlest runs, while White Corries has the steepest.

These two centres are more informal than the others. Nevis Range, Glenshee and Cairngorm offer good facilities and runs for skiers of all abilities, including nursery slopes.

Ski centres are usually open from December to April, depending on the amount of snow cover. Unfortunately, snow is not wholly reliable in Scotland but when it does snow, the skiing is exhilarating. Hotels and guesthouses in the ski areas offer weekend and midweek packages, and there are ski schools in all the areas. The best advice is to keep an eye on the weather and take your chance as it arises.

Cross-country or Nordic skiing is a popular, informal sport in Scotland. Given good snow cover, there are many suitable areas, ranging from the Southern Uplands to the hills of the north and west, as well as hundreds of miles of forest trails all over Scotland.

Downhill skiing on the Scottish slopes

DIRECTORY

SAFETY IN THE MOUNTAINS

Scotland has a good network of volunteer mountain rescue teams. Calls for rescue should be made to the police on **999**.

Weather Forecasts
Highlands & Northwest
☎ *(0891) 112235.*

Grampians & Cairngorms
☎ *(0891) 112236.*

Argyll, Perthshire & Southern Uplands
☎ *(0891) 112237.*

Glenmore Lodge
Aviemore,
Inverness-shire PH22 1QU.
☎ *(01479) 861256.*
FAX *(01479) 861212.*

Mountaineering Council of Scotland
4a St Catherine's Rd,
Perth PH1 5SE.
☎ *(01738) 638227.*
FAX *(01738) 442095.*

Hillphones
Operating in certain areas, a recorded message, updated daily, gives information on which walking routes are affected by stag shooting and stalking, with a forecast of stalking activity over the next few days.

The service operates from 1 August to 20 October, and is organized by the Mountaineering Council of Scotland, Scottish Natural Heritage and all participating estates. It covers the following areas:

Drumochter
☎ *(01528) 522200.*

Glen Dochart/Glen Lochay
☎ *(01567) 820886.*

Glen Shee
☎ *(01250) 885288.*

Grey Corries/Mamores
☎ *(01855) 831511.*

North Arran
☎ *(01770) 302363.*

South Glen Shiel
☎ *(01599) 511425.*

SKI CENTRES

www.ski.scotland.net

Cairngorm
Aviemore, Inverness-shire.
☎ *(01479) 861261.*

Glenshee
Cairnwell, Aberdeenshire.
☎ *(013397) 41320.*

The Lecht
Strathdon, Aberdeenshire.
☎ *(01975) 651440.*

Nevis Range
Torlundy, Inverness-shire.
☎ *(01397) 705825.*

White Corries
King's House,
Glencoe, Argyll.
☎ *(01855) 851226.*

Other Outdoor Activities

S COTLAND HAS A FEW surprises up its
sleeve for people who still associate
the country with old-fashioned tourist
images. While traditional pursuits such
as deerstalking or salmon fishing still
thrive, they are now complemented by a
wide range of more contemporary sports
including mountain biking and even surf-

**Dunkeld
fishing fly**

ing. Flanked by the North Sea and the Atlantic, Scotland
has ample water for sailing, windsurfing and fishing,
while horse riding and cycling present excellent ways
to explore the country's varied and dramatic landscapes.

**Splendid catch of the day from the
River Tweed, southern Scotland**

Mountain biking on low-level tracks

CYCLING AND MOUNTAIN BIKING

C YCLING AROUND Scotland is
one of the best ways to
view the country. The trails of
the Highlands are near perfect
mountain bike territory and a
lot of the forest road network
has been opened to mountain
bikers – contact the **Forest
Enterprise** for details. There
is also an expanding national
cycle path network to explore.

Edinburgh has a system of
cycle paths on old train tracks.
**Edinburgh Central Cycle
Hire** is just one of many hire
shops in the city. The **Scottish
Cyclists Union** has information on cycling events and
races in and around the capital.

A *Cycling in Scotland* book-
let is available from tourist
offices. For details of cycling
trips in Scotland, contact the
Cyclists Touring Club and
Scottish Cycling Holidays.

FISHING

A LTHOUGH SCOTLAND is most
associated with salmon
fishing, there are opportunities
for sea angling, coarse fishing,
and game fishing for trout too.

The **Salmon and
Trout Association**
has information on
game fishing – the
season runs from
mid-February to the
end of October. For
coarse fishing and
sea angling a land-
owner's permission
is required before
casting off. The
**Scottish Federa-
tion for Coarse
Angling** and
**Scottish Federation of Sea
Anglers** provide all the nec-
essary information. Contact the
**Scottish Anglers National
Association** for general advice.

HUNTING

T HE TRADITION of recreational
hunting can be traced back
to the mid-1800s, when Queen
Victoria and Prince Albert set
up residence in Balmoral on
Deeside. It became fashionable
for British aristocrats to spend
the autumn shooting in Scotland. Large parts of the Highlands became sporting estates.

Scotland is recognized as providing Europe's best game-
shooting and deerstalking. Red
deer and grouse are plentiful,
while many estuaries and firths
are wintering grounds for birds.

Over the last 30 years or so,
hunting in Scotland has also
attracted overseas visitors. For
information on gun licensing
and where to shoot, contact
the **British Association for
Shooting and Conservation.**

PONY TREKKING AND HORSE RIDING

T HERE ARE MORE than 60 trekking and riding centres
across Scotland, catering to a
wide range of abilities, including trips deep into the Highlands for experienced riders.
Some offer accommodation,
tuition and trail riding, others
provide trekking by the hour.
The **Trekking and Riding
Society of Scotland** has a
complete list of all the centres.

Pentland Hills Icelandics,
south of Edinburgh, offers
rides on rare Icelandic ponies.
On Deeside is the **Glen Tanar
Equestrian Centre**, and visitors to the Western Isles should
try **Uig Trekking** on Skye.

Visitors taking in the Scottish scenery on horseback

SAILING

SCOTLAND IS A country of firths, islands and sea lochs, and the best way to explore them is by boat. You do not necessarily have to be a skilled sailor to do this, as some companies now offer supervised yachting holidays for novices. Visitors also have the option of chartering a yacht. Centres such as **Port Edgar Marina** near Edinburgh or the **Scottish National Watersports Centre** on Cumbrae in the Firth of Clyde offer tuition for beginners, while experienced sailors will find serviced moorings for their own craft in beauty spots up and down the west coast and among the islands.

Kayaking on Loch Eil in the shadow of magnificent Ben Nevis

Wooden sailboat in the Sound of Sleat, just off the Isle of Skye

WATERSPORTS

SURFING IS NOT an activity normally associated with Scotland, but a good wetsuit and a sense of determination are all that is needed. Pease Bay in East Lothian is a popular spot, as are some north coast locations such as Dunnet Bay by Thurso and the northwest tip of Lewis. September to October is the best time for the waves. Windsurfing is also a favourite activity. The **Scottish Windsurfing Association** has information on sites across the country. The top venue is the remote island of Tiree, which hosts a major windsurfing event in October every year.

Canoes and kayaks can be rented on lochs and in sheltered bays. The **Scottish Water Ski Centre** has details on the best places to water ski.

DIRECTORY	FISHING	HUNTING	Uig Trekking

Uig Trekking
Uig Hotel,
Uig, Isle of Skye
IV51 9YE.
(*(01470) 542205.*

CYCLING AND MOUNTAIN BIKING

Cyclists Touring Club
69 Meadrow, Godalming,
Surrey GU7 3HS,
England.
(*(01483) 417217.*

Edinburgh Central Cycle Hire
13 Lochrin Place,
Edinburgh EH3 9QX.
(*(0131) 228 6333.*

Forest Enterprise
21 Church St,
Inverness IV1 1EL.
(*(01463) 232811.*

Scottish Cycling Holidays
87 Perth St, Blairgowrie,
Perthshire PH10 6DT.
(*(01250) 876100.*

Scottish Cyclists Union
The Velodrome,
Meadowbank Sports
Centre, 139 London Road,
Edinburgh EH7 6AD.
(*(0131) 652 0187.*

FISHING

Salmon & Trout Association
The Lagg,
Aberfeldy,
Perthshire PH15 2EE.
(*(01887) 829238.*

Scottish Anglers National Association
Caledonia House,
South Gyle,
Edinburgh EH12 9DQ.
(*(0131) 339 8808.*

Scottish Federation for Coarse Angling
8 Longbraes Gardens,
Kirkcaldy,
Fife KY2 5YJ.
(*(01592) 642242.*

Scottish Federation of Sea Anglers
Caledonia House,
South Gyle,
Edinburgh EH12 9DQ.
(*(0131) 317 7192.*

HUNTING

British Association for Shooting and Conservation (Scotland)
Trochry,
Dunkeld,
Perthshire PH8 0DY.
(*(01350) 723226.*

PONY TREKKING AND HORSE RIDING

Glen Tanar Equestrian Centre
Glen Tanar Estate,
Aboyne,
Royal Deeside AB34 5EU.
(*(01339) 886448.*

Pentland Hills Icelandics
Rodgersrigg Farm,
Carlops,
Midlothian EH26 9NG.
(*(01968) 661095.*

Trekking and Riding Society of Scotland (TRSS)
Boreland, Fearnan,
Aberfeldy,
Perthshire PH15 2PG.
(*(01887) 830274.*

SAILING

Port Edgar Marina
South Queensferry,
Edinburgh
EH30 9SQ.
(*(0131) 331 3330.*

Scottish National Watersports Centre
Cumbrae KA28 0HQ.
(*(01475) 530757.*

WATERSPORTS

Scottish Water Ski Centre
Town Loch,
Townhill,
Dunfermline KY12 0HT.
(*(01383) 620123.*

Scottish Windsurfing Association
Caledonia House,
South Gyle,
Edinburgh EH12 9DQ.
(*(0131) 317 7388.*

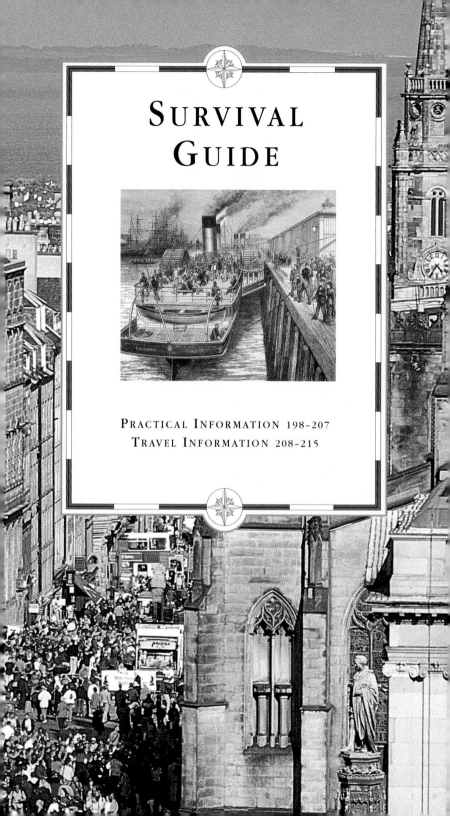

SURVIVAL
GUIDE

PRACTICAL INFORMATION 198-207
TRAVEL INFORMATION 208-215

PRACTICAL INFORMATION

To ENJOY SCOTLAND FULLY, it is best to know something about the workings of everyday life. The range of facilities for tourists in Scotland has never been better – indeed tourism has become a major part of the country's economy – and the Scottish Tourist Board is continually promoting better services around the country. This chapter gives advice about when best to visit Scotland; customs and immigration requirements; where to find tourist

Logo of the Scottish Tourist Board

information; what to do or whom to turn to if things go wrong; banking and communications; and how to get around the country by public and private transport, including ferries to the islands.

Whether or not you find Scotland an expensive country will depend on the exchange rate between the pound and your own currency. Visitors travelling to Edinburgh from London will find that costs are generally lower in Scotland's capital.

Visitors' Centre in Callander, at the heart of the Trossachs

WHEN TO VISIT

SCOTLAND'S CLIMATE is highly unpredictable *(see pp36–9)*. Weather patterns shift all the time, and the climate can differ widely in places only a short distance apart. Whatever your destination, always pack a mixture of warm and cool clothes and carry an umbrella.

Scotland's towns and cities are all-year destinations, but many attractions open only between Easter and October. The main family holiday months, July and August, and public holidays *(see p38)* are always busy. Hotels are crammed at Christmas and New Year, particularly in Edinburgh for the Hogmanay street party *(see p39)*. Spring and autumn offer a moderate climate and a lack

of crowds. Whatever the time of year, it is wise to get an up-to-date weather forecast before you set off on foot to remote hills or mountainous locations. Walkers and climbers can be surprised by the weather, and the Mountain Rescue services are frequently called out due to unexpectedly severe conditions. Weather reports are given on television and radio, in newspapers and by a weather phone service *(see p193)*.

INSURANCE

IT IS SENSIBLE to take out travel insurance before travelling, to cover cancellation or curtailment of your holiday, theft or loss of money and possessions, and the cost of any medical treatment *(see p202)*. If your country has a reciprocal medical arrangement with the UK you can obtain free treatment under the National Health Service. Australia, New Zealand and everywhere in the European Union (EU) has this arrangement. North American health plans, and student identity cards may give some protection against incurred costs, but always check the small print.

If you want to drive a car in Scotland, it is advisable to take out fully comprehensive insurance. You must carry a valid driver's licence. If you are not an EU citizen, you must have an international driver's licence, available through the AAA for those in the US.

Sign for the Mountain Rescue

ADVANCE BOOKING

OUT OF SEASON, you should have few problems booking accommodation or transport at short notice, but in high season always try to book ahead if possible. Before travelling, contact the British Tourist Authority (BTA) in your country, or a travel agent, for advice and information.

CUSTOMS AND IMMIGRATION

A VALID PASSPORT is needed to enter the United Kingdom. Visitors from the European Union (EU), the United States, Canada, Australia and New Zealand do not require visas to enter the UK, nor any inoculations or vaccinations. Once within the UK, visitors are free to travel to and from Scotland, England, Wales and Northern Ireland without passing any other frontier formalities.

When you arrive at any international air or sea port in the UK, you will find separate queues at immigration control: one for EU nationals and several others for everyone else. Scotland is a member of the EU, which means that anyone arriving from an EU member country can pass through a blue channel. Random checks are still made, however, for illegal goods, especially drugs.

Standard tourist information sign

◁ **The busy Royal Mile in Edinburgh, with the Firth of Forth in the distance**

Travellers entering from outside the EU have to pass through the usual customs channels. Go through the green channel if you have nothing to declare over the customs allowances for overseas visitors, and the red channel if you have goods to declare. If you are unsure of importation restrictions, go through the red channel. Full details of these restrictions are available from HM Customs and Excise in London. Beware – never carry luggage or parcels through customs for someone else.

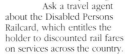

STB brochure

TOURIST INFORMATION

THERE ARE TWO centres of the Scottish Tourist Board (STB) in Scotland, one in Edinburgh and one in Inverness. The STB also has a base in central London. In addition to these, every region of Scotland has its own tourist board, providing information about local accommodation, entertainment and places of interest. Smaller, subsidiary tourist information offices can be found in many towns and public places, and at some of the principal locations of historical interest. Look out for the tourist information symbol, indicating an office. The **British Tourist Authority** operates offices overseas.

DISABLED TRAVELLERS

THE FACILITIES on offer in Scotland for disabled visitors are steadily improving. An increasing number of buildings now offer easy wheelchair access. This information is given in the headings for each entry throughout the guide. Given advance notice, ScotRail *(see p211),* ferry or coach (long-distance bus) staff will help any disabled passengers. Ask a travel agent about the Disabled Persons Railcard, which entitles the holder to discounted rail fares on services across the country.

Specialist tour operators, such as **Holiday Care Service**, cater for the physically handicapped visitor. You can contact them for details on (01293) 774535. **Hertz Rent A Car** offers hand-controlled vehicles without any extra cost *(see p215).* For permission to use any disabled parking space, you need to display a special sign in your car.

For general information on facilities for disabled travellers, contact **RADAR** on (0171) 250 3222. Visitors from the US can telephone the **Society for the Advancement of Travel for the Handicapped (SATH)** on (212) 447 7284 before leaving. They publish *ACCESS to Travel,* a magazine full of information.

Tobermory harbour on the Isle of Mull, popular with tourists

Glamis Castle, one of the castles charging admission to visitors

TRAVELLING WITH CHILDREN

PUBLIC HOLIDAYS and school holidays (mid-July–August) have most to offer in the way of children's entertainment. Many places have activities suitable for children over the Christmas period, particularly pantomimes. Discounts for children and family tickets are available for travel, theatre and other entertainments.

Choose accommodation that welcomes children (see pp164–73), or opt for self-catering (efficiency apartments). Many hotels provide baby-sitting or baby-listening services, and offer reductions or free accommodation for the very young.

Nowadays restaurants are better equipped for children; many provide highchairs and special menus (see pp174–83). Pubs often admit children, if accompanied by an adult. The legal drinking age is 18.

Playing with interactive exhibits at Edinburgh's Museum of Childhood

ADMISSION CHARGES

THESE VARY WIDELY, from a nominal fee to a more substantial charge for popular attractions. Reductions are often available for groups, senior citizens, children or students. The majority of local churches, museums and art galleries are free, unless a special exhibition is showing, but donations are often expected. Some attractions in Scotland are run privately, either as a commercial venture or on a charitable basis.

OPENING HOURS

MANY SHOPS in Scotland open on Sundays, particularly in the city centres. Monday to Friday hours are around 9:30am to 5:30pm, but shop hours do vary, opening late one evening a week – usually on a Thursday. Museums and art galleries generally open for fewer hours on Sundays, and in Glasgow many of the attractions close on Tuesdays. Most places close on public holidays, especially on Christmas Day and New Year's Day.

VAT AND REFUNDS

VALUE ADDED TAX (VAT) is charged at 17.5 per cent on most goods and services – exceptions include food, books and children's clothes. VAT can be redeemed by non-residents when leaving the UK. Refunds will be given if goods are faulty and are returned with the receipt as proof of purchase.

STUDENT TRAVELLERS

FULL-TIME STUDENTS who have an International Student Identity Card (ISIC) are often entitled to discounts on travel, sports facilities and entrance fees. North American students can also get medical cover but it may be very basic (see p202). ISIC cards are available from **STA Travel**, or the **National Union of Students**. Inexpensive accommodation is also available (out of term) at the university halls of residence in the main cities. This is a good way of staying in central locations when on a tight budget.

Student ISIC card

An **International Youth Hostel Federation** card enables you to stay in one of Scotland's many youth hostels. Contact the **Scottish Youth Hostels Association** direct.

The Edinburgh headquarters of the National Trust for Scotland

NATIONAL TRUST FOR SCOTLAND

MANY OF SCOTLAND'S historic buildings, parks, gardens, and vast tracts of countryside and coastline are cared for by the **National Trust for Scotland** (NTS). Entrance fees are often relatively high compared to fees at other sights, so if you wish to visit several NTS properties it may be worth taking out annual membership, which allows free access thereafter to all NTS properties. Beware, however, that many NTS properties close in the winter.

Typical newspaper stand, Glasgow

MEDIA

NATIONAL newspapers in Scotland fall into two categories: serious broadsheets, such as Edinburgh's *The Scotsman* or Glasgow's *The Herald*; and tabloids, heavy on gossip, such as *The Sun* or *The Daily Record*. Weekend newspapers, such as *Scotland on Sunday*, are more expensive than dailies, with supplements of all kinds, including sections on arts, restaurants, entertainment, travel and reviews.

Specialist periodicals can be bought from newsagents on just about every topic thinkable. There are a few foreign magazines and newspapers available in large towns, often at main train stations and in some of the larger book stores.

The BBC (British Broadcasting Corporation) operates two TV channels and produces some of the best television programmes in the world, without commercial breaks. The BBC's three main rivals are ITV, Channel 4 and Channel 5. The BBC owns a number of radio stations from the popular Radio One to the middle-brow Radio Four. There are many local Scottish radio stations.

ELECTRICITY

THE VOLTAGE IN Scotland is 220/240 AC, 50 Hz. The electrical plugs have three square pins and take fuses of 3, 5 and 13 amps. In order to use your foreign appliances, such as hair dryers, you will need an adaptor. Most hotel bathrooms have two-pronged sockets for electric shavers.

SMOKING AND ALCOHOL

IT IS NOW FORBIDDEN to smoke in many public places in Scotland. These include most public transport systems, taxis, some train stations, theatres and cinemas. The exception to the anti-smoking trend is pubs. ASH (Action on Smoking and Health) can give advice on smoke-free venues – call (0171) 935 3519. There is a general ban on drinking in public in Greater Glasgow and the Clyde Valley area. This ban is usually lifted for the New Year street party at Hogmanay (31 December).

CONVERSION CHART

Britain is officially metricated in line with the rest of Europe, but imperial measures are still in common usage, including road distances (measured in miles). Imperial pints and gallons are 20 per cent larger than US measures.

Imperial to metric
1 inch = 2.5 centimetres
1 foot = 30 centimetres
1 mile = 1.6 kilometres
1 ounce = 28 grams
1 pint = 0.6 litres
1 gallon = 4.5 litres

Metric to imperial
1 millimetre = 0.04 inch
1 centimetre = 0.4 inch
1 metre = 3 feet 3 inches
1 kilometre = 0.6 mile
1 gram = 0.04 ounce
1 kilogram = 2.2 pounds

TIME

SCOTLAND IS ON Greenwich Mean Time (GMT) during the winter months – that is, five hours ahead of Eastern Standard Time and ten hours behind Sydney. From the middle of March to the end of October, the clocks go forward one hour to British Summer Time (which is one hour ahead of GMT). To check the correct time, you can dial 123 to contact the Speaking Clock service.

A selection of Scottish newspapers

Personal Security and Health

**Pharmacy
sign**

L IKE ANY OTHER country, Scotland has its share of social problems, but it is very unlikely that you will come across any violence. If you do encounter difficulties, do not hesitate to contact the police for help. The UK's National Health Service (NHS) can be relied upon for an emergency or routine treatment. However, you may have to pay for treatment if your country has no reciprocal arrangement with the UK. Below is some guidance for enjoying a trouble-free visit.

HOSPITALS AND MEDICAL TREATMENT

A LL VISITORS to Scotland, especially those from outside the European Union (EU), are strongly advised to take out medical insurance against the cost of emergency hospital care, repatriation and specialists' fees. Emergency medical treatment in an NHS Accident and Emergency department is free, but additional medical care could prove very expensive. Visitors from the US should check with their insurance companies before leaving home to be sure they are covered if medical care is needed.

EU residents and nationals of some other Commonwealth and European countries are entitled to free medical treatment under the NHS, though the process is bureaucratic. Before travelling, obtain an E111 form that confirms that your country of origin has adequate reciprocal health arrangements with the UK. Some treatments are not covered, however, and repatriation is not included, so medical insurance is preferable.

If you need to see a dentist while staying in Scotland, you will have to pay. The cost will vary depending on your entitlement to NHS treatment. Emergency dental treatment is available in some hospitals.

PHARMACISTS

Y OU CAN BUY a wide range of medicines without prescription from pharmacies in Scotland. Boots is the best-known and largest supplier, with branches in most towns.

A traditional, privately owned pharmacy in Leith, Edinburgh

Many medicines are available only with a doctor's prescription, which you must take to a dispensing chemist (pharmacist). Either bring your own supply or ask your doctor to write out the generic name of the drug (as opposed to the brand name). If you are entitled to an NHS prescription, you will be charged a standard rate; without this, you will be charged the full cost. Ask for

a receipt for any insurance claim. Some pharmacies stay open until midnight. Doctors' surgeries (offices) are usually open mornings and early evenings. Hospital Accident and Emergency departments are always open.

THE MIDGE

B EING BITTEN BY midges is one of the most common hazards for visitors to Scotland. The chance of encountering these tiny biting flies is particularly heightened around lochs and on the coast, as they love damp conditions. They breed between April and October, and are at their worst at the start and end of the day. There is no way of escaping them altogether, but to ensure that you suffer only the minimum of bites, apply insect repellent (such as Autan) and avoid sitting near bright lights after dark. If they really are a nuisance you may want to invest in a midge net.

CRIME AND SUITABLE PRECAUTIONS

S COTLAND IS NOT a dangerous place for visitors, and it is most unlikely that your stay will be blighted by crime. There are, however, practical steps that can be taken to help you avoid loss of property or personal injury. Take good care of your belongings

Woman police constable   Police constable   Traffic police officer

Police patrol car with the familiar yellow stripe and blue light

at all times. Make sure your possessions are adequately insured before you arrive. Never leave them unattended in public places. Keep your valuables well concealed, especially in crowds. In cinemas or theatres, keep handbags on your lap, not on the floor. It is advisable not to carry too much cash or jewellery with you; leave it in the safe in the hotel instead. Pickpockets tend to frequent crowded places like bustling markets, busy shops and rush-hour public transport.

By far the safest way of carrying large amounts of cash around is in traveller's cheques *(see p205)*. Or you can withdraw small amounts of cash from cashpoints (ATMs). If you are travelling alone at night try to avoid deserted and poorly lit buildings and places such as back streets and car parks.

WOMEN TRAVELLING ALONE

I T IS NOT UNUSUAL in Scotland for women to travel unaccompanied, or to visit a bar or restaurant with a group of female friends. Nor is it especially dangerous. But caution is advisable in deserted places, especially after dark. Try to avoid using public transport when there is just one other passenger or a group of young men. It is best to summon a licensed taxi *(see p215)* rather than walk through a lonely area of a city at night, especially if you do not know the area well. It is illegal to carry any offensive weapons, including knives, guns, mace or tear-gas, even for self-defence. Personal alarms are permitted however.

Ambulance

Fire engine

POLICE

T HE SIGHT of a traditional British bobby patrolling the streets in a tall hat is now less common than the police patrol car, usually with wailing sirens and flashing lights. But the old-fashioned police constable does still exist in Scotland, particularly in rural areas and crowded city centres, and continues to be courteous, approachable and helpful. Unlike in many other countries, the police in Scotland do not carry guns. If you are lost, the traditional advice to ask a policeman or woman still applies. Traffic wardens may also be able to help with directions.

In a crisis, dial 999 to reach police, fire and ambulance services who are on call 24 hours a day. Calls are free from any public or private phone, but they should only be made in real emergencies. In Scotland's coastal areas this number will also put you in touch with Britain's voluntary coastguard rescue service, the RNLI (Royal National Lifeboat Institution).

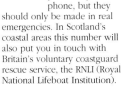

Logo of the Royal National Lifeboat Institution

LOST PROPERTY

I F YOU ARE unlucky enough to lose anything or have anything stolen, go straight to the nearest police station to report your loss. If you want to claim on insurance for any theft, you will need a written report from the local police. All of the main bus and train stations have lost property centres. Most hotels disclaim all responsibility for valuables not kept in their safe.

It is advisable to make photocopies of your vital documents such as passports and travel papers. If you lose your passport, contact your embassy or consulate in either Edinburgh or London *(see p201)*.

DIRECTORY

POLICE, FIRE AND AMBULANCE SERVICES

📞 999. Calls are free (24-hour phoneline).

HOSPITAL ACCIDENT AND EMERGENCY DEPARTMENTS

Aberdeen Royal Infirmary
📞 (01224) 840506.

Edinburgh Royal Infirmary
📞 (0131) 536 4000.

Glasgow Royal Infirmary
📞 (0141) 211 4484.

Inverness Raigmore
📞 (01463) 704000.

Perth Royal Infirmary
📞 (01738) 473838.

EMERGENCY DENTAL CARE

Edinburgh Dental Hospital
📞 (0131) 536 4900.

DISABLED HELPLINE

The Disability Helpline
📞 (0345) 123456.

Banking and Local Currency

VISITORS TO SCOTLAND usually find that the high-street banks (major banks) offer them the best rates of exchange. However, if you do find yourself having to use one of the hundreds of privately-owned bureaux de change that are found at nearly every major airport, train station and tourist area, check the commission and minimum charges carefully before beginning any transaction. Credit cards and traveller's cheques are the safest methods of bringing currency with you to Scotland.

One of many banks to offer bureau de change facilities

BUREAUX DE CHANGE

ALTHOUGH BUREAUX de change are often more conveniently located than banks and have longer opening hours, the exchange rates can vary considerably and commission charges can be high.

The reputable firms such as **Exchange International**, **Thomas Cook** and **American Express** offer good exchange facilities. Exchange International has just one branch, in Edinburgh's Waverley train station; both Thomas Cook and American Express have branches throughout Scotland.

BANKS

BANKS GENERALLY offer the best rates of exchange for visitors. Every large town and city in Scotland should have a branch of at least one of the following banks – Bank of Scotland, Royal Bank of Scotland, TSB Scotland, Girobank and Clydesdale.

Most banks have a cashpoint (ATM) from which you can obtain money with a bank or credit card and your personal identification number (PIN). Some of the most modern machines have easy-to-read computerized instructions

in several languages. Cardholders from principal English banks, such as NatWest, HSBC, Lloyds and Barclays, can withdraw money from certain banks in Scotland. Check that your bank card is compatible with the cashpoint you are using or you may be charged a fee or have your card rejected.

You can also obtain money by contacting your own bank and asking them to wire cash to the nearest Scottish bank. Branches of Thomas Cook or American Express will do this for you. Visitors from the US can have cash dispatched through **Western Union** to a bank or post office. Take your passport as proof of identity. Banking hours vary from bank to bank, but the minimum opening times are 9:30am to 3:30pm Monday to Friday.

CREDIT CARDS

CREDIT AND STORE cards are widely accepted throughout Scotland, but some smaller shops, guesthouses and cafés may not take them. VISA is the most widely used card, but MasterCard, Access, Diners Club and American Express are also accepted. For a small fee you can get cash advances with a credit card at any bank displaying the card sign.

EUROCHEQUES

AS WITH NORMAL cheques, Eurocheques can be written for an exact amount in sterling and guaranteed with a Eurocheque card. If the amount is above the card guarantee limit, additional Eurocheques can be written.

Scottish Banks
Most British high-street banks, especially the Scottish banks (Royal Bank of Scotland, Bank of Scotland and Clydesdale), have branches in the majority of Scotland's towns and cities. Most banks offer exchange facilities, but proof of identity may be required and the commission charges will vary.

Royal Bank of Scotland logo

Clydesdale Bank logo

Bank of Scotland logo

NatWest logo

DIRECTORY

EXCHANGE FACILITIES

Exchange International
[*(0131) 557 2784.*

Thomas Cook
[*(0141) 201 7200.*

American Express
[*(0141) 221 4366.*

Western Union
[*(0800) 833833.*

CURRENCY AND TRAVELLER'S CHEQUES

BRITAIN'S CURRENCY is the pound sterling (£), which is divided into 100 pence (p). There are no exchange controls in Britain, so you may bring in and take out as much cash as you like. Scotland has its own notes that are legal tender throughout Britain (with the exception of the £1 note), though they are not always accepted in England and Wales. Bank of England and Northern Ireland notes can be used throughout Scotland. Ask for some small notes when changing money, as they are easier to use. Traveller's cheques are a safer alternative to carrying large amounts of cash. Be sure to keep the receipts separate from the cheques so you can easily obtain a refund if your cheques are lost or stolen. Some high-street banks issue traveller's cheques free of commission to their account holders, but the normal charge is around 1 per cent.

Bank Notes
Scottish notes are produced in denominations of £1, £5, £10, £20, £50 and £100. Always get small denominations, as some shops may refuse the larger notes. Although Scotland has a £1 note, the English £1 coin, and all Bank of England currency, is legal tender.

£100 note

£20 note

£10 note

£5 note

£1 note

Coinage
Coins currently in use are £2, £1, 50p, 20p, 10p, 5p, 2p and 1p. The same coins are produced and accepted throughout the UK.

2 pounds (£2)   1 pound (£1)   50 pence (50p)

20 pence (20p)   10 pence (10p)   5 pence (5p)   2 pence (2p)   1 penny (1p)

Using the Telephone

Modern BT phone box

THE TELEPHONE SYSTEM in Scotland is efficient and inexpensive. Public payphones are located throughout the country. In urban areas, phone boxes can be found in shopping precincts, train and bus stations and on streets. Rural phone boxes are more scarce, but are often located by bus stops and in villages. Most pubs and public buildings also have payphones. As well as BT, several companies now offer cheap phonecards that use a PIN number. These can be bought at newsagents.

TELEPHONE DIRECTORIES

YELLOW PAGES are regional telephone directories that list local businesses and services by type. There are also local directories, such as *The Thomson Local*, that list private and business phone numbers. All of these can be found at most hotels, post offices and libraries. **Talking Pages** is a telephone service run by BT (formerly British Telecom), which gives you the number of a specific kind of shop or service in any area you want.

Yellow Pages logo | **Talking Pages logo**

CHARGES

TELEPHONE CHARGES depend on when, where and for how long you talk. The cheapest time to call is between 6pm and 8am Monday to Friday, and throughout the weekend.

USING A CARD PHONE

1 Lift the receiver and wait for the dial tone.

2 Insert a phonecard, picture side up.

3 Display shows how many units are left. Minimum charge is one unit.

4 Some phones also accept credit cards. Insert horizontally, with the arrow (if any) facing forward, and slide through.

5 Dial the number and wait to be connected.

6 When your phone card runs out, you will hear a bleeping noise. To continue press the button; the old card will be ejected so you can insert a new one.

7 If you want to make a further call, do not replace the receiver; instead press the follow-on call button.

USING A COIN PHONE

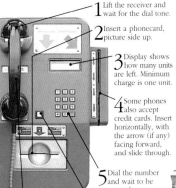

1 Lift the receiver and wait for the dial tone.

2 Insert the money. Normally any combination of 10p, 20p, 50p and £1 coins can be used.

3 Dial the number and wait to be connected.

4 The display indicates how much money you have put in and the credit left. A rapid bleeping noise means your money has run out. Insert more coins.

5 If you want to make a further call, do not replace the receiver; instead press the follow-on call button.

6 When you have finished speaking, replace the receiver. Any coins that were not used will be returned. Coin phones do not give change, however, so use 10p and 20p coins for shorter calls.

Phonecard and logo displayed by shops selling phonecards

Sending a Letter

The distinctive Post Office sign

BESIDES MAIN POST OFFICES that offer all the mail services available, there are many sub-Post Offices in news-agents, grocery stores and general information centres, particularly in more isolated areas and smaller towns. In many villages the Post Office is also the only shop. Post Offices are usually open from 9am to 5:30pm Monday to Friday, and until 12:30pm on Saturday. Mailboxes – in all shapes and sizes but always red – are found throughout cities, towns and villages.

A rural mailbox, embedded in a stone wall

A rural Post Office in Scotland

MAIL SERVICES

STAMPS CAN BE BOUGHT at many outlets, including supermarkets and petrol stations. Hotels often have mailboxes at their reception. When writing to a Scottish address always include the postcode. Letters and postcards can be sent either first or second class within the UK.

1st class aerogramme

2nd-class stamp 1st-class stamp

Greetings stamps featuring characters from children's fiction

First-class service is more expensive but quicker, with most letters reaching their destination the following day (except Sunday); second-class mail takes a day or two longer.

POSTE RESTANTE

LARGE URBAN Post Offices have a poste restante service where letters can be sent for collection. To use the service be sure to print the surname (last name) clearly so it will be filed correctly. Send it to Poste Restante followed by the address of the Post Office. To collect your mail you will have to show your passport or other form of identification. Mail will be kept for one month. One of the most central Post Offices in Edinburgh is the one situated in the St James Centre, EH1, close to the main bus station. This Post Office also offers the poste restante service.

MAILBOXES

THESE MAY BE either free-standing "pillar boxes" or wall safes, both painted bright red. Some pillar boxes have separate slots, one for overseas and first-class mail, another for second-class mail. Initials on older mail boxes indicate who was monarch at that time.

Mailboxes are often embedded in Post Office walls. Collections are usually made several times a day during weekdays (less often on Saturdays and rarely on Sundays and public holidays); times are marked on the box.

Pillar box

MAILING ABROAD

ALL MAIL SENT within Europe goes via airmail while surface mail can be used for letters and packages sent outside Europe. Overseas mail rates are classed by weight.

Aerogrammes go first class anywhere in the world and cost the same regardless of destination. They take about three to four days to reach European cities, and between four and seven days for destinations elsewhere.

The Post Office offers an express delivery service called **Parcelforce International**. Available from most main Post Offices it is comparable in price to many private companies such as **DHL**, **Crossflight** or **Expressair**.

Crossflight
(*(01753) 776000.*

DHL
(*(0345) 100300.*

Expressair
(*(0181) 897 6568.*

Parcelforce International
(*(0800) 224466.*

EMAIL

THE INTERNET has made email a popular and affordable form of communication. Many towns have cyber cafés where you can access the Internet.

TRAVEL INFORMATION

A S THE UK IS an international gateway for air and sea traffic, travelling to Scotland poses few problems. There are direct flights from North America and continental Europe. Coach travel from Europe via the ferries is a cheap, albeit rather slow form of transport. Travelling by train using the Channel Tunnel is an efficient way of crossing to the UK. Travelling within Scotland itself is fairly easy. Internal flights are

A British Airways plane in mid-flight

available between the cities on the mainland, and also to the island groups. Another easy way to island-hop is to take the ferries. There is an extensive network of roads in urban areas and renting a car can be the best way of travelling around. The inter-city rail network is limited in Scotland, though a small network of trains serves the country. Travelling by coach is the cheapest option; there are services between most cities.

Check-in desks at Glasgow International Airport

INTERNATIONAL FLIGHTS TO AND FROM SCOTLAND

E DINBURGH AND Glasgow are the principal airports in Scotland. The five other international airports are Dundee, Prestwick, Aberdeen, Inverness and Sumburgh on Shetland. **Air France**, **British Midland** and **KLM UK** (formerly AirUK) offer direct flights from continental Europe. Glasgow and Edinburgh have the most frequent services, with direct and indirect flights to many major

European destinations including Paris, Dublin, and Brussels.

A number of transatlantic airlines offer direct services to Glasgow airport, including **British Airways, American Airlines, Continental Airlines** and **Air Canada**. Flights to Edinburgh and Glasgow are available from long-haul destinations such as North Africa, South Africa, Australia and the Far East. These are routed via a European capital, often Brussels or Amsterdam.

A more economical option can be to fly to London and take a cheap domestic flight north. These flights can cost as little as £29 one way.

The airports at Glasgow, Edinburgh, Aberdeen and Prestwick all offer up-to-date facilities, including 24-hour banking, shops, cafés, hotels and restaurants. Edinburgh is currently undergoing a major programme of development and renovation. Expect some disruption at the airport until work is completed in June or July of the year 2000.

TRAVELLING WITHIN THE UK FROM SCOTLAND

F LIGHTS FROM Scotland to other British destinations operate from all the mainland international airports. British Airways offers

Express services to London's Heathrow and Gatwick airports. British Midland also flies direct to Heathrow. **easyJet, Ryanair** and KLM UK operate between Scotland and the English airports of Luton, Stansted and London City. There are also direct flights to other major cities in the UK, including

Logo for British Airways' budget airline

Passengers from abroad passing through International Arrivals

AIRPORT	ℹ INFORMATION	DISTANCE TO CITY CENTRE	TAXI FARE TO CITY CENTRE	PUBLIC TRANSPORT TO CITY CENTRE
Aberdeen	(01224) 722331	7 miles (11 km)	£10–12	Bus: 30 min Taxi: 20 min
Edinburgh	(0131) 333 1000	8 miles (13 km)	£12–15	Bus: 25 min Taxi: 20 min
Glasgow	(0141) 887 1111	8 miles (13 km)	£12–15	Bus: 25 min Taxi: 20 min
Prestwick	(01292) 479822	29 miles (47 km)	£30–40	Train: 45 min Taxi: 40 min

The smart new terminal at Glasgow International Airport

Manchester, Newcastle upon Tyne, Leeds, Birmingham, Belfast and Cardiff, but the cost of these flights can sometimes outweigh the time saved.

↑ 🛪 **Domestic departures**
   International departures
ℹ️ **Airport information**
   Toilets

Sign directing passengers to locations within an airport

← ⓘ **HM Customs enquiries**

Directions to the department for information on customs

TRAVELLING WITHIN SCOTLAND BY AIR

Scotland's size means that internal air travel is quick, but it can prove an expensive mode of travel compared to rail, coach or car. There are good air connections between the Highlands and central Scotland. When travelling to the islands off the coast of Scotland, flying becomes a particularly viable option. **British Regional Airlines** and **Loganair**, both subsidiaries of British Airways, provide regular flights from all the major cities on the mainland to the Western Isles, Orkney Islands and Shetland Islands.

TRANSPORT FROM THE AIRPORTS

Scotland's main international airports lie on the outskirts of Glasgow, Edinburgh and Aberdeen, where there are efficient transportation links. Taxis are the most convenient form of door-to-door travel, but they are also fairly expensive. Coaches or buses provide cheaper transport to the town centres, though during rush hour or heavy traffic, coaches, buses and taxis may be slow. **National Express** as well as **Scottish Citylink** *(see p211)* provide direct coach services from the major airports to various destinations.

Prestwick International is served by its own train station; a service runs to Glasgow city centre every half an hour.

AIR FARES

Air fares to Scotland are usually at their highest from June to September. The best deals are available from November to April, excluding the Christmas period – if you want to travel then, you should book well in advance.

Apex (Advance Purchase Excursion) fares are often the best value, though they must be booked a month ahead and are subject to restrictions, such as minimum and maximum stays and no refunds. Charter flights offer even cheaper seats, but with less flexibility.

Promotional fares are often available, and it is worth checking direct with the airlines for special offers. Cheap deals are sometimes offered by package operators and are advertised in newspapers and travel magazines. Students, those under 26 years old and senior citizens may be eligible for a discount. Children and babies travel for less.

If you choose a discount fare, always buy from a reputable operator, and check with the airline to ensure your seat has been confirmed. Packages may also be worth considering for cost-savings, even if you enjoy independent travel. Airlines and tour operators can put together a great range of flexible deals to suit your needs, sometimes with car rental or rail travel included. This can often be cheaper than arranging transport once you have arrived. A small airport tax is imposed on all those departing from British airports.

Rental car collection point at Glasgow International Airport

DIRECTORY

AIRLINE INFORMATION

Air Canada
📞 *(0990) 247226.*
www.aircanada.ca

Air France
📞 *(0181) 742 6600.*
www.airfrance.com

American Airlines
📞 *(0345) 789789.*
www.aa.com

British Airways
📞 *(0345) 222111.*
www.british-airways.com

British Midland
📞 *(0345) 554554.*
www.iflybritishmidland.com

British Regional Airlines
📞 *(01624) 826000.*

Continental Airlines
📞 *(0800) 776464.*
www.flycontinental.com

easyJet
📞 *(0990) 292929.*
www.easyjet.com

KLM UK
📞 *(0990) 074074.*
www.klmuk.com

Loganair
📞 *(0141) 848 7594.*

Ryanair
📞 *(0541) 569569.*
www.ryanair.ie

Travelling by Rail and Coach

Scotland has a privatized rail network, ScotRail, that covers most of the country and is generally efficient and reliable. A half-hourly shuttle service operates between Edinburgh and Glasgow, and lines radiate from both cities, with frequent services to many Scottish destinations and to most parts of England. Journey times to London are just over four hours from Edinburgh and just over five hours from Glasgow. Scotland also has a good coach (long-distance bus) service that is generally cheaper than the trains, although journeys can be slow. Weekend rail and coach services are popular, so book ahead.

The Flying Scotsman, one of the many swift inter-city train services

The new Virgin Superfast train at Edinburgh's Waverley station

TRAIN TICKETS

Allow plenty of time to buy your ticket, and always ask about any special offers or reduced fares. There are four types of discounted fares for adults. Apex (Advance Purchase Excursion) and SuperApex tickets are available in limited numbers on some inter-city routes. SuperApex fares must be purchased 14 days in advance, and Apex at least a week in advance. Savers can be used at weekends and on most weekday trains outside rush hours. Supersavers cannot be used on Fridays, or on any peak-hour service to, from or through London. First-class tickets cost about one-third more than standard fares, and returns are cheaper than buying two singles.

RAIL PASSES

If you plan to travel a lot by train, it is a good idea to buy a rail pass. These can be purchased from agents such as **Rail Europe**, which operates in Europe, the US and Canada. There are different passes available to suit every need. The Freedom of Scotland pass allows unlimited rail travel around the country for a set

period. The Highland Rover permits travel on the West Highland lines and the Inverness-to-Kyle line. The Festival Cities Rover, available during the Edinburgh International Festival in August, is for use between Glasgow's Queen Street and Edinburgh's Waverley station on any three out of seven consecutive days. The passes are also valid on some coach and ferry services and on the Glasgow Underground (see p96).

One-third price discounts are available for 16- to 25-year-olds using a Young Person's Rail Card. The Senior Railcard and Disabled Railcard entitle the holder to a one-third discount on most fares. Those aged 5 to 15 travel for less, and there are also family tickets.

A leaflet about the steam train

GENERAL TIPS

Britain's fastest and most comfortable trains are those on the inter-city routes. These popular services book up quickly. It is always advisable to reserve your seat in advance, especially if you want to travel at peak times such as Friday evenings and Sunday afternoons. Inter-city trains are fast, with a limited number of stops. The trip from Edinburgh to Glasgow, for example, takes around 50 minutes. A reduced service is usually in operation on Sundays and public holidays. Porters are often scarce at British stations, although trolleys are usually available for passengers to help themselves. If you are disabled and need assistance, contact the relevant train company before the day you travel.

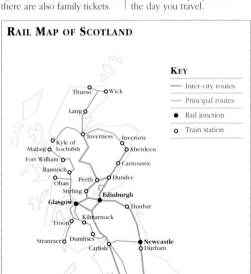

RAIL MAP OF SCOTLAND

KEY
— Inter-city routes
— Principal routes
● Rail junction
○ Train station

SCENIC TRAIN RIDES

WHEN MOTOR transportation made many rural railways redundant in the mid-20th century, picturesque sections of track, and many of the old steam engines, were rescued and restored to working order. Tourist offices or train ticket offices can provide you with information on where the lines are, and how much it will cost to take a ride on the trains.

Ride the Jacobite steam train from Fort William to Mallaig, passing over a spectacular viaduct at Glenfinnan; or take the Strathspey Steam Railway from Aviemore to Boat of Garten.

The Jacobite steam train on its picturesque journey to Mallaig

INTERNATIONAL COACH TRAVEL

ALTHOUGH TRAVELLING by coach (long-distance bus) is cheap compared with other methods of transport, it is not the most comfortable way of crossing Europe. If you have a lot of spare time, however, and want to stop off en-route at other destinations, it can be a convenient mode of transport. The ticket usually covers all parts of the journey, including the ferry or Channel Tunnel.

NATIONAL COACH NETWORK

THE LARGEST coach operators in Scotland are **Scottish Citylink** and **National Express**, which runs services only between the main cities and to destinations in the rest of Great Britain. Buy a reserved ticket to guarantee a seat.

Discounts are available for full-time students or anyone under 25 with a coach pass. Over-50s and children aged between 5 and 15 years also qualify for reductions. Under-5s travel free on Scotland's national coaches. The Tourist Trail

Pass is ideal for those planning to cover many destinations over a limited period. It allows unlimited travel on all National Express services in Scotland and the rest of Britain. You can buy the pass from most coach travel agents in the US via **British Travel Associates**, or in the UK at major international airports, at Glasgow's Buchanan Bus Station and at Edinburgh's St Andrew Square Bus Station. The Scottish Explorer Pass, available from Scottish Cityline agents and from Glasgow Airport, allows travel only within Scotland.

COACH AND BUS TOURS

DOZENS OF COACH tours are available in Scotland, catering for all interests, age groups and a host of different destinations. They may last anything from a couple of hours for a city tour to several days for a national tour.

Frames offers a six-day tour from London, via St Andrews and Loch Ness. It also provides tours of Edinburgh, the Highlands and the Isle of Skye. The Edinburgh-based **Scotline Tours** and **Timberbush Tours** offer half- and full-day tours, while **Prestige Tours** and **Rabbie's Trail Burners** offer tours of three days or more.

Ask at your hotel or tourist office for details of local bus and coach tours. Most major towns and cities offer open-top bus tours. Local buses are a cheap way to get about. The **Trossach Trundler**, a 1950s bus, provides a summer service around the Trossachs.

In the more remote rural areas not served by public transport, **Royal Mail** operates the Postbus. Fare-paying passengers travel in the postal delivery van – an interesting way to travel around.

The Trossach Trundler bus, which leaves Callander four times a day

Open-top bus tour on the Royal Mile in Edinburgh

DIRECTORY

UK AND OVERSEAS RAIL NUMBERS

Disabled Information
(*(0345) 443366.*

Lost Property
(*(0141) 335 3276 (Glasgow).*

National Rail Enquiries
(*(0345) 484950.*

Rail Europe
(*(0990) 848848 (UK).*
(*(303) 443 5100 (US).*
(*(905) 602 4195 (Canada).*

ScotRail Telesales
(*(0345) 550033 (for bookings).*

COACH AND BUS INFORMATION

British Travel Associates
(*(800) 327 6097 (US only).*

Frames
(*(0171) 837 3111.*

National Express
(*(0990) 808080.*

Prestige Tours
(*(0141) 886 1000.*

Rabbie's Trail Burners
(*(0131) 226 3133.*

Royal Mail
(*(0131) 228 7407.*

Scotline Tours
(*(0131) 557 0162.*

Scottish Citylink
(*(0990) 505050.*

Timberbush Tours
(*(0131) 555 4075.*

Trossach Trundler
(*(01877) 330969.*

Travelling by Ferry

IF YOU ARE travelling to Scotland from continental Europe by foot, car, coach or train, you will need to cross the English Channel or North Sea by ferry or Channel Tunnel. Ferry services operate between several ports on the Continent and Scotland and England, while the Channel Tunnel provides a nonstop rail link from France and Belgium. Fares between ferries and the Channel Tunnel are fiercely competitive. Island-hopping by ferry is an enjoyable and economical way to visit the beautiful islands situated off the coast of Scotland.

Logo of a Scottish ferry company

A car ferry travelling from Oban to Lochboisdale on South Uist

TRAVELLING DIRECT TO SCOTLAND BY FERRY

DIRECT WEEKLY ferry services to Scotland are available through **P&O Scottish Ferries**. Operating from June to August, the ferries run from the Norwegian port of Bergen to Aberdeen, via Lerwick on the mainland of Shetland. Fares vary greatly according to the season, time of travel and duration of stay. There are faster, express crossings, which cost more than standard crossings.

From Northern Ireland, there are two routes available. **Seacat** and **Stena Line** both run frequent services between Belfast and Stranraer, while

P&O European Ferries offers several daily crossings between the ports of Larne and Cairnryan, just north of Stranraer.

SERVICES TO ENGLAND FROM THE CONTINENT

A NETWORK OF ferry services regularly crosses the North Sea and the English Channel from northern Europe to ports in the UK. Of those travelling to the north of England, **P&O North Sea Ferries** runs a daily crossing from Rotterdam or Zeebrugge to Hull, and **Scandinavian Seaways** runs from Hamburg, Gothenburg and Amsterdam to Newcastle.

An alternative way to travel to Scotland from the Continent via England is the Channel Tunnel, which links the UK with France. Passengers travelling by coach or car board the **Eurotunnel** train, and remain in their vehicle throughout the 35-minute journey from Calais to Folkstone. For those travelling

Ferry timetable and fares

on foot, the **Eurostar** train runs frequent services between Paris, Brussels, and London.

Any visitors from outside the European Union should allow plenty of time for immigration control and customs clearance at British ports *(see pp198–9)*.

ISLAND-HOPPING IN SCOTLAND

SCOTLAND HAS just under 800 islands scattered off its coastline, and travelling by ferry is a wonderful way to experience their rugged beauty. The islands can be roughly divided into two main groups: the Hebrides, situated off the west coast, and Orkney and Shetland, lying to the northeast of the mainland. **Caledonian MacBrayne** has 30 ships, linking 23 of the westerly isles to the mainland and to each other. Destinations include Arran, Islay, Mull, Barra, Lewis, Harris, Skye, Raasay, Coll, Tiree and Eigg. The summer timetable runs from Easter to mid-October with a reduced service for the rest of the year. Most of the routes have two or three trips a day, but some have only one, so be sure to call ahead and check. Single, return and five-day tickets are available.

In addition, there are two special travel tickets. Island Hopscotch tickets are valid on a choice of fifteen routes for one month from the date of the first journey. The Island Rover gives you the freedom to choose your own route between the islands for 8 or 15 consecutive days from the date of the first journey. Although the Island Rover ticket is valid on all of Caledonian's services, it does not ensure a place on any particular sailing, and it is advisable to make vehicle

Passengers on the deck of a ferry leaving Tobermory on the Isle of Mull

A Caledonian MacBrayne ferry leaving the port of Mallaig

reservations. The northeastern islands of Orkney and Shetland are served by P&O Scottish Ferries. The principal crossing to Orkney from the mainland is a daily one from Scrabster, near Thurso, to Stromness, though this service does not operate on Sundays between November and March. The main crossing to Shetland departs Mondays to Fridays from Aberdeen, and the sailing times are subject to change between January and March.

During the summer, **John o' Groats Ferries** run a 45-minute crossing to Burwick on South Ronaldsay, the most southerly of the Orkney isles. They also offer day trips to Orkney from John o' Groats. Bookings are recommended.

CRUISES

A CRUISE IS A leisurely way to see the many different Scottish islands. Caledonian MacBryane offers an overnight cruise, as well as various non-landing, evening cruises which include a three-course dinner. These depart from a number of locations on the west coast.

It is also possible to take a cruise on some of Scotland's lochs and rivers. **Caledonian Discovery** offers seven-day cruises along the Caledonian Canal from Fort William to Inverness, allowing stops each day for outdoor activities such as canoeing, windsurfing, hill walking and cycling. Beds and meals are provided on board.

Cruising on Loch Ness with Caledonian Discovery's *Fingal of Caledonia*

CAR FERRY ROUTE	[INFORMATION	DAYS	LAST CHECK-IN	JOURNEY TIME
Aberdeen–Lerwick (Shetland)	(01224) 589111	Mon–Fri	1 hour	14 hrs
Ardrossan–Brodick (Arran)	(01294) 463470	daily	30 mins	55 mins
Kennacraig–Port Ellen (Islay)	(01880) 730253	daily	45 mins	2 hrs, 10 mins
Kilchoan–Tobermory (Mull)	(01688) 302017	Mon–Sun	none	35 mins
Mallaig–Armadale (Skye)	(01687) 462403	daily	30 mins	30 mins
Oban–Castlebay (Barra)	(01631) 566688	Mon, Wed–Sat	45 mins	5 hrs, 15 mins
Oban–Craignure (Mull)	(01631) 566688	daily	30 mins	40 mins
Scrabster–Stromness (Orkney)	(01224) 589111	daily	1 hour	1 hr, 45 mins
Uig (Skye)–Tarbert (Harris)	(01470) 542219	Mon–Sat	30 mins	1 hr, 45 mins
Ullapool–Stornoway (Lewis)	(01854) 612358	Mon–Sat	45 mins	2 hrs, 45 mins

Travelling by Car

I N SCOTLAND, AND THE REST of the UK, driving is on the left-hand side of the road, and distances are measured and signposted in miles. A network of toll-free motorways exists in the south and between Edinburgh and Glasgow; using these can reduce travelling time. In the larger towns traffic density can cause delays, and during public holiday weekends heading north to the Highlands is often slow work. Rural Scotland, with its striking scenery, is an enjoyable place to drive, and the roads to even the remote parts are generally good.

No stopping

Speed limit (mph)

No entry

No right-turn allowed

Railway level crossing

Yield to all vehicles

One-way traffic

Gradient of a road

The A68 dual carriageway from Northern England to Scotland

WHAT YOU NEED

T O DRIVE IN Scotland you need a current driving licence, with an international driving permit if required. In any vehicle you drive, you must carry proof of ownership or a rental agreement, plus insurance documents.

A motorway sign

ROADS IN SCOTLAND

P EAK RUSH-HOUR traffic can last from 8–9:30am and 5–6:30pm on weekdays in the cities. Radio Scotland and local radio stations broadcast regular reports of road conditions throughout the day. You can also contact **AA Road Watch** for information on road conditions. You can save vital travel time by knowing which routes should be avoided.

Outside the cities, a good touring map is essential; the AA or RAC motoring atlases are straightforward to use. For exploration of more remote areas, the Ordnance Survey series is the best. Such areas often have only single-track roads with passing places that demand careful driving.

On all road maps, motorways are indicated by an M followed by a number, such as the M8. Major roads, which are often dual (2-lane) carriageways, are labelled A roads. Secondary roads, often less congested than A roads, are called B roads. There are fewer roads in the Highlands.

Disabled drivers can contact the **AA Disability Helpline** for general motoring information.

ROAD SIGNS

S IGNS ARE NOW generally standardized in line with the rest of Europe. Directional signs are colour-coded: blue for motorways, green for major (A) roads and white for minor (B) roads. In the Highlands and islands, road signs display both English and Gaelic names. Brown signs with a blue thistle give visitor information on attractions and tourist centres. Warning signs are usually triangles in red and white, with easy to understand pictograms. Watch for electronic notices on motorways that warn of road works, accidents or dangerous driving conditions.

Level crossings at train tracks often have automatic barriers. If the lights are flashing red, it means a train is approaching; you are required to stop.

RULES OF THE ROAD

S PEED LIMITS are 50–65 km/h (30–40 mph) in built-up areas and 110 km/h (70 mph) on motorways or dual carriageways – look out for speed signs on other roads. It is compulsory to wear seatbelts in Scotland. Severe penalties are imposed for drinking and driving – see the *UK Highway Code Manual* for legal limits.

PARKING

C OIN-OPERATED parking meters are in force during working hours (usually 8am–6:30pm Mon–Sat). Some cities have "park and ride" schemes, where you take a bus from an out-of-city car park into the centre. Other towns have a "disc" parking scheme; ask the tourist office or a local newsagent for a disc to mark your arrival time. Many car parks operate on a pay-and-display system. Avoid double yellow lines at all times; you can park on single lines at evenings

Parking meter

and weekends, but check roadside signs for variations to the rule. Traffic wardens will not hesitate to ticket, clamp or tow away your car if in breach of the rules. If in doubt, find a car park. Outside urban and popular visitor areas, parking is not such a problem. Look out for the letter P, which indicates legal parking spaces.

It is best to avoid driving in Edinburgh, as cars have limited access to the centre and the vast majority of sights can be reached on foot. Taxis, which you can hail on the street or find waiting at a taxi rank, are another option. Licensed cabs must display a "For Hire" sign. Mini-cabs must display a card proving the identity of the licensed driver. If there is no meter, ask the fare in advance.

One of Glasgow's black cabs

FUEL

NORTH AMERICAN visitors to Scotland may find petrol (gasoline) very expensive, particularly at motorway service stations. Large supermarkets often have the lowest prices. Petrol is sold in three grades: diesel, 4-star (regular) and unleaded. Most modern cars use unleaded petrol. Diesel and unleaded fuel are cheaper than 4-star. Most petrol stations are self-service but instructions at the pumps are easy to follow. Green hoses denote unleaded fuel pumps.

BREAKDOWN SERVICES

BRITAIN'S MAJOR motoring organizations, the **AA** (Automobile Association) and the **RAC** (Royal Automobile Club), provide a comprehensive 24-hour breakdown service. Both offer reciprocal assistance for members of overseas motoring organizations – before arrival check with your own group to see if you are covered.

The busy M8 motorway on the outskirts of Glasgow

You can contact the AA or RAC from roadside SOS phones on all motorways. Most car rental agencies have their own cover, which includes membership of either the AA or the RAC while you are driving. Even if you are not a member of an organization, you can still call out a rescue service, although it will be expensive. Always take the advice given on the insurance policy or rental agreement. If you have an accident that injures you or damages a vehicle, contact the police straight away.

CAR RENTAL

RENTING A CAR can be costly, but one of the more competitive companies is **Hire for Lower**. Others include **Arnold Clark**, **Budget**, **Hertz Rent A Car**, **Europcar** and **National Car Rental**. Many companies require a credit card number or a substantial cash deposit as well as your driving licence and passport. The normal age requirements are over 21 and under 70. Major airports, train stations and city centres have car rental outlets.

MOTORAIL

**RAC and AA
logos**

IF YOU DO NOT want to drive the long distance from London to Scotland, **Motorail** is an overnight train service that transports your car between London (Gatwick and Heathrow) and Edinburgh, Glasgow or Inverness, leaving you to travel by air or train.

General Index

Acknowledgments

DORLING KINDERSLEY would like to thank the following people whose contributions and assistance have made the preparation of this book possible.

EDITORIAL AND DESIGN
MANAGING EDITORS Fay Franklin,
Louise Bostock Lang
MANAGING ART EDITOR Annette Jacobs
SENIOR EDITOR Helen Townsend
EDITORIAL DIRECTOR Vivien Crump
ART DIRECTOR Gillian Allan
PUBLISHER Douglas Amrine
PRODUCTION Jo Blackmore
PICTURE RESEARCH Brigitte Arora
DTP DESIGNERS Maite Lantaron, Lee Redmond
MAPS Ben Bowles, Rob Clynes (Colourmap Scanning, London)
MAP CO-ORDINATOR David Pugh
Hilary Bird, Claire Folkard, Alrica Green, Carolyn Hewitson, Jessica Hughes, Donnie Hutton, Marie Ingledew, Elly King, Sue Megginson, Clare Pierotti, the Scottish Tourist Board (especially Vineet Lal), Pamela Shiels and Stewart Wild.

ADDITIONAL PHOTOGRAPHY
Joe Cornish, Andy Crawford, Philip Dowell, Chris Dyer, Andreas Einsiedel, Peter Gathercole, Steve Gorton, Paul Harris, Dave King, Cyril Laubscher, Brian D. Morgan, Ian O'Leary, Stephen Oliver, Tim Ridley, Kim Sayer, Karl Shore, Clive Streeter, Mathew Ward, Stephen Whitehorne.

PHOTOGRAPHIC AND ARTWORK REFERENCE
Aerographica: Patricia & Angus Macdonald; London Aerial Photo Library.

PHOTOGRAPHY PERMISSIONS
City of Edinburgh Council Heritage and Arts Marketing/ People's Story Museum; Royal Botanic Garden, Edinburgh; House for an Art Lover, Glasgow; Glasgow School of Art; Glasgow Botanic Gardens.

PICTURE CREDITS
t = top; tl = top left; tlc = top left centre; tc = top centre; trc = top right centre; tr = top right; cla = centre left above; ca = centre above; cra = centre right above; cl = centre left; c = centre; cr = centre right; clb = centre left below; cb = centre below; crb = centre right below; bl = bottom left; b = bottom; bc = bottom centre; bcl = bottom centre left; br = bottom right; d = detail

The publisher would like to thank the following individuals, companies and picture libraries for their kind permission to reproduce their photographs.

ABERDEEN TOURIST BOARD: 51cra; ABERDEEN UNIVERSITY LIBRARY: The George Washington Wilson Collection 161t; ACTION PLUS: 12t; AEROGRAPHICA: Patricia & Angus Macdonald 14t/b, 15tl, 16cra; ALLSPORT: Craig Prentis 36b; T & R ANNAN & SON (D): 101br.

BRIDGEMAN ART LIBRARY, London/New York: 25t, 146b, 147b (d); City of Edinburgh Museums & Galleries 26bl; Fine Art Society, London 101 clb; Robert Fleming Holdings Limited, London 43c; National Gallery of Scotland, Edinburgh 40; National Museet Copenhagen 42c; Collection of Andrew McIntosh Patrick, UK 101cla; Smith Art Gallery and Museum, Stirling 120b; South African National Gallery 101cra; Trinity College Library, Dublin 42t; BRITISH AIRWAYS: 208t.

LAURIE CAMPBELL: 16clb/bl, 127b, 157t/c; BRUCE COLEMAN: 158br, 159bl/bcr/br; Peter Evans 140tl; Gordon Langsbury 14lt; Hans Reinhard 116tl; Dr. Frieder Sauer 152t; COLLECTIONS: Michael St. Maur Sheil 159cr; DOUG CORRANCE: 10, 21br, 27b, 28c, 28cc, 29br, 32bl, 38t, 52, 90t, 108cl/b, 110, 133b, 139t, 144b, 146t, 147t, 186c, 187ca/cb/b, 190br, 192cl, 194tr/b, 198c, 212b; ERIC CRICHTON PHOTOS: 21cl/cr; CROWN COPYRIGHT: Historic Scotland 60 tr/c, 121c; Ordnance Survey/Photo, Scotland in Focus 192tl.

EDINBURGH FESTIVAL FRINGE SOCIETY: Andy Manzie, Royal Blind School, Edinburgh 36t; EMPICS: 109r; ET ARCHIVE: Bibliothèque Nationale, Paris 6–7; MARY EVANS PICTURE LIBRARY: 7 (inset), 24t/c/b, 44c, 45cr, 86bl, 88c, 123b, 153br, 163 (inset), 197 (inset). LOUIS FLOOD: 26br.

GARDEN PICTURE LIBRARY: John Glover 20tr; GLASGOW MUSEUMS: Art Gallery & Museum, Kelvingrove 102t, 134b, 150b; Burrell Collection 104–105 except 104tl; Saint Mungo Museum of Religious Life and Art 99b; Museum of Transport 22br, 23bl, 102c; RONALD GRANT ARCHIVE: 25c; V. K. GUY LTD: Mike Guy 16cla, 34cl, 133t, 3 (inset); Paul Guy 2–3; Vic Guy 118–119.

ROBERT HARDING PICTURE LIBRARY: 130t, 193b; Van der Hars 142t; Michael Jenner 160c; Julia K. Thorne 18bl; Adina Tovy 18br; Andy Williams 126; Adam Woolfitt 140tr; DENNIS HARDLEY: 34cr, 35t/cb, 80, 82, 84c/b, 90b, 91t, 113, 114t/b, 115b, 136b, 137b, 156b, 161b, 199b; GORDON HENDERSON: 17cra, 34t, 35ca/b, 148c, 157b, 158t/cl, 159t, 160b, 213t; HOUSE OF LORDS RECORD OFFICE: Reproduced by permission of the Clerk of the Records 45t; HULTON GETTY COLLECTION: 23cra, 46t, 92tl, 117br, 149c; (c) HUNTERIAN ART GALLERY, UNIVERSITY OF GLASGOW: 103tl; Mackintosh Collection 94, 101crb; HUTCHISON LIBRARY: Bernard Gerard 13t; ANDREW LAWSON: 20bl, 21tl/tr, 156t. MUSEUM OF CHILDHOOD, Edinburgh: 58b.

NATIONAL GALLERIES OF SCOTLAND: Scottish National Gallery of Modern Art *Study For Les Constructeurs: The Team At Rest* by Fernand Leger 1950 (c) ADAGP, Paris and DACS, London, 1999 69t; NATURAL HISTORY PHOTOGRAPHIC AGENCY: Bryan & Cherry Alexander 37tr; Laurie Campbell 11t, 17b1a, 36c; Manfred Danegger 17br/bra; Scottish National Portrait Gallery 63t; NATIONAL MUSEUMS OF SCOTLAND: 62b; NATIONAL PORTRAIT GALLERY, London: 64b; NATIONAL TRUST FOR SCOTLAND: 50b, 56b, 92tr, 93tl/tr/br, 124b, 125c, 200cr; Lindsey Robertson 93bl; Glyn Satterley 100br; NATURE PHOTOGRAPHERS: William Paton 158bl; Paul Sterry 159bcl; NATWEST: 204br; NETWORK PHOTOGRAPHERS: Laurie Sparham 12b. ORTAK JEWELLERY, Edinburgh: 74ca, 106t.

PA NEWS: 29t/bl; Chris Bacon 39c; Roslin Institute 23br; (c) 1996 POLYGRAM FILMED ENTERTAINMENT: 25b; POWERSTOCK/ZEFA: 18c.

REX FEATURES: J. Sutton Hibbert 47c; ROYAL BOTANIC GARDEN, Edinburgh: 21bl; ROYAL COLLECTION (c) 1999, HER MAJESTY QUEEN ELIZABETH II: 27tc; ROYAL PHOTOGRAPHIC SOCIETY: 23tl.

SCIENCE PHOTO LIBRARY: M-SAT Ltd 8; SCIENCE & SOCIETY PICTURE LIBRARY: Science Museum 23crb; ALASTAIR SCOTT: 15b, 17cla, 29cb, 191b, 195l; SCOTTISH HIGHLAND PHOTO LIBRARY: 17tc, 135t; PHIL SHELDON GOLF PICTURE LIBRARY: 188tr; James Shuttleworth: 211c; STILL MOVING PICTURE COMPANY: Gordon Allison 28br; Marcus Brooke 15tr; Wade Cooper 47t; Doug Corrance 28t, 81b, 130b, 185cl, 190cl, 194c; Peter Davenport 16br; Distant Images 89t; Derek Lairs 41c; Robert Lees 39b, 186t, 191t; Paisley Museum 89b; Ken Paterson 67t; David Robertson 20cl, 149b; Glyn Satterley 187t; Colin Scott 29cl; Scottish Tourist Board 28bl, 140br, 141c, 184c, 185t; Paul Tomkins/STB 160t, 184b, 186b; Stephen J. Whitehorne 117t; Harvey Wood 139b. TRON THEATRE: Keith Hunter 108cr.

CHARLIE WAITE: 131t; DAVID WARD: 134t; STEPHEN J. WHITEHORNE: 1, 17tl, 29cra, 34b, 37c, 62tl, 63c, 66b, 83, 111b, 115t, 132t, 148b, 161c, 175c, 184t, 192b, 193t, 195r, 205t, 207cl, 213c.

Front Endpaper: DOUG CORRANCE: cl, br; ROBERT HARDING PICTURE LIBRARY: Andy Williams tl; DENNIS HARDLEY: bl; HUNTERIAN ART GALLERY, UNIVERSITY OF GLASGOW: Mackintosh Collection tr. Jacket: all special photography Joe Cornish; Steve Gorton, Paul Harris, Clive Streeter, Stephen J. Whitehorne except DOUG CORRANCE: tl, bl, tl (back), bottom spine; DENNIS HARDLEY: t; STILL MOVING PICTURE CO: Scottish Tourist Board br (back), Stephen J. Whitehorne cla.

DORLING KINDERSLEY SPECIAL EDITIONS

DORLING KINDERSLEY books can be purchased in bulk quantities at discounted prices for use in promotions or as premiums. We are also able to offer special editions and personalized jackets, corporate imprints, and excerpts from all of our books, tailored specifically to meet your own needs.

To find out more, please contact:
(in the United Kingdom) – SPECIAL SALES, DORLING KINDERSLEY LIMITED, 9 HENRIETTA STREET, COVENT GARDEN, LONDON WC2E 8PS; TEL. 020 7753 3572;

(in the United States) – SPECIAL MARKETS DEPARTMENT, DORLING KINDERSLEY, INC., 95 MADISON AVENUE, NEW YORK, NY 10016.

Scottish Vocabulary

Gaelic is a Celtic language that is still spoken as a second language in the Highlands and Western Isles of Scotland. Estimates put the figure of Gaelic speakers throughout the country at around 80,000. The last decade has seen something of a revival of the language, due to the encouragement of both education and broadcasting authorities. However the majority of people are most likely to come across Gaelic today in the form of place names. Words such as glen, loch, eilean and kyle are all still very much in use. English remains the principal language of Scotland. However the country's very distinct education, religious,

political and judicial systems have given rise to a rich vocabulary that reflects Scottish culture. Many additional terms in current usage are colloquial. English as spoken by the Scots is commonly divided into four dialects. Central Scots can be heard across the Central Belt and the southwest of the country. As around a quarter of the population lives within 32 km (20 miles) of Glasgow, West Central Scots is one of the most frequently heard subdivisions of this dialect. Southern Scots is spoken in the east of Dumfries and Galloway and the Borders; Northern Scots in the northeast; and Island Scots in the Orkney and Shetland Islands.

PRONUNCIATION OF GAELIC WORDS

Letters	Example	Pronunciation
ao	craobh	this is pronounced similar to **oo**, as in cool
bh	dubh	"h" is silent unless at the beginning of a word in which case it is pronounced **v**, as in vet
ch	deich	this is pronounced as in the German composer Bach
cn	cnoc	this is pronounced **cr**, as in creek
ea	leabhar	this is pronounced **e**, as in get or **a**, as in cat
eu	sgeul	this is pronounced **ay**, as in say or **ea**, as in ear
gh	taigh-òsda	this is silent unless at the beginning of a word, in which case it is pronounced as in get
ia	fiadh	this is pronounced **ea**, as in ear
io	tiocaid	this is pronounced **ee**, as in deep or **oo**, as in took
rt	ceart	this is pronounced **sht**
th	theab	this is silent unless at the beginning of a word in which case it is pronounced **h**, as in house
ua	uaine	this is pronounced **oo**, as in poor

WORDS IN PLACE NAMES

ben	mountain
bothy	farm cottage
brae	hill
brig	bridge
burn	brook
cairn	mound of stones marking a place
close	block of flats (apartments) sharing a common entry and stairway
craig	steep peak
croft	small plot of farmland with dwellings in the Highlands
dubh	black
eilean	island
firth	estuary
gate/gait	street (in proper names)
glen	valley
howff	a regular meeting place, usually a pub
kirk	a Presbyterian church
kyle	a narrow strait of river
links	golf course by the sea
loaning	field
loch	lake
moss	moor
Munro	mountain over 900 m (3,000 ft) high
strath	valley/plain beside river
wynd	lane
yett	gate

FOOD AND DRINK

Arbroath smokie	small haddock that has been salted and then smoked
breid	bread
clapshot	mashed turnips and potatoes
clootie dumpling	rich fruit cake
Cullen skink	fish soup made from smoked haddock
dram	a drink of whisky
haggis	sheep's offal, suet, oatmeal and seasonings, usually boiled in the animal's intestine
Irn-Bru	popular soft drink
neeps	turnips
oatcake	a savoury oatmeal biscuit
porridge	a hot breakfast dish made with oats, milk and water
shortie	shortbread
tattie	potato
tattie scone	type of savoury pancake made with potato

CULTURAL TERMS

Burns Night	25 January is the anniversary of the birth of the poet Robert Burns, celebrated with a meal of haggis
Caledonia	Scotland
ceilidh	an informal evening of traditional Scottish song and dance
clan	an extended family bearing the same surname (last name)
first foot	the first person to enter a house after midnight on New Year's Eve
Highland dress	Highland men's formal wear including the kilt
Hogmanay	New Year's Eve
kilt	knee-length pleated tartan skirt worn as traditional Highland dress
Ne'erday	New Year's Day
pibroch	type of bagpipe music
skean-dhu	a small blade tucked into the outside of the sock on the right foot worn as part of the traditional Highland dress
sporran	pouch made of fur worn to the front of the kilt
tartan	chequered wool cloth, different colours being worn by each clan

COLLOQUIAL EXPRESSIONS

auld	old
auld lang syne	days of long ago
Auld Reekie	Edinburgh
aye	yes
bairn	child
barrie	excellent
blether	chat
bonnie	pretty
braw	excellent
dreich	wet (weather)
fae	from
fitba	football
hen	informal name used to address a woman or girl
ken	to know; to have knowledge
lassie	a young woman/girl
lumber	boyfriend/girlfriend
Nessie	legendary monster of Loch Ness
Old Firm	Celtic and Glasgow Rangers, Glasgow's main football teams
wean	child
wee	small

DORLING KINDERSLEY *TRAVEL GUIDES*

TITLES AVAILABLE

THE GUIDES THAT SHOW YOU WHAT OTHERS ONLY TELL YOU

COUNTRY GUIDES

AUSTRALIA • CANADA • FRANCE • GREAT BRITAIN
GREECE: ATHENS & THE MAINLAND • THE GREEK ISLANDS
IRELAND • ITALY • MEXICO • PORTUGAL • SCOTLAND
SOUTH AFRICA • SPAIN • THAILAND

REGIONAL GUIDES

BARCELONA & CATALONIA • CALIFORNIA
FLORENCE & TUSCANY • FLORIDA • HAWAII
JERUSALEM & THE HOLY LAND • LOIRE VALLEY
MILAN & THE LAKES • NAPLES WITH POMPEII & THE
AMALFI COAST • PROVENCE & THE COTE D'AZUR • SARDINIA
SEVILLE & ANDALUSIA • SICILY • VENICE & THE VENETO
GREAT PLACES TO STAY IN EUROPE

CITY GUIDES

AMSTERDAM • BERLIN • BUDAPEST • DUBLIN • ISTANBUL
LISBON • LONDON • MADRID • MOSCOW • NEW YORK
PARIS • PRAGUE • ROME • SAN FRANCISCO
ST PETERSBURG • SYDNEY • VIENNA • WARSAW

TRAVEL PLANNERS

AUSTRALIA • FRANCE • FLORIDA
GREAT BRITAIN & IRELAND • ITALY • SPAIN

DK TRAVEL GUIDES CITY MAPS

LONDON • NEW YORK • PARIS • ROME
SAN FRANCISCO • SYDNEY

DK TRAVEL GUIDES PHRASE BOOKS

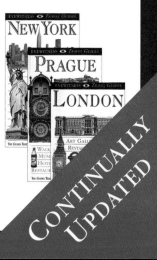

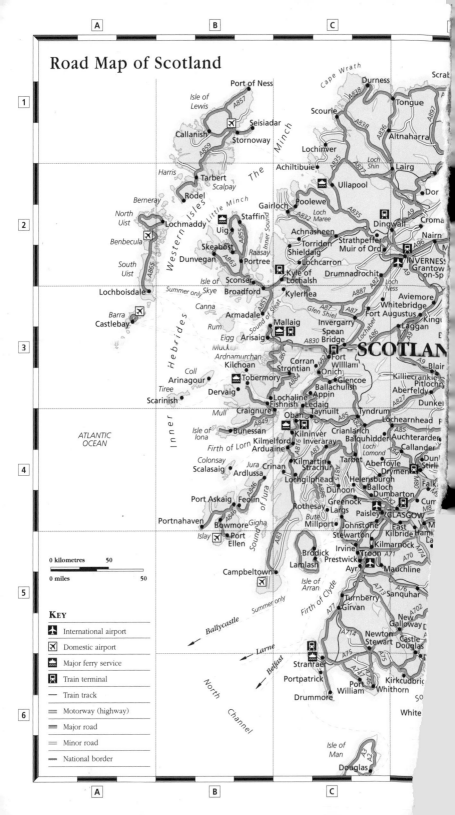